THE
GOVERNMENT
AND POLITICS
OF JAPAN

THE GOVERNMENT AND POLITICS OF JAPAN

Hitoshi Abe
Muneyuki Shindō
Sadafumi Kawato

Translated by James W. White

UNIVERSITY OF TOKYO PRESS

Translation and publication of this volume were assisted by grants from the Japan Foundation.

This volume is a translation of *Gaisetsu Gendai Nihon no Seiji*, published by University of Tokyo Press in 1990.

ISBN 4–13–037021-9
ISBN 0– 86008–501–5
Printed in Japan

CONTENTS

Contents

Part 5   The Political Culture

TABLES AND FIGURES

TABLES

FIGURES

TRANSLATOR'S INTRODUCTION

This book is the first to offer to readers of English a general introduction to contemporary Japanese politics from a Japanese perspective. The authors, all academic political scientists, are intimately familiar with the study of politics, both Japanese and American, in the United States; at the same time, they bring to the subject a variety of emphases and preoccupations which set them apart from foreigners who study Japan. In many instances these differences have little influence on the aspects of Japanese politics they describe and explain here, or on the way they set them forth. Nevertheless, their perspective does lend this book a distinctive quality in several respects, and readers will learn not only from what the authors cover, but also from how they choose to cover it.

In the first place, this book begins with and places heavy relative emphasis on *governmental institutions*. The discipline of political science, in Japan, has grown out of the disciplines of law—especially constitutional law—and public administration. A concern for the institutional arenas in which politics takes place is unsurprisingly central, in contrast to American texts, which begin more often with discussions of popular political culture and political behavior and their historical roots. This does not mean, as the reader will see, that political behavior is in any way slighted. It does diminish the typically American danger of reducing political institutions to the behavior of their members, and it also facilitates portrayal of the independent existence of institutions and their influence on political actors. At times this will challenge the reader, as when one encounters all of the different types of national government subsidies for which local political leaders must apply. But it also conveys an accurate impression of the very real complexity of the institutional framework within which these actors must operate, and the ways in which institutions influence their behavior.

An institutional perspective also does not mean that the less formal aspects of government are slighted. Indeed, much of the operation of formal Japanese political institutions is informal: the extralegal "administrative guidance" offered by bureaucrats to their clients, the preference for particular solutions over general legal precedents and principles, the delegation of central government functions to local government, the widespread governmental use of citizen advisory councils with vague legal powers, and the close—and sometimes corrupt—interrelationships among interest groups, elected politicians, and public officials based on old school ties, social and kinship connections, and economic interests. Again, one must not exaggerate the differences between Japan and, for example, the United States. Still, the point is often made that government in Japan takes place to a distinctive extent outside the formal regulations and structures laid down by law, and one can see ample evidence of this tendency here.

A final institutional arena of particular note in any overview of Japanese politics is *local government*, a dimension which receives more attention here than in either the average text on U.S. government or in texts on Japanese politics written by foreigners. The reasons are quite simple. The first is empirical: in a unitary state such as Japan, local government is far more a part of national politics than is the case in a federal system such as that of the United States, and Japanese observers are closely aware of this fact. Japan is a far more centralized country than the United States, and many local government activities are mandated and paid for by the national government—and sometimes even carried out by national government bureaucrats on temporary assignment to municipal or prefectural governments. The easy conclusion—that local governments are simply appendages of Tokyo—does not follow, as the authors note, but the American tendency to look separately at national and local politics is still a misplaced focus in Japan.

The second reason for the relatively strong emphasis on local government here is normative, and derives from my next point: the salience in Japan of questions of democracy. The authors, like many Japanese, see the overconcentration of political power in Tokyo as a serious constraint on the operation of democratic procedures and institutions at the local level. Therefore, much more than Americans, they evaluate the democratic quality of Japanese politics in terms of the relationships between center and locality. The Japanese name of the field itself—*chihō jichi*, which means local "autonomy," not local "government"—reveals the importance of local politics to the overall evaluation of democratic politics in Japan.

Thus the third distinctive aspect of this book is its concern for the *quality of democracy*. For the first two or three decades after the war Western authors, too, focused on the question of whether or not Japan had successfully instituted democratic political forms and procedures, and what the prospects were that democracy would take deep root. But in the last decade or so this focus has faded from foreign texts on Japan, especially those written by Americans: democracy in Japan tends to be taken as a given. Japan might be efficient or not, stable or not, elitist or pluralist, but it certainly seems democratic.

Japanese observers are less sure. The difference, I think, is that most Americans focus on "procedural" democracy: free elections, competitive parties, civil rights, constitutional protections, the rule of law, and so on. The Japanese themselves are more likely to view democracy in "substantive" terms: do the people really have meaningful political choices and equal opportunities to participate; is government really representative, accountable, and open; are wealth and power really equitably distributed; and is political conflict accepted as a legitimate part of politics, freely initiated and fairly resolved? The authors occasionally address this difference directly, as when they discuss the difference between a largely procedural "democracy" and a much more normative "liberalism," as defined in Japan. Often, however, they seem to be more critical of Japan than Americans are, although this critical posture reflects to some degree their distinctive focus on democracy, not simple cynicism.

Their critical focus is apparent also in the approach to *nationalism* taken here. Texts on American politics are unlikely to devote an entire chapter to the subject, and American texts on Japanese politics do not do so either, presumably on the assumption that the genie of Japanese ultranationalism, with its tragic history, is back in the bottle once and for all. The misgivings of Japan's neighbors, and their anxieties when they observe Japan's military growth, are routinely covered, at least in studies of Japanese foreign policy. But nationalism does not seem to be much of a potential future problem among a people who, according to opinion surveys, are as pacifist as any in the world.

The Japanese people themselves are not so sanguine. The devastating role played by nationalism in Japan's recent history is a living memory for many of its people still, and the acute sense of national identity—an ever-present, painfully sharp awareness of Japaneseness in contrast to the rest of the human race—which was manipulated into prewar nationalism is unweakened. The susceptibility of this identity to different expressions—national inferiority at one time, national confidence at another—and some of its intellectually less attractive—albeit apolitical—manifestations during the postwar period make it an ongoing concern for the Japanese themselves, and we see here the disquieting position it holds in the political culture.

Overall, then, this text takes a singularly *critical* position vis-à-vis contemporary Japanese politics. Highly critical studies of Japanese politics and economics are hardly lacking, but introductory texts by Americans tend to avoid the sorts of value judgments which the Japanese themselves need not fear. Here we have clear evaluations of the prewar period, in which the potential for militarism and autocracy is seen as an intrinsic part of the Meiji system, and of the postwar period also, with its rampant political corruption and factionalism, bureaucratic unaccountability, and overconcentration of power in the hands of both government and big business.

But the perspective here is balanced. It is not a naive idealism in which Japanese democracy is criticized for falling short of some standard which neither it nor any other real-world government can achieve. The tradeoffs, contradictions, and tensions of democracy, and the price one pays for it, are acknowledged here, such as the impossibility of ever achieving complete equality and the frustration and conflict which this fact entails. Nor is it the sort of knee-jerk cynicism which informs many critical foreign studies of Japan. The authors clearly recognize the magnitude and value of the postwar changes in the political life of the people, and the capacity of the people to work to improve this life further: to push government, to demonstrate, to litigate, and not simply to lie back and enjoy a system devised for them by the U.S. Occupation. And their ability to appreciate and criticize at the same time is not peculiarly Japanese—it was, after all, Winston Churchill who evaluated democracy as the worst form of government of all, except for all the others.

But there is a distinctively Japanese impetus behind the choice of policy issues chosen for closer examination in Part 3. Both the budget process and administrative reform not only provide vivid examples of the interaction of parties, institutions of local and national government, interest groups, and citizens, and the strengths and weaknesses of the system but in ways observable in other countries as well. They also reflect the preferences of Japanese political leaders, visible for a century, for small government which delegates, guides, induces, and subcontracts rather than actually trying to do everything itself. The "big government" which came under criticism in the 1980s was already leaner—in terms of budget, levels of taxation, and number of personnel—than that of most other industrial democracies. But a never-ending search for low-cost efficiency, in a period of slowed economic growth, has nevertheless led to repeated attempts to bring the budgetary process under control and refine the structure and operation of government.

One should note that budgetary severity and administrative reform do not, however, signify any new willingness on the part of the central government to relinquish real power. It wants smaller government and cheaper government (how better to woo the voters than with tax cuts?), not weaker government. Hence the authors' concern for deconcentration of power, and their observation of the fact that, in devolving functions to local government, the state has unwittingly provided them with a leverage and room for maneuvering which it never intended and which quite contradict the conventional view of local government as wholly dependent on Tokyo.

The importance of the third policy dilemma dealt with here is self-evident, given Japan's history—the problematic role of nationalism, and the acute attention paid to the issue by Japan's neighbors. Japan has wrestled mightily with the issue of defense. In a chapter written especially for the English edition of this book, we see how today—almost fifty years after the end of the Pacific War—the issue is far from resolved, as the rancorous parliamentary debate and aroused public opinion surrounding Japanese participation in UN peace-keeping operations makes clear. The leading opposition party, the Socialists, are to this day unable to agree among themselves whether the Japanese military is constitutional or not. In the 1980s the defense issue seemed to have faded from the scene, but with the Gulf War, the end of the Cold War, and the apparent efforts of North Korea to develop nuclear weapons, it is back on the front burner, and will remain there for some time to come.

In their concern for governmental institutions, local government, democracy, nationalism, critique, and policy focus, then, Professors Abe, Shindō, and Kawato bring a distinctive perspective to this book. The book was a cooperative enterprise; however, primary responsibility for chapters 1, 2, and 18 through 21 lay with Abe Hitoshi; Shindō Muneyuki was in charge of chapters 3 through 12 and 17 while Kawato Sadafumi oversaw chapters 13 through 16. I would like to thank all three of these scholars, with whom it was a pleasure to work on this project. Thanks are also very much in order to the Japan Foundation, the support of which made possible both the translation and publication of this book. I have profited greatly from a critical reading of my translation by Margaret McKean of Duke University and Richard Samuels of MIT, both appropriately jaundiced of eye but neither responsible for any remaining errors, and especially from the professionalism, patience, and enduring good spirits of Nina Raj of the University of Tokyo Press.

Finally, two notes: Japanese names are presented in this book in Japanese order, that is, with surname first, except when cited as the authors of English-language sources. And, in calculating the yen figures given here in dollars, one may note that the exchange rate in mid-1993 was approximately ¥110 = U.S.$1.

James W. White

PART 1

THE NATIONAL GOVERNMENT: PARLIAMENT AND THE BUREAUCRACY

CHAPTER 1

FROM THE MEIJI STATE TO THE POSTWAR CONSTITUTION

POLITICS AND THE STATE

The subject of this book is Japanese politics, but before our subject is addressed, the term "politics" itself deserves definition. Politics is a term with myriad definitions. The most useful one for our purposes is: human activity directed at the regulation and resolution of conflict, and the maintenance of order, in society. When so defined, politics may be considered a quintessentially modern type of activity. In premodern society, people lived their lives within intimate collectivities, such as family and community. The social traditions and customs in accordance with which people lived, and by means of which conflict was regulated, were firmly established and largely unquestioned, and were not often thought of as having been humanly created or as subject to human control or manipulation. Social order seemed to exist naturally and immutably in the form of traditional family and community rules, and there was neither the necessity nor the possibility for people consciously to remake this order, that is, to engage in politics.

When modern society emerged, however, the cohesion and conformity existing in these social collectivities declined and it became less and less possible to maintain social order and stability without some form of conscious effort. Thus, politics has become in the modern age an enterprise that is absolutely essential to society. Moreover, the difficulty in complex modern societies of coordinating conflicting interests and maintaining social order and stability has created a need for elaborate organization. In any type of group, when the membership grows beyond a certain threshold, the problems of conflict resolution and regulation become so complex that there will inevitably be movement toward the organization and institutionalization of political processes. The same process holds true for whole societies, and the organizational manifestation of society as a whole, in its attempts to maintain order and regulate conflict, is the state. In that politics involves conflict regulation for whole societies, it is accurate to say that contemporary politics unfolds primarily within the framework of the state.

In the case of Western Europe, the earliest form of modern state was the absolute state, which appeared during the sixteenth and seventeenth centuries. With authority concentrated in the hands of the monarch, the absolute state was a political system that tried to construct a new form of social order in societies moving toward disorder, following the political decline of feudalism and the social disintegration of traditional collectivities in the face of commercial and industrial development and the unchecked spread of modern warfare. The absolute, or early modern, state was a response to the increasing need for protection against internal and external threats to security and social stability. This state was a hybrid: in that an individual monarch ruled, it still possessed the premodern quality of a medieval monarchy, but, in that it was a centralized response to the problems of national security and the creation of social order, it also constituted the point of departure of the modern state.

The first modern state in Japanese history was the Meiji state, established in 1868 after the overthrow of the Tokugawa Shogunate. The Meiji state was a modern state with the goals of national security and domestic social and political order. Moreover, it was established by new political forces, with the lower strata of the warrior aristocracy, or samurai, at their core, who were intent upon modernization. These forces installed the emperor as the putative sovereign[1] and claimed merely to exercise power in his name. (We shall look at his real function in a moment.) One may thus say that modern politics in Japan began with the Meiji state. Our objective is to study the politics of contemporary Japan, but because the heritage of the Meiji state lives on in various forms in contemporary politics, we must begin our study by looking at the special characteristics of the Meiji state.

PREMODERN QUALITIES OF THE MEIJI STATE

The first characteristic of the Meiji state to note is the fact that the premodern collectivities that had constituted the foundation of Tokugawa society did not disintegrate at the time of the Meiji Restoration. Nor were they, as in Europe, excluded from the political system; rather they survived socially and were in fact incorporated into and preserved in the state. In the case of Western Europe, the growth of absolute states was simultaneously the process of decay of the pre-modern community. It was because the community was in a process of disintegration that it was necessary to create a new type of state, and the creation of the state in turn required the elimination of competing power centers such as free cities, religious orders—and communities. In the case of Japan, however, what made the creation of a state necessary was not the disintegration of traditional collectivities but rather the crisis brought on by the imperialist encroachment into Asia of the states of Europe and the United States during the nineteenth century. Japan was pressed into state-building by the urgent need to build a nation-state in order to resist foreign pressure.

In order to create a nation-state, it is necessary to create a nation, that is, a populace that identifies with, supports, and accepts conflict regulation and taxation by a state that takes precedence over traditional institutions, such as village and family. In light of the fact, however, that in nineteenth-century Japan the great majority of the people were living in agricultural villages in which the premodern community and family survived largely intact, the task of leading the people to understand the concepts of "nation" and "state" promised to be difficult indeed. The strategy chosen was to bring them to an understanding of the state by likening it to the most prevalent social institution (and the one that constituted the basis of the village), that is, the family. According to the official government analogy, just as the family has a head, the father, so also does the state have a head, the emperor; and the people in the state were to fulfill their loyalty to the emperor just as they would fulfill their filial obligations to the father in a family. This concept, which merged the ideas of political loyalty and filial piety, became the ideological core of the prewar Japanese "family state."

The Meiji state was rooted in the concept of the family state, but one of the characteristics of the concept was that, since the state was viewed as the family writ large and the ideal of the family was that of a totally harmonious whole, the state had to attempt to eliminate the possibility of confrontation and conflict from society. The ideal family was intrinsically free of conflict and dissension; since the state was a macrocosm of the family, it, too, should be free of disharmony. Insofar as politics is, more than anything else, related to conflict and dissension both as cause and cure, this meant that the Meiji state was, at least in theory, an apolitical state.

Of course, in actuality, even the Meiji state was unable to avoid conflict and disharmony. Within a few years of the Restoration, open splits emerged in the regime, and a major—albeit unsuccessful—aristocratic rebellion erupted in 1877. On the popular level, a wave of protests against governmental oligarchy swept the country in the 1870s, and, in the 1880s, the Freedom and Popular Rights Movement demanded more open government and greater popular political participation. Moreover, resistance to the government's policies of state-led national economic development and militarization[2] was continuous. Nevertheless, at least on the level of ideology and political myth, the concept of the family state emphasized that Japan was a unique country in which harmony was revered and conflict unknown. In addition, insofar as traditional collectivities were preserved alongside the Meiji state, the family-state concept was not simply a fiction but was supported by reality. This is because the natural village, where the majority of the people lived, was, like the family, a place where everyone supposedly lived in peace and harmony and in which there was neither room nor need for conflict to occur. Therefore, the Meiji government tried strenuously to idealize rural life and maintain the village community. Consequently, the regime established a comprehensive system of local government that, although designed to subordinate local communities to central government rule, sought also to preserve their traditional ways of maintaining social order.

Even after the dissolution of the Meiji state following World War II, this apolitical legacy of the Meiji state lives on, a strong undercurrent in popular views of politics. Typically, the Japanese excel at devising stratagems for denying, avoiding, or suppressing confrontation, but not at the mutual negotiation and compromise needed to resolve conflict once it arises. On the one hand, one may note the prevalence of *nemawashi*, an elaborate process of informal consensus-building before decisions are formally taken that has been described as a quintessentially Japanese way of reaching decisions and a stereotypical way of avoiding conflict.[3] On the other hand, one can also cite innumerable neighborhood conflicts that, uncontainable by conventional conflict-regulation rituals, have degenerated into petty, vicious squabbles, illustrating the underdevelopment of generally accepted political processes of conflict regulation and resolution among the people.

MODERN QUALITIES OF THE MEIJI STATE

The Meiji government tried to stabilize the state it had established by preserving the traditional village community and the family collectivity. At the same time, it tried to enhance the modern outward appearance of the state by promulgating a modern European-type constitution in 1889 and establishing a parliamentary system in 1890. But here, too, Japan displayed strikingly different features from the constitutional states of America and Europe.

The difference is exemplified by the transcendent status of the emperor under the Meiji Constitution. According to the Constitution, the emperor was a "divine and inviolable" being, and all sovereign powers—administrative, legislative, and judicial—were vested in the throne. It did not stop at making the emperor the absolute embodiment of political authority—he was also the embodiment of absolute spiritual authority. The absolute monarchs of Europe ruled by divine *right*, but under the Meiji Constitution the Japanese emperor *was* divine. Not only did the Constitution declare the emperor to be the son of the gods and himself a living god whose commands the people were unequivocally to obey, it sought also that the emperor should be revered by the people in the depths of their hearts. Even everyday popular morality was the object of manipulation and control by imperial decree, as exemplified by the Imperial Rescript on Education of 1890, in which all the nation's schoolchildren were adjured to study hard and obediently for the benefit of the throne and empire.

In this manner, the absolute authority of the emperor was established in principle; political reality, however, did not remotely resemble direct imperial rule. The emperor was a legitimating facade in whose name government power was exercised. The emperor supposedly made and executed policy with the "counsel" and "cooperation" of institutions like parliament, the cabinet, the Elder Statesmen, or *genrō*, and the Senior Advisors, or *jūshin*,[4] who in fact ruled. But this charade was actually a source of stability: when political negligence, failure, or blunders occurred, these were not laid at the feet of the monarch but rather were attributed to mistakes on the part of these advisers and counsellors, who could be fired without compromising the integrity of the ultimate sovereign, the emperor. This sort of political arrangement did bear some similarity to constitutional monarchy in Western Europe, especially Britain, where the monarch, or "dignified" organ of government, reigned and legitimized the actual rule by the "efficient" organs of government such as parliament and cabinet. Also, there was conscious emulation: the "organ theory of the emperor" developed in 1911 by constitutional scholar Minobe Tatsukichi, according to which the emperor was just another organ of government rather than a transcendent being, was an attempt to interpret the Meiji Constitution in a manner as close as possible to Western constitutional monarchism.

But such theoretical attempts were in vain, because at the same time that the Meiji Constitution paralleled constitutional European monarchy in some ways, the apotheosis of the throne and the inculcation of worshipful loyalty to the emperor in the hearts of the people went far beyond any European concept of constitutional monarchy. Criticism of the imperial system was a serious crime—and advocacy of its alteration a capital one—and academic research that questioned the imperial system was forbidden, too. The emperor's portrait hung in every school, and everyone was required to act respectfully and do obeisance when in its presence.

How does one explain this apparent political schizophrenia? Why was it that on the one hand aspects of constitutional monarchy were embraced, while at the same time the absolutization of the emperor was attempted? One view is that the drafters of the Meiji Constitution hoped to stabilize the state by installing the emperor as the "axis" of the state.[5] In other words, in order to guarantee the stability of Japan as a modern state—a state only recently and precariously built after much effort and amid many dangers—they felt it necessary to establish some political bonding agent or anchor, commonly embraced by all the people, which would bind the people loyally to the state—in a sense, an axis around which all political institutions and affairs would revolve. They hoped that the throne would perform the function of such an axis. As long as the emperor was possessed of qualities of nobility and intellect far surpassing those of ordinary people, it should have been relatively easy to instill in the people feelings of reverence for the throne. It could not be assured, however, that any given emperor would be so inspirational. Given this danger, it was essential to exclude the emperor from the reality of government and turn the throne into a depersonalized "axis," or "dignified" organ of government, independent of the qualities of any individual emperor. One way to achieve this goal was to deify the emperor utterly and create an absolute monarch "without peer in any nation of the world"—and also without imperfect human qualities.

POSTWAR DEMOCRATIZATION

The aspects of constitutional monarchy present in the Meiji Constitution, in concert with broad currents of social, economic, and international change, in due course contributed to the post–World War I emergence of the period known as "Taishō democracy." With the rise of the military in the 1930s, however, a movement to exploit its absolutist aspects and establish an autocratic political system grew stronger, and ultimately a totalitarian regime came to power. This totalitarian regime ultimately led Japan into a reckless military adventure and was destroyed in World War II. After the war, Japan was occupied and ruled by an allied army (in reality, dominated by U.S. forces). Under the Occupation a variety of reforms were carried out in order to dismantle the prewar Japanese political system. The objectives of these reforms were demilitarization and democratization: to demilitarize Japan completely and thus to eliminate Japan permanently as a threat to any country and, to minimize the possibility that another military dictatorship could ever emerge, to establish a political system in accordance with the will of the people. In that demilitarization also eradicated the premodern and pro-military characteristics of the Meiji state, it served to promote the democratization of Japan as well.

The Occupation's democratization policies included the elimination of the Home Ministry; the popular election of prefectural governors; the dissolution of the financial conglomerates, or *zaibatsu*; the purge of wartime leaders in politics, public administration, and business; land reform; the legalization of labor unions; and education reform. Each of these policies had a significant impact on postwar Japanese politics.

First, the dismantling of the Home Ministry, which had controlled the police, elections, and local government, and the popular election of prefectural governors (who had previously been appointed by Tokyo), dealt a fatal blow to the Meiji state's system of centrally concentrated, nonrepresentative government and opened the way for the establishment of a modern system of autonomous local government. Since the tradition of centrally concentrated authority was extremely strong in Japan, however, even reforms such as these were insufficient to fully democratize local government. As we shall see, even today, local autonomy is compromised by powerful influences from the central government.

Dissolution of the zaibatsu, a small number of huge business conglomerates each under the control of a central holding company, contributed to the modernization of business enterprise by making independent the subsidiaries and component companies of the four major zaibatsu and giving freer play to their respective competitive and managerial capabilities. Moreover, the purge of wartime leaders brought a wave of youthful elements into management and made possible enhanced innovation in enterprise management. This reform may be cited as one of the contributing causes of the subsequent high-speed growth of the Japanese economy.

Land and labor reforms contributed to the same end. The amount of land any individual could own was limited, and large landowners were forced to sell their excess land to the government, which resold it, primarily to those who had previously farmed it as tenants. Workers were given the right to organize, bargain collectively, and strike if necessary to achieve their aims. These reforms dramatically raised the incomes of farmers and workers and, by increasing their purchasing power, made possible the expansion of the domestic market necessary for rapid economic growth. Moreover, and crucially, by conferring upon millions of farmers and workers rights of landed property and freedom of association and expression, the reforms contributed to the growth of a middle class aware of the necessity of these rights to their own economic prosperity, family security, personal happiness, and political freedom. Thus, they created a huge constituency in firm support of democratic politics.

Finally, decentralization of the education system (with significant powers devolving from the Education Ministry to local boards of education) and democratization of its content (including the elimination of all pro-emperor and pro-military material), coupled with the traditional enthusiasm for education, caused popular educational levels to rise dramatically and thus enhanced the ability of the people to participate intelligently and responsibly as citizens in a democratic society.

The culmination of these policies of democratization was the promulgation in 1947 of a new Japanese Constitution. The Meiji system of transcendent imperial sovereignty was abolished and the principle of popular sovereignty was established, with the emperor becoming merely a symbol of national unity. The transition from a centrally concentrated to a locally decentralized system of authority was best exemplified by the fact that in the new Constitution an entire chapter was devoted to the subject of the authority of local governments.[6] Moreover, in the Meiji Constitution the "rights of subjects" had been recognized but effectively nullified, in that their exercise was guaranteed only insofar as consistent with one's duties as a subject. In addition, the principle of "selfless devotion to the state" had been universally inculcated, constituting a further constraint on the exercise of individual rights. By contrast, the postwar Constitution guarantees a broad variety of individual rights to the citizenry as basic and inviolable. Moreover, the Constitution is now the supreme law of the land—amendable only by the will of the people—and the Supreme Court is the court of last resort in a newly independent judiciary,[7] with the power to decide the constitutionality of all laws and government actions. Finally, the sovereign will of the people is to be expressed only by them, through the ballot box, and by their freely elected representatives. Thus, one may say that, in postwar Japan, it is the Constitution itself that is designed to be the binding and stabilizing axis of national politics.

LIMITATIONS OF DEMOCRATIZATION

Without question, the constitutional and extraconstitutional reforms of the Occupation contributed to the modernization and democratization of Japanese politics; nevertheless, they clearly had their limits.

First, although the abolition of the prewar emperor system and creation of a new polity with a merely symbolic throne clearly marked a major transition, the fact that the emperor system was retained, even if only as a symbol, represented continuity with the prewar period. At the very least, this facilitated the survival of archaic and unreconstructed popular attitudes and facilitated the continuation of old ideas of domination within a democratic institutional framework.

Second, although a great many wartime political leaders were purged by the Occupation, the civil service bureaucracy, which had constituted the institutional heart of the autocratic government since the Meiji era, managed to avoid suffering any serious blows at all. The purge of wartime leaders had extended into the civil service and entailed significant personnel changes, but it did not go so far as to weaken the functions of the bureaucratic system as a whole. Quite the contrary; the Occupation chose to rule Japan indirectly, through the bureaucracy. As the institution in charge of direct, day-to-day administration of the country, the bureaucracy actually *increased* its influence during the Occupation.

Third, since the Occupation army reigned supreme from 1945 until 1952 and enacted both constitutional and extraconstitutional reforms unilaterally, Japan was from the beginning unable to play any autonomous role vis-à-vis democratic reform. Moreover, with the intensification of the Cold War in Asia, the Occupation's policy of democratization was transformed. The initial democratization policy had the aim of weakening Japan's power by destroying the old agencies and relationships of control, but the situation in Asia following the communist victory in China in 1949, and especially after the outbreak of war in Korea in 1950, required that Japan's strength be revived. From this point on began the so-called reverse course, characterized by the strengthening of the central government, revival of the Japanese military capability, and a broad retreat from the liberal economic and political reformism of the early Occupation period.

Fourth, change in popular consciousness lagged far behind the pace of change in political institutions. The transformation of attitudes always requires more time than the transformation of institutions, and, in the case of Japan, in particular, there was every reason to expect that to sweep away the old consciousness inculcated for over half a century under the prewar emperor system and to create a new political culture compatible with a democratic constitution would take a long time indeed. The time that elapsed between the inception of democratization and its diversion into the "reverse course" was exceedingly short, however, and there was never sufficient time to transform popular consciousness completely.

Finally, although parliamentary supremacy was expressly established by the new Constitution, before the routines of parliamentary politics took firm root, an intense ideological confrontation between Left and Right came to dominate parliamentary politics. As a result, parliament often became an arena for sterile and vituperative partisan conflict, and it is difficult to credit parliament with setting an example—much less with making adequate efforts to build popular understanding—of democratic processes of policymaking through constructive debate.

Despite these limitations, however, Japan's postwar Constitution has, in fact, become widely accepted by the people and has endured without amendment or serious challenge up to the present, testimony to the fact that a political system with a democratic constitution as its stabilizing axis is gradually taking root in Japan. In the chapters that follow, we shall examine various aspects of Japan's contemporary constitutional framework and the political system that it embraces.

NOTES

1. In fact, they claimed simply to have "restored" the emperor to his rightful position of rule, after 268 years during which the shogun (whom they labeled a usurper) had actually exercised sovereign power.

2. The slogan for these two policies was *fukoku-kyōhei*: "a rich country and a strong military."

3. The term itself means "root-binding," and refers to the digging of a ring around a tree to be moved and then the gradually binding of its roots into a ball so that, when moving day arrives, all is in order and perfectly prepared. An English approximation is "laying the groundwork" or "maneuvering behind the scenes" to gain one's objective."

4. Both of these groups were informal, extraconstitutional advisory bodies to the throne. The Elder Statesmen were the former leaders of the Restoration and the early Meiji state; the Senior Advisors were a group of former premiers.

5. The Meiji leaders' assumption was that Christianity had played such an axial role in European states.

6. By contrast, the Meiji Constitution did not refer to local government at all.

7. Previously, the judiciary had been subject to the Justice Ministry.

CHAPTER 2

PARLIAMENT AND THE LEGISLATIVE SYSTEM

THE JAPANESE PARLIAMENT

Parliamentary government began in Japan with the Imperial Diet, first elected in 1890 under the terms of the Meiji Constitution.[1] According to the Meiji Constitution, legislative authority derived from imperial sovereignty, but the constitutional provision that "the emperor shall exercise legislative power with the approval of the Imperial Diet" meant that the actual exercise of legislative power was in the hands of parliament. Parliament comprised two houses: a popularly elected House of Representatives and a House of Peers, which included members of the imperial family, aristocrats, imperial appointees, and others, predominantly of high social position. Apart from the House of Representatives' prerogative to consider the budget first, the powers of the two houses were equal. Thus, even though the House of Representatives tried to represent the will of the people, it could be thwarted by the non-elective House of Peers. Reform of the House of Peers in order to remedy this situation later became a major political aim during the 1910s and 1920s, when popularly backed political parties dominated parliament.

But the House of Peers was not the House of Representatives' only rival. Legislation passed by parliament was subsequently debated in the Privy Council, the stronghold of the old feudal domain factions and the bureaucrats; then it required imperial approval, only then becoming law. During these subsequent stages, amendments, qualifications, and conditions were frequently attached to legislation. Moreover, the emperor had the power to issue general and emergency decrees (although the latter required subsequent parliamentary approval), and it was his sole prerogative to appoint the premier, whose cabinet ministers could be anyone he selected. The Imperial

Diet possessed the appearance of a modern parliament, but its authority was thus severely constrained.

Under the postwar Constitution, Japan's parliament is known as the National Diet. The Diet is the supreme organ of state power and the sole national legislative body (Article 41). In principle, bills become law when passed by both houses of parliament; the emperor promulgates laws, but this act of state is required of him by the Constitution and is a pure formality. Under the Constitution, parliament, apart from legislating law, also possesses the authority to approve the budget, approve treaties, and initiate amendments to the Constitution itself. Moreover, the prime minister is now chosen by parliament, of which a majority of the members of his cabinet must be members.

Thus, the Constitution gives the legislative branch precedence over both the executive and judicial branches. But the Constitution, based on the principle of separation of powers and mutual checks and balances among the three branches, also stipulates procedures by which the executive and judiciary can restrain parliament. For example, it gives the executive the power to dissolve parliament and gives the courts the power of judicial review. Nevertheless, parliament, as the sole organ whose members have been elected by and are representatives of the sovereign people, occupies a position superior to that of the other branches. Thus, parliament is the supreme organ of state power.

BICAMERAL PARLIAMENTARISM

Japan's parliament is bicameral, composed of a House of Representatives and a House of Councillors. The bicameral legislative system emerged in medieval England, when a house was created in parliament for each of society's two orders, lords and commons; the system is used today in most modern legislative systems. The rationale for the second house is that it adds prudence to legislative deliberations and creates checks and balances within the legislature. Originally, however, there was a conservative intent behind the arrangement: to prevent "tyranny of the majority" by opposing the lower house (which represented the majority of the people) with an upper house based on a nondemocratic, nonelectoral principle of representation such as status or occupation. Consequently, with the spread of modern democracy, many countries have either gone to unicameral legislatures or unequal bicameral systems, with the lower house dominant.

In Japan, as noted, the Meiji Constitution established a bicameral system with coequal houses. During the formulation of the postwar Constitution, the U.S. Occupation initially proposed a unicameral legislature, but, at the strong request of the Japanese government, eventually adopted a bicameral system. Under the present bicameral system, there are only slight differences between the terms of the two houses' members, rules of candidacy, and electoral systems, for example. In fact, both houses have become dominated by political parties, and the checks and balances between the two houses have almost ceased to function. The only real justification for the system now is that it serves to check runaway legislative impulses.

Today's House of Representatives and House of Councillors are unequal in power. In addition to the right of prior deliberation of the budget, the lower house has the predominant power to effect a vote of no confidence in the cabinet, approve budgets and treaties, appoint the prime minister, and extend parliamentary sessions. Bills become law after approval by both houses, but the House of Representatives can override the upper house with a two-thirds majority (Article 59). When the lower house is dissolved, the House of Councillors may, in a crisis, call itself into emergency session, but this action must be subsequently ratified by the House of Representatives (Article 54).

The House of Councillors, after the first postwar election, was dominated by independents, including a number of nonpartisan men of learning and experience, and was thus qualitatively different from the House of Representatives. Subsequently, however, it became increasingly partisan and more and more similar to the House of Representatives. For this reason, there are many who assert that the upper house is no longer relevant, but insofar as it elaborates and publicizes the deliberative process, it does serve to stimulate public attention and inform public opinion. Moreover, given its domination by political parties, elections for the upper house, like those for the lower house, have become opportunities to gauge public opinion and seek a popular mandate. The crushing defeat of the Liberal Democratic Party (LDP) in the 1989 House of Councillors election, after a new consumption tax was introduced, epitomized this role. Finally, since the LDP lost its majority in the upper house in 1989, that house became a powerful check on the government, belying the charge of irrelevance. Lately, a number of questions concerning the upper house—such as the holding of elections for both houses on the same day (as happened in 1980 and 1986) and the introduction in 1983 of proportional representation into its electoral system (see chapter 14)—have stirred debate. The first, however, was simply an LDP tactic to boost its own vote, and the second has, if anything, made the house more partisan than before. Thus, from the perspective of strengthening the upper house's raison d'être as a less partisan, more reflective and deliberate chamber, they were all questionable decisions.

TWO TYPES OF REPRESENTATION

One defining characteristic of a democratic legislature is that it is composed of representatives elected by the people. But what, or who, do the legislators actually represent?

The dominant view in contemporary democratic societies, including Japan, is that legislators represent the interests of the people as a whole. Accordingly, the fact that a member of parliament (MP) was elected from one constituency or another is simply coincidental— what the MP should represent in parliament is not simply the interests of the people in his or her constituency but those of the people as a whole. Of course, it is not necessarily clear exactly what the interests of the people as a whole are, but ideally it is the duty of the legislator to imagine that such a general public interest does exist and to try to recognize and articulate it. This view of the representative as "trustee" of the entire national interest predominates in Japan and the industrial democracies of Western Europe.

Opposed to this view is the ideal of the representative as a "delegate" who is sent to parliament with the sole duty of representing directly the interests of the voters in his or her constituency. In the United States, where the tradition of direct democracy is strong, the original legislative principle—epitomized in the New England town meeting—was one of universal participation in collective decisions. In this tradition, representation is only an expedient adopted when large populations make direct democracy impossible. The duty of a representative is to act faithfully on behalf of the demands of those who elected him or her. Thus, the United States is the exception in that it has a system in which the representative as delegate reflects the dominant view.

Insofar as a legislature attempts to seek generally acceptable and beneficial policies through its debates, it may well be easier for an assemblage of trustees, seeking to define and pursue a common national interest, to reach unity than an assemblage of delegates, each of whom is likely to insist on local interests. This may be the reason trusteeship is the ideal in most democracies outside the United States. The Japanese Constitution's stipulation that "both Houses shall consist of elected members, representative of *all the people*" (Article 43; italics added) accords with this idea.

It probably comes as no surprise to learn, however, that in fact, behind the principle of trusteeship, there are many MPs who operate more according to the ideal of the local delegate. This tendency is especially strong in contemporary Japan. Certainly, even beyond the fact that one of an MP's paramount interests is his or her own reelection, it is inevitable that every MP will at times act as a delegate. When legislators focus exclusively on local interests, however, parliament loses its ability to agree or to lead, and it becomes impossible to give coherent direction to affairs of state through parliamentary deliberations. Therefore, it is important to recognize that an MP should not exclusively follow one principle or the other but, rather, must pursue both of these two potentially contradictory paths.

PARLIAMENT AS A LEGISLATIVE BODY

A legislature performs multiple functions; among them, the most important are the *integrative* function and the *legislative* function. In the past, these two functions were closely intertwined: it was expected that parliament as a legislative body would, through its legislative debates, serve to resolve conflicts, temper opposition, and integrate the body politic. The legislative function has been transformed today, and this transformation has influenced the integrative function. In today's Japanese parliament, how is the legislative function performed?

First, both MPs and the cabinet are empowered to introduce legislation. The Constitution makes no provision for the cabinet to introduce legislation, but Article 5 of the Cabinet Law states that the prime minister, as the representative of the cabinet, may introduce legislation to parliament. Bills may be introduced by individual MPs or by the cabinet into either house of parliament. Upon submission, the speaker of that house sends the bill to the appropriate standing or special committee. Either house's steering committee, however, may designate a bill as especially important and introduce it directly into a plenary session; moreover, in emergencies, by decision of the house, the stage of committee deliberation may be bypassed.

Presently, there are 20 standing committees in the House of Representatives and 17 in the House of Councillors, as shown in table 2.1. The standing committees, with the exception of the budget, audit, steering, and house discipline committees, correspond to the ministries of the cabinet. For example, the jurisdiction of the House of Representatives' Cabinet Committee includes all matters pertaining to the cabinet, the National Personnel Authority, the Imperial Household Agency, the Management and Coordination Agency (formerly the Prime Minister's Office), the Hokkaidō Development Agency, the

TABLE 2.1   Standing Committees of the Diet

Committee	Number of members	
	House of Representatives	House of Councillors
Cabinet	30	19
Local Administration	30	19
Judicial Affairs	30	19
Foreign Affairs	30	19
Finance	40	22
Education	30	19
Health and Welfare	40	19
Agriculture, Forestry, and Fisheries	40	21
Commerce and Industry	40	19
Transportation	30	19
Communications	30	19
Labor	30	19
Construction	30	19
National Security	40	—
Budget	50	45
Audit	25	30
Steering	25	25
Disciplinary Measures	20	10
Science and Technology	25	—
Environment	25	—

Defense Agency, and the Okinawa Development Agency; that of the Foreign Affairs Committee covers everything concerning the Foreign Ministry; and that of the Committee on Commerce and Industry includes the Ministry of International Trade and Industry (MITI), the Economic Planning Agency (EPA), and the Fair Trade Commission (FTC). The number, size, and functions of special committees are determined at the time of their establishment.

Committee deliberations begin with an explanation of the major features of proposed legislation and continue with interpellation of government and other witnesses, debate, and revision, after which bills are voted on. Presentation of the government's position on bills is the task of the relevant cabinet minister, assisted by ministry officials. In fact, it is these officials who provide most of the substance of the government's replies to committee interpellations. Public hearings are a common part of committee deliberations, but they are not utilized as fully in Japan as they are in the United States or Germany, where they are a key component of committee operations. Bills not brought to a vote in committee during a session of parliament expire with the end of that session.

Bills passed by committee are reported to the full house by the committee chair. In the full house they are again the subject of interpellation, debate, and revision, and then voted on. There are three forms of voting in parliament: unanimous voice vote, standing vote, and roll call. Bills passed by one house of parliament are sent to the other for consideration; when a bill is passed by one but not the other, it can still become law in one of three ways. First, when the House of Councillors revises and then passes a bill previously passed by the House of Representatives, the bill becomes law if the lower house passes the revised version during the same session of parliament. Second, if the upper house rejects, revises, or fails within 60 days to vote on a bill, it becomes law if passed again in the original version by the lower house by a two-thirds' majority. Third, the bill becomes law if passed by a joint committee of both houses. Such joint committees were never convened between 1953 and 1989; since the LDP lost control of the upper house in 1989, however, they have been convened a number of times.

After a bill becomes law, the speaker of the house that last passed it sends it via the cabinet to the emperor for promulgation. Promulgation is reported in the official gazette within 30 days, and at that point it assumes the force of law.

CHARACTERISTICS OF THE LEGISLATIVE PROCESS

Among the special characteristics of Japan's legislative process, the first to note is that bills submitted to parliament by the cabinet account for the great majority of proposed legislation. Between the first postwar session of parliament in 1947 and the 112th in 1988, cabinet submissions accounted for 68 percent of all bills submitted, with members' bills accounting for 32 percent. Moreover, when one looks only at bills passed, fully 85 percent were cabinet submissions and only 15 percent were members' bills.

Not only do cabinet-proposed bills outnumber members' bills— qualitatively, too, they account for most of the important legislation. In parliamentary systems such as Japan's, it is normal for the executive branch to play this sort of leading role in the legislative process. Although few laws result from members' bills, one should note that they have included some very important legislation. Not only were the Diet Law, the Public Office Election Law, and other laws governing parliament itself the result of members' bills, but so also were many laws promoting regional development for the purpose of either correcting interregional socioeconomic disparities or eliminating the harmful effects of the administrative standardization so dear to the hearts of central government planners and bureaucrats. Such acts as the Northwest Coast Development Promotion Law, the Central Japan Regional Development Law, the Remote Islands Promotion Law, the Mountain Villages Promotion Law, and the Law for Special Measures for Promoting Underpopulated Regions—all of whose names indicate their purpose—were the result of members' bills. One should also note that a number of laws addressing new social problems, such as parental leave legislation and regulation of the consumer loan industry, were the result of members' bills.

The second characteristic of the legislative process is that committee proceedings have become the heart of the process, with house plenary sessions losing much of their meaning. In many European and North American legislatures, bills are "read" multiple times to the full house, with the aim of making house deliberations important, but, in Japan, bills are presented but once. In a "three-reading" system, for example, upon its first submission to the legislature, a bill is presented and its major features explained in general outline; at the second reading, the bill is debated in general terms and accepted or rejected for committee consideration. If it is accepted, it goes through the committee process; if voted out of committee, it returns to the full house for a third "reading," or debate and decisive vote. Under the prewar constitution, the three-reading system was used in the Japanese parliament. Under this system, discussion of each bill in the full house is quite time consuming, but it is hoped that serious deliberation will result. Under the one-reading system, one can expect speedier deliberations, but the full house is less able to restrain or countermand the deliberations of the committees, which are far more susceptible to influence from special-interest and pressure groups.

The sharp imbalance between Japan's parliamentary committees and plenary sessions becomes clearer in comparison with other countries. Between 1970 and 1974, the House of Representatives met in plenary session 50 times per year on the average, for a total of 82 hours; the House of Councillors met 34 times for 63 hours. During the same time, the British House of Commons met 167 times per year for 1,528 hours and the House of Lords 112 times for 730 hours, while the U.S. House of Representatives met 164 times annually for 766 hours and the Senate 183 times for 1,146 hours. The number of committee meetings and the time thus spent were far greater in Japan: between December 1981 and December 1982 the House of Representatives met 45 times for a total of 47 hours, while 352 standing committee sessions consumed 1,170 hours. The House of Councillors met 35 times in plenary session, for a total of 46 hours; at the same time, its standing committees convened 291 times for a total of 878 hours. From such data one can see how full house sessions are becoming little more than a shadow of the legislative ideal.[2]

ROLE OF BUREAUCRATS IN THE LEGISLATIVE PROCESS

The third characteristic of the legislative process is the historical influence of executive-branch civil servants, which continues to this day. What is the manner in which civil servants exercise this influence? For our purposes it is sufficient to note that their influence is conspicuous at three different legislative stages: drafting, deliberation, and implementation.

First, although some important legislation is drafted by MPs, the majority of laws are based on cabinet-submitted bills, and such bills are ordinarily drafted by civil servants. The procedure varies considerably, but most such bills originate in discussions within government ministries and agencies—specifically, in discussions among department heads and their assistants and the chief clerks in that branch of the agency. As a concrete proposal is worked out, the matter also becomes the subject of discussion with the bureau head and other administrative officials, and is eventually formalized in the form of a draft proposal (*ringi-sho*) (see chapter 4). Once this draft has been agreed on by the whole agency, the next step is to negotiate the agreement of other concerned ministries. Subsequently, the proposal is considered by the Cabinet Legislative Bureau, which drafts it into the legally proper form of a legislative proposal. After a proposal has thus been formalized, it is presented to the ruling party for examination; once approved there it is submitted to the cabinet and finally adopted as a government-sponsored bill. Along the way, deliberation by advisory councils (*shingikai*) (see chapter 5) may also occur; nevertheless, it is clear that the greatest influence on the preparation of legislation is exercised by the bureaucrats.

As for legislative deliberation, one can also see the influence of civil servants at work in many aspects of the parliamentary process. First, the functional jurisdictions of the standing committees of both houses of parliament correspond to those of the ministries and agencies of the executive branch. This correspondence serves to promote mutual understanding, coordination, and communication between government bureaucrats and their parliamentary counterparts on corresponding committees. Of course, these relationships can also become paths of reciprocal influence, lobbying, and logrolling among

MPs and civil servants. Needless to say, the participation of civil servants as assistants to the minister in responding to committee questioning works to strengthen their influence. The influence of executive-branch civil servants is, in fact, demonstrated most clearly during committee deliberations, although it is a minor factor in full sessions of the house. In other words, the centrality of parliamentary committees to the legislative process enhances the influence of the bureaucracy in that process.

Finally, at the implementation stage of the legislative process, the civil servants of the executive branch do not stop at simply applying laws passed by parliament: under the pretext of "fleshing out" the law, they, in fact, make rules themselves. These rules take the concrete form of ordinances (*seirei*), announcements (*kokuji*), notifications (*tsūtatsu*), and so forth. Ordinances are orders issued by the cabinet for the purpose of enforcing the provisions of laws, and are of two types: executive orders, which spell out in detail the procedures for enforcing laws, and delegatory orders, which specify details of the actual content of laws. The latter form of ordinance is also known as "delegatory legislation," reflecting the fact that, as administrative functions have grown, there has been a trend for parliament simply to legislate the main points of a law, with the elaboration of concrete detail left to the cabinet. In Japanese law, wholesale delegation of legislative authority is not permitted, but in specified and limited circumstances it is permissible. In addition to cabinet ordinances (and for the purpose of implementation of both laws and ordinances), there are ministerial ordinances, but they are subordinate to cabinet actions. It is clear, however, that, as forms of administrative legislation, they too serve to supplement, and thus in effect to make, laws.

Announcements and notifications were not originally designed to be directly binding upon the citizenry; announcements formally publicized the particulars of ministerial and agency decisions, while notifications were orders or instructions from high-level agencies to lower-level ones that interpreted laws regarding the exercise of authority. They were thus intended to set standards internal to government, but in fact they have a great impact on the lives of the people. Thus, contemporary Japanese law as a parliamentary product simply sets forth basic frameworks, purposes, and goals, entrusting the determination of the details essential to enforcement to cabinet and ministerial ordinances, announcements, and notifications. By performing this "administrative legislation," the bureaucrats of the executive branch shape and control basic policy, and should they so desire, can on occasion even render it wholly ineffectual.

RECENT CHANGES

The postwar heyday of the influence of civil servants over the legislative process lasted until the 1970s. By the 1980s, it was clear that their power had begun to wane. Of course, the powers and functions of the executive branch are great today as before; as we have noted, their current role in the initiation, deliberation, and execution of the law cannot be overlooked. Nevertheless, parliament no longer simply bestows legislative legitimacy upon bills drafted by the bureaucracy; it has acquired a real role in the legislative process. As criticism of the administrative state has strengthened and arguments for "small government" have come to the fore in the advanced industrial democracies, one can see a trend toward shrinkage of the functions of the bureaucracy and expansion of those of the legislature, amounting in some cases to a "legislative restoration." Japan is no exception to this general trend. In light of the fact that Japan's parliament has been weak ever since the Meiji era, however, it is more accurate to speak of the attainment for the first time of parliament's true function than of a legislative restoration.

In accounting for the enhanced role of parliament, one should note changes occurring in both the legislative and executive branches. In the executive, as the relationships and rivalries between administrative agencies have become increasingly complicated, it has become impossible for the traditionally highly narrow and competitive ministries to coordinate their own interrelationships; hence, there has been no alternative but to look to some outside agency to perform this coordinating function. Moreover, it has become rarer than before for civil servants to feel strongly that they are servants of the public interest and to act with a sense of mission to realize that interest. This used to be one source of the political aura and influence of the bureaucrats but, as their political environment has become larger and more complex, the concept of the public interest has become more and more ambiguous, and the bureaucrats' sense of mission has become correspondingly less coherent and weaker. In any case, the reduction of the political influence of the bureaucrats vis-à-vis the legislative process is unmistakable.

Among the changes in the legislative branch, the most important is the extraordinary growth of the power of the Liberal Democrats. During what sometimes seemed like the eternal domination of party politics by the LDP—from 1955 to 1993—many of its politicians (the *zoku giin*) (see chapter 6) gained lengthy ministerial experience, thus acquiring a capacity for and competence in governing rivaling that of the civil servants. Even though the influence of the administration remained strong, the ruling party acquired power sufficient to control it at times. When the bureaucrats prepared draft legislation, it was common for them to submit it to the LDP's Policy Affairs Research Council (PARC) to gain party assent, and party MPs were able at this stage to demand revisions. Not only were significant revisions sometimes made after PARC deliberation; there was also a considerable body of draft legislation that, unable to obtain PARC approval, never saw the light of day. Moreover, even in legislation drafted exclusively by civil servants one could frequently discern between the lines the desires of LDP MPs.

At the same time that one could see the increasing role of the ruling party in the origins of legislation, a slight increase in the influence of the opposition parties at the deliberative stage of legislation was also visible. It is rare for this to take the form of direct revision of bills in parliament: as long as the LDP controlled a stable majority in parliament it could override any and all opposition. In contrast to the confrontational style that characterized interparty relations in parliament until the early 1970s, however, LDP-opposition relationships thereafter took on a much more cooperative and mutually conciliatory coloration.[3] As a result of the diminished ideological distance between the parties, it became possible to anticipate the smooth operation of parliament on the basis of cooperation between ruling and opposition parties, although whether or not this cooperation will characterize the LDP now that it is the opposition remains to be seen.

The growing influence of the opposition even before 1993 was most directly visible in the management of the parliamentary calendar. In comparison with other parliamentary democracies, Japanese legislative sessions are short, so that parliament must consider and pass a great volume of legislation in a limited time. The ability to delay —as even a minority can—becomes a significant weapon, since how the deliberation of any given bill, and the day-to-day deliberative schedule of this plethora of bills, is determined is a major factor in the passage or defeat of each bill. The cooperation of the opposition is thus essential to the expeditious completion of the legislative mission. It was necessary, therefore, for both civil servants and the LDP to seek the agreement of the opposition through prior consultations, and it was common for the interests of the opposition to be incorporated into the content of legislation during this process. One cannot yet tell whether the LDP in opposition will wield the weapon of delay as did its predecessors, or whether the present government will compromise as did the LDP. In any case, it is a fact that the voice of the political parties in the legislative process has become greater and that this has strengthened the position of parliament in the legislative process as well.

NOTES

1. The official translation of the Japanese word for national legislative assembly, *kokkai*, is "Diet," a German term adopted by the framers of the Meiji Constitution.

2. Fukase Chūichi, "Nihon no Rippō Katei no Tokushoku" (Characteristics of the Japanese Legislative Process), *Jurisuto* 805 (1 January, 1984): 21.

3. For example, in 1965, the Japan Communist Party (which one would expect to be the most vehemently anti-LDP) consented to only 3 percent of the legislative bills introduced by the cabinet; by 1979 this proportion had risen to 69 percent. The proportion for the other opposition parties for the period 1965–87 was similarly high: New Liberal Club, 94 percent; Democratic Socialist Party, 84 percent; Kōmeitō, 78 percent; and Japan Socialist Party, 68 percent. This trend became especially remarkable during the period 1973–79, when the Diet was moving from confrontational to cooperative interparty relationships.

CHAPTER 3

PARLIAMENT AND CABINET

POPULAR SOVEREIGNTY AND THE
PARLIAMENTARY SYSTEM

A cabinet form of government was established in Japan in December 1885. At its outset, the Meiji regime had adopted a conciliar form of the executive branch that went all the way back to the Heian period (794–1185), but in order to modernize (read "Westernize") its administrative system, at least formally, it introduced cabinet government. With this step the regime hoped to institutionalize a system based on the supreme executive power of the sovereign emperor before convoking the Imperial Diet, planned for 1890.

According to the Meiji Constitution, promulgated in 1889, "The respective Ministers of State shall give their advice to the Emperor, and be responsible for it" (Article 55). Accordingly, the Imperial Edict of Cabinet Organization put the premier in the position only of first among equals. Each cabinet minister bore individual responsibility to advise the emperor, thus denying the principle of collective cabinet responsibility and reducing the power of both the premier and parliament. Moreover, the Constitution stipulated that the Army and Navy ministers were to be appointed by their respective services and had to be officers in active service. Consequently, there was inherent in this legal framework the dangers of cabinet fragmentation and collapse, as well as of undue military influence.

The postwar Japanese Constitution, promulgated in 1947, established a system true to the principles of parliamentary and cabinet government. The prime minister was to be chosen *by* and *from among* the members of parliament, which, as the elected representatives of the now-sovereign people, constituted the supreme organ of state power. Cabinet ministers, a majority of whom must also be MPs, are now appointed by the prime minister. In its exercise of executive power, the cabinet is collectively responsible to parliament, and in the event of a vote of no confidence in the government by the House of Representatives, the cabinet has 10 days within which either to dissolve parliament or resign.

In this manner, with the transfer of the locus of sovereignty, a system of responsible cabinet government, dependent only upon the confidence of parliament, was established. But the cabinet is not unilaterally dependent on parliament: not only does the cabinet submit legislation, the budget, treaties, and appointments to parliament, it can also respond to a vote of no confidence by dissolving parliament. For its part, parliament exercises its powers of administrative oversight through deliberation of the bills submitted to it and supervision of the daily actions of the cabinet. In this respect, there are mutual checks and balances inherent in the system of parliamentary/cabinet government. On the other hand, this form of government is inevitably drawn into the maelstrom of partisan politics, with both good and bad consequences for parliament. Cabinet and parliamentary "politics" in contemporary Japan must be considered within this context.

CABINET GOVERNMENT IN A PREDOMINANT-PARTY SYSTEM

Party politics in postwar Japan began as a competitive party system. From the merger of the conservative parties in 1955 until 1993, however, the party system was consistently dominated by the LDP. Party systems have been classified into seven types. In the "predominant-party" type of system, "parties other than the major one not only are permitted to exist, but do exist as legal and legitimate —if not necessarily effective—competitors of the predominant party. . . . A predominant-party system is such to the extent that, and as long as, its major party is consistently supported by a winning majority . . . of the voters."[1] This description neatly fits the Japanese party system between 1955 and 1993.

The permeation of the ruling party by corruption became increasingly apparent in the late 1980s, however, epitomized by the Recruit scandal of 1989, to which the public reacted with outrage. Support for the LDP plummeted in the House of Councillors election of July 1989, and it lost a majority of seats there for the first time since the founding of the party. Nevertheless, the LDP managed to maintain a majority of seats in the more powerful House of Representatives in the general election of February 1990. Although the LDP's control was seriously diluted, it is fair to say, however, that the Japanese party system still fit the model of a predominant-party system until the LDP lost control of the lower house in July 1993. Throughout, cabinet government in Japan was to a large extent controlled by the internal politics of the ruling party, in addition to parliamentary politics. Let us look now at this situation with reference to several aspects of cabinet government in the post-1955 period.

From the first House of Representatives election in April 1946 to the most recent, in July 1993, there have been 19 general elections in postwar Japan, with 13 since the conservative merger in 1955. Of these 13, the general election of 1976 came as the result of the house fulfilling its entire four-year term; all the others came as the result of dissolutions of the house.

Article 69 of the Constitution specifies dissolution of the lower house as one response the cabinet can make to passage of a motion of no confidence by that house. With a single predominant party, however, it was rare for the terms of Article 69 to be applied, since no opposition party or parties held enough seats to pass such a motion. Most postwar dissolutions have invoked, rather, Article 7, which allows the emperor to dissolve parliament with the advice and consent of the cabinet.

In 1948, during the tenure of the second Yoshida cabinet—which enjoyed only minority support in the House of Representatives—one constitutional scholar argued that the *cabinet* had the power, under Article 7, to dissolve parliament without need of a parliamentary vote of no confidence.[2] This interpretation set off a vigorous debate about whose prerogative parliamentary dissolution really was. Even today there is disagreement as to the constitutionality of such a dissolution, but under the terms of Article 7, dissolution of parliament has in fact become standard practice. Thus, even when major political confrontation like that caused by the Recruit scandal or the 1988–89 debate over tax reform erupts and the opposition parties call for a dissolution and new elections "to seek a judgment by the people," they actually appeal to the cabinet on the basis of Article 7.

Our aim here is not to debate further the constitutional propriety of parliamentary dissolution under the terms of Article 7. One could say that the flexible utilization of this type of dissolution introduces a healthy, plebiscitary element into policy debate. On the other hand, as the terms "consultative dissolution," "collusive dissolution," and "snap dissolution" suggest, dissolution has on occasion been used as a technique of ruling and opposition party wheeling and dealing or of ruling party coercion vis-à-vis the opposition. The people, therefore, unsurprisingly, no longer see a prime minister and cabinet as being electorally "purified" or legitimated when they dissolve parliament and are then reelected. To the extent that the people are aware of these compromises and deals, this tendency will become stronger.

Moreover, the cabinet's exercise of the power of dissolution has thus far been governed by the internal political dynamics of the ruling party. In a predominant-party system, where the president of the LDP became prime minister with little concern for the attitudes of parliament, dissolution was a move in the drama of prime ministerial succession. If the prime minister and his allies tried to strengthen their intraparty legitimacy with a dissolution followed by an electoral "appeal to the people," other intraparty forces tried to obstruct the move. Conversely, intraparty groups that did not support the prime minister tried to create a situation in which he had to resign by pushing him to dissolve parliament when they knew the party stood to lose parliamentary seats in the election to follow (even though the LDP would remain in power). Moreover, some of the opposition parties on occasion became participants in these stratagems. On the other hand, whenever a situation emerged in which the legitimacy of the ruling party was *really* called into question, the LDP simply installed a new prime minister and cabinet without dissolving parliament, thus hoping to clean up after the party's political failures and restore its image. Such "political cosmetic surgery" made the continuation of one-party dominance possible until the early 1990s, when an unprecedented string of scandals and the LDP refusal to implement meaningful political reforms finally cost the party its parliamentary majority.

Some of the pathologies of cabinet government under one-party predominance are reflected in the selection and terms of office of cabinet ministers. Since 1955 the average term of office of a cabinet minister has been only one year. On one or more occasions during his own term of office the typical prime minister has used his powers of appointment and dismissal of ministers to "reorganize" his cabinet. Needless to say, the reason for frequent cabinet reshuffles is simply to strengthen the intraparty base of the party president-cum-prime minister; they are unrelated to the parliamentary process. Until 1993 cabinet selections were made on the principle of factional balance among the major factions within the LDP.[3] This procedure, which developed under prime ministers Ikeda Hayato and Satō Eisaku in the 1960s and early 1970s, called for each faction, regardless of whether it supported the prime minister, to receive cabinet posts equivalent to the number of MPs in it. A comparison of the actual number of portfolios awarded to each faction in each cabinet since Ikeda's time with the predicted number of portfolios that would be awarded if cabinets were formed in proportion to the size of each faction has demonstrated a precise correspondence between the two.[4]

The frequency with which cabinets are reshuffled and the interfactional and interparty equity with which portfolios are awarded spread the opportunities for access to prestige and authority (and indebtedness to the prime minister) widely and evenly, thus preventing division within the ruling party or coalition. As this process of cabinet selection has become institutionalized, however, a very clear precedent of experience and prior posts has been created within which any MP who wishes to attain a cabinet post must proceed.[5] No matter how superior one's qualities, it is extremely rare for a freshman MP—at least under LDP rule—to become a cabinet minister. It can be argued that the institutionalization of this intraparty seniority system has hurt the party's ability to make maximum use of MPs of talent and capability,[6] and has sapped the vitality of the cabinet as well.

CABINET GOVERNMENT AND THE ADMINISTRATIVE BUREAUCRACY

Under a predominant-party system, cabinet government largely reflected the internal politics of the ruling party. Such a situation gave rise to a variety of problems in the relationships between both the cabinet as an institution and individual ministers, on the one hand, and the civil service on the other. As already noted, in a predominant-party system the cabinet does not derive its authority and legitimacy from having won the mantle of rule in electoral battle with its partisan competitors. This makes it very difficult to control the bureaucracy by wielding the symbolic political weapon of a popular mandate, a weapon that the current ruling coalition does have at its disposal. Moreover, in that the appointment, dismissal, and tenure of ministers are as capricious as described above, it is inevitable that ministerial control of the civil service, whose members are in office for life, is severely restricted. Ministers come and go so fast that bureaucratic wits refer to them as "Minister What's-his-name." And this transience may offset the power of the ruling coalition's mandate.

Of course, the bureaucrats cannot ignore the importance of either ministers or the cabinet. For this reason civil servants provide frequent briefings for ministers, hoping that by so doing the influence of their own agency will be enhanced. For their part, ministers attempt to realize the interests of their own factions, their constituents, and their favorite interest groups, by communicating them to the civil service—backed, of course, by the political clout of their ministerial position. This sort of collusive, mutually manipulative, apolitical process may make life easier for both politicians and bureaucrats, but, as economic friction with foreign countries increases, it raises the anxiety and mistrust with which Japan is regarded internationally. It may be that one of the reasons Japanese politics is seen as having deteriorated into a parochial fixation with domestic issues, with an utterly inadequate international perspective, is that the cabinet system, in the absence of alternation between ruling parties, simply fell victim to intraparty rivalry, party-bureaucracy collusion, and interest-group politics.

NOTES

1. Giovanni Sartori, *Parties and Political Systems*, Cambridge, Cambridge University Press, 1976, pp. 195–96.

2. Miyazawa Toshiyoshi, "Kaisan no Kenpōteki Imi" (The Constitutional Meaning of Dissolution), *Asahi Shinbun*, 8 November 1948.

3. After the 1993 election, the cabinet was formed on the principle of balance among the parties that made up the ruling coalition. The following were the results of that election and the cabinet posts appointed by party.

Party	Seats	Cabinet posts
Liberal Democratic Party	223	0
Japan Socialist Party	70	6
Shinsei	55	5
Kōmeitō	51	4
Japan New Party	35	1
Democratic Socialist Party	15	1
Japan Communist Party	15	0
Sakigake	13	1
Social Democratic League	4	1
Independents	30	0
Nonpoliticians	—	2

4. Ishikawa Masumi, *Dēta: Sengo Seiji Shi* (Data: Postwar Political History), Iwanami, 1984, p. 219.

5. An MP's first term in parliament is a time of familiarization. During their second term, the MP should become a director or political affairs assistant on a standing committee. In the third term, the MP should be chair of a committee of the LDP's Policy Affairs Research Council, and, in the fourth, an assistant to the LDP secretary general or a bureau chief in the party secretariat. Such a record will, by the fifth term, qualify an MP for a cabinet post. In the general election of 1983, 259 LDP candidates were elected; of the 34 MPs who thus won a sixth term, 24 (71 percent) had cabinet experience, as did 19 of the 22 who won a seventh term (86 percent). Of the 23 who then began their fifth term, only 4 had had cabinet experience, and only 1 of the 32 fourth-termers had done so.

6. Sasaki Takeshi, *Jimintō wa Saisei Dekiru no ka?* (Can the LDP Regenerate Itself?), Nihon Keizai Shinbun, 1989, p. 62.

CHAPTER 4

THE CIVIL SERVICE BUREAUCRACY

FORMATION OF THE MODERN JAPANESE BUREAUCRACY

The German sociologist Max Weber described bureaucratic rule as the truest form of rational-legal authority.[1] Bureaucratic administration is also perhaps the ideal institutional vehicle for the rule of law that emerged from the popular revolutions of the modern age. The reason for this is that the formulation and execution of law, so necessary to modern democracy, are not necessarily in and of themselves rational. Law implemented by bureaucratic agencies, however, partakes in the process of the rationality—the objectivity, precision, stability, promptness, and efficiency—characteristic of the internal processes of bureaucratic organizations. This is the reason that bureaucratic organization has been broadly adopted in modern societies—not only in public administration but also in corporations, schools, churches, and other large-scale social organizations.

In Japan, a Weberian type of civil service bureaucracy was adopted, at least in form, soon after the Meiji Restoration. A bureaucratic administrative structure was established in Japan between 1885—when the cabinet system was established—and 1899. In replacing a more traditional conciliar executive with a cabinet system, and integrating it with the administrative apparatus, the Meiji government put into place the institutional framework within which parliament would be established and by which its unpredictable democratic impulses could be restrained. But institutions alone would not suffice; the modernization of Japan also created the need for administrative personnel with specialized knowledge and training. In 1886, a Faculty of Law was therefore established at Tokyo Imperial University for the express purpose of preparing government officials, and its graduates were appointed to the higher civil service without having to take the standard civil service examination. In

1893, this special privilege was abolished, and new rules for administrative appointments and edicts on civil service examination established, at least formally, the principle of recruiting administrative talent according to merit. Moreover, an examination system was introduced for entry to the Foreign and Justice ministries. Finally, in 1899, the influence of partisan politics on the administrative recruitment process was strictly circumscribed, and a disciplinary code and a detailed set of regulations governing official roles, advancement, duties, and prerogatives were adopted, completing the institutional and personnel structure of a modern system of public administration.

Thus, the civil service system established around the turn of the century was based on a merit system and did, in fact, open the door to public service widely to society. At the same time, however, under the principle of imperial sovereignty, officials, once appointed, were expected to serve the throne with selfless loyalty. Government officials were not the *public* servants found in countries that had undergone the democratic revolutions of the modern era; rather, they were exclusively servants of the emperor. Thus, as the old saying that "officials are revered, the people are despised" implies, an almost feudalistic status relationship of arrogance and subservience grew up between public officials and society. Moreover, within the civil service, sharp status distinctions differentiating officials personally appointed by the emperor, appointed in his name, or approved by him, and junior officials were introduced in addition to distinctions based on function.

Despite its meritocratic procedures and criteria, this system of public administration became the object of widespread patronage under the party governments of the 1920s. Given its own immaturity and ineptitude as well as the radical upheavals of the domestic and international environment during the 1920s, however, party government did not survive. With this disarray of parties and parliament in the background, a band of self-styled "progressive bureaucrats" pushed to the fore. They wanted to eliminate what they saw as inept, corrupt party government and create a more coherent, disciplined organization to lead the political administration, free of partisan squabbling and democratic constraints. Ultimately, they threw in with the military and created a dictatorship. This signified the extraordinary politicization of an officialdom ideally sworn to selfless service to the throne, and it is to this type of politicized civil servant with a distinct political agenda that the word *kanryō*—the Japanese equivalent of "bureaucrat," which became common usage at that time—refers.

TRANSFORMATION OF SOVEREIGNTY AND THE IDEA OF THE PUBLIC SERVANT

The fundamental transformation of sovereignty after the war also brought a fundamental transformation in the position of government officialdom. Under popular sovereignty, civil administrators became *public* servants, that is, employees of the citizenry. Additionally, they lost their special status. Personnel administration became subject to the Public Service Act, and was managed by an autonomous National Personnel Authority in order to guarantee its political neutrality. This transformation of political principles did not, however, bring instant changes in bureaucratic behavior. At the time, Tsuji Kiyoaki, a scholar of public administration, advised four requisites for a system of public service capable of efficiently performing administrative functions in a way consistent with democratic control by the people: (1) the number of political appointees should be increased, at least to the level of vice-minister; (2) procedures for the impeachment of civil servants should be instituted; (3) means of democratic control of the National Personnel Authority should be instituted; and (4) political activity by lower-level civil servants should be permitted.[2]

None of these recommendations has ever been implemented. Indeed, since the functions of the postwar Japanese bureaucracy have grown in conjunction with the growth of the welfare state, the absence of such structures of democratic control over the bureaucracy has meant that the civil service has been at increasing risk of running completely out of control.

ADMINISTRATIVE GUIDANCE AND THE BUREAUCRACY

One very effective method of policy implementation possessed by the Japanese civil service is the practice known as administrative guidance (*gyōsei shidō*). According to a former director of the Cabinet Legislative Bureau, administrative guidance ideally "refers to a practice by which administrative agencies attempt to get specific individuals, corporations, organizations, etc., to do their bidding in regard to the application or execution of law in a specific administrative area. This is done not by autocratically commanding or coercing them, or even by guiding, advising, or suggesting, on the basis of some legal rationale, that they do something 'voluntarily.' Rather, with no basis at all in law, it elicits spontaneous agreement and cooperation from the other party by letting it know what the administrative organ hopes or wishes to see done or realized."[3] This often-quoted definition of the concept contains much value. Nevertheless, there are some ways in which the definition does not reflect reality.

One can distinguish between two types of administrative guidance: first are courses of action that civil servants recommend when approached with applications for approvals, and that will soon be required by law. Second is policy guidance, offered when there is no clearly applicable provision in the law relevant to the matter at hand: for example, in the coordination of production in industries like petroleum refining, steel manufacturing, or agriculture, or when advising local governments to adjust the salaries of their personnel. In any of these cases, however, administrative guidance is not simply a matter of generating "spontaneous agreement and cooperation" in accordance with an expression of "hopes or wishes." It is backed by the informal or indirect threat of sanctions: approval of a pending request may be revoked or some benefit such as financing or a subsidy may be withheld. The above definition is correct, however, in suggesting that administrative guidance is not simply a matter of bureaucratic coercion. In the words of a senior Finance Ministry official, on occasion industrial sectors also ask the bureaucrats for "a bit of guidance, please," when they have failed to resolve conflicts of interest among their members. They thus entrust conflict resolution to the bureaucrats.[4]

In any event, the concrete direction of administration is often determined through administrative guidance. Indeed, administrative guidance is the very core of postwar Japanese public administration. In Japanese administration, utterly extralegal administrative guidance is a source of authority on a par with—indeed, superior to—discretionary application of the law to specific cases. And the commonality of interests between administrators and the private sector that both results from and leads to administrative guidance both makes possible the bureaucrats' expectations of a comfortable second career after they leave public service and gives rise to official corruption. Insofar as administrative guidance is central to administrative behavior, the rationality of bureaucratic organization described by Max Weber assumes a very different form in contemporary Japan. It has been argued that administrative guidance has contributed a major element of stability to administration, economic growth, and society in Japan. In a time of increasing economic friction between Japan and its trading partners, however, administrative guidance is seen as a nontariff trade barrier and, as a type of government-business collusion, is severely criticized by foreign countries.

THE RINGI SYSTEM AND BUREAUCRATIC DECISION-MAKING

How, then, are the outward signs of administrative purpose—including but not limited to administrative guidance—internally arrived at? In the past, the decision-making process in the Japanese bureaucracy has been discussed under the concept of the *ringi* system. Tsuji Kiyoaki explains the concept as follows. In the *ringi* system, policy plans and proposals are originated by administrators at the very bottom of the bureaucratic hierarchy, and written up in a specified form (a *ringi* document, or *ringi-sho*) for approval by superior officials. It is circulated in sequence to all officials under whose jurisdiction the matter in question falls and then begins to work its way up the administrative hierarchy, being approved at each step, finally reaching the person at the top empowered to give it final approval. The problems with this process are, first, that it takes a *ringi-sho* a long time to work its way up to the final arbiter, and thus invites inefficiency. Second, by the time the form reaches the top, it has been signed by anywhere from dozens to over 100 bureaucrats, each of whom reads it but none of whom has more than "one signature's worth of responsibility" for its contents, thus diffusing—if not completely camouflaging—accountability. Third, this bottom-up decisional process has been so solidly institutionalized that even if top civil servants want to exercise leadership they have almost no room to do so: a thoroughly circulated *ringi* form has all the appearance of a unanimous ministerial decision. Thus, the leadership of top bureaucrats is seriously compromised.[5]

It is unquestionable that the *ringi* system of decision-making has been internalized by the bureaucracy. One must keep in mind, however, that the simple term "decision-making" comprises everything from day-to-day administrative business to matters involving important policy evaluations. Moreover, there are decisions for which even a pro forma *ringi* process is inappropriate, such as decisions on draft budget requests and the compilation of materials for ministerial interpellations in parliament. Recent research has made it clear that, although the *ringi* process described above applies to routine business and discretionary administrative actions, when it comes to matters requiring important policy judgments, thorough discussion takes place among relevant officials, especially top administrators, *before* the *ringi* process is initiated. It is only after such discussion is concluded that the agreed-upon items are incorporated into a *ringi-sho* and begin their trip through the approval cycle.

Moreover, there are a variety of expediting devices, such as altering the sequence or number of approvals necessary, that can be resorted to in order to speed up the whole process. Consequently, the negative aspects of the process described above do not necessarily affect the whole administrative decision-making process.

These devices may also have the effect of reducing the diffusion of administrative responsibility. From the perspective of the people, however, there is another problem regarding the diffusion of responsibility. In the administrative system, authority derives less from one's position in the hierarchy than from one's membership in administrative units such as bureaus, departments, and sections. As a result, collective considerations take precedence over functional ones, leading to intense sectionalism both within and between government agencies. Although the coordinating effects of the *ringi* system and of ministry-wide staff organs (personnel, archives, accounting, and so forth) reduce the damage from this sort of group consciousness within specific ministries, inter-agency coordination and integration are exceedingly difficult in the state's administrative apparatus as a whole. Moreover, the fact that not only ministries but even bureaus and departments act monolithically hinders organizational self-assessment either before or after the fact. The result is an administrative style that depends too much on formal planning and not enough on a creative response to problems arising in the course of political events.

NOTES

1. Bureaucracy, as opposed to rule by an individual, a council of elders, or a hereditary nobility, etc., is a hierarchical, rule-governed form of administration in which:
   (a) offices have fixed powers and duties;
   (b) an official's power derives solely from the position held;
   (c) these powers and duties, and administrative procedures, are themselves determined by formal rules; and
   (d) offices are filled by persons with specified qualifications.
See H.H. Gerth and C. Wright Mills, *From Max Weber*, New York, Oxford University Press, 1981, p. 196.
2. Tsuji Kiyoaki, "Kōmuinsei no Igi to Genkai" (The Significance and Limits of the Public Service System) (1949), reprinted in his *Shinpan Nihon Kanryōsei no Kenkyū* (A Study of the Japanese Bureaucracy), University of Tokyo Press, 1969, pp. 3–58.
3. Hayashi Shūzō, "Iwayuru Gyōsei Shidō ni tsuite" (On the So-called Administrative Guidance), *Gyōsei to Keiei* 4 (1962): 17.
4. Tanimura Yutaka, in Ōkita Saburō, *Nihon Kanryō Jijō* (The Japanese Bureaucrat), TBS Britannica, 1984, p. 162.
5. Tsuji, *Shinpan Nihon Kanryōsei no Kenkyū*, pp. 155ff.

CHAPTER 5

ADVISORY COUNCILS

DEVELOPMENT OF ADVISORY COUNCILS

One major actor in the planning process, which has also come in recent years to add flexibility to administration, is the advisory council. Such appointive councils, or *shingikai*, are consultative organs to agencies of the executive branch, and are found in contemporary Japan in large numbers in both national and local government. Typically, their members include representatives of the major parties, business, labor, powerful interest groups, academia, and the general public. The legal origins of national-level advisory councils lie in Article 8 of the National Administrative Organization Act (NAOA), although each is created through a separate ordinance of establishment. Although referred to generically as *shingikai*, their individual titles, scales, and functions are not uniform. Local governmental advisory councils, further, include some whose establishment is mandated by national ordinances and some that are established autonomously. On this level, too, there are a variety of names for such councils. But this structural, functional, semantic, and legal variety should not mask their ubiquity.

Advisory councils did not become common until after World War II. A small number of consultative committees were recognized by the prewar state, but they were exceptional. As we have seen, the Meiji modernization produced a state with a very powerful bureaucracy. Under imperial sovereignty, public officials were servants of the emperor, and it was unnecessary to take any broad measures—such as public consultation—to legitimize their coordination of public interests.

Although under the postwar constitution the administrative bureaucracy became the repository of even greater specialized knowledge, its status changed diametrically, from that of imperial servant to *public* servant. For the first time the bureaucracy had to worry about its relationship with parliament, now the highest agent of popular sovereignty. So the bureaucracy, wishing to preserve and enhance its prestige and authority, had to develop some system of its own for responding to (and thus being able to claim to express) the "will of the people." A system of advisory councils—"a flexible policy of response to change in its environment"—was the bureaucracy's solution.[1]

In fact, when NAOA took effect in 1949 there were already 352 advisory councils in existence. In that year the number dropped by roughly half, to 184; still, this number represented a dramatic increase from the prewar period. The number of councils has fluctuated between 200 and 280 since that time; in 1991 their number stood at 212. As this number suggests, advisory councils have been established as a means of turf defense and image enhancement not only by each ministry but also by individual bureaus within ministries.

In general, it was expected that the advisory council system would resolve conflicts of popular interest on specific issues and, by articulating publicly supported policy recommendations, exert influence over the executive branch. Moreover, according to a survey of the attitudes of civil servants, the bureaucrats also see the advisory councils as ensuring equity in policy.[2] One should also not forget, however, that the executive impetus behind the development of the postwar advisory council system was a desire to counteract the diminished authority of the civil service after World War II and to generate public trust in the impartiality and openness of the bureaucracy. Thus, one should not be surprised to find that the public function and the *actual* role of advisory councils do not precisely coincide.

POLICY FORMATION AND THE ORGANIZATION AND FUNCTIONS OF ADVISORY COUNCILS

The 212 advisory councils attached to the agencies of the national government vary greatly in objectives, functions, and scope. They have been defined broadly according to two types of functions. The first type were councils of "inquiry" or "advice," which conducted inquiries into important issues and policy questions, either in response to a request from their parent agency or on their own initiative, usually resulting in policy recommendations to the parent agency. The second type were "judicial" or "authorizing" councils, whose primary functions were to adjudicate between contradictory public views of policy and to evaluate and authorize test and professional standards and qualifications, to determine official compensation, for example, in order to ensure equity in the application of law. Although this definition is slightly arbitrary, it seems clear that, for example, the Land Appraisal Committee, the Certified Public Accountants Examination Board, and the Central Pharmaceutical Affairs Council (attached to the National Land Agency, the Finance Ministry, and the Ministry of Health and Welfare, respectively) all belong to the second category.

Although one should not underestimate the influence of the second type of advisory council vis-à-vis the decision-making processes of administrative agencies, the core of the debate concerning the role of advisory councils in contemporary Japanese politics focuses on advisory councils of the first type. But it is no simple matter to evaluate the influence of advisory councils in the policy process, because even among the advisory councils of inquiry there is wide variety. For example, such councils as the Investigatory Commission on the Constitution (in session 1957–62) and the first and second Ad Hoc Commissions on Administration (1962–64 and 1981–83) dealt with constitutional revision and administrative reform, issues of fundamental importance in postwar politics, and as such were of special significance. One may also include the Eighth Election System Council, established in 1989, in this category.

Even when one excludes such extraordinary advisory councils as these, there are, among those remaining, a number that focus on the operation and reform of systems central to the state, such as the Tax Commission, the Fiscal System Council, the Social Security Commission, and the Council on Local Government, and others that focus on major national economic and social policies, such as the National Land Development Council. In addition, there are a large number of advisory councils whose jurisdictions cover narrower policy areas. All of these myriad advisory councils, each in accord with its own procedures, have made their own contributions to the coordination of social interests and infusion of specialized knowledge into administration. One can see such contributions in, for example, the role of the Social Security Commission in the development of the pension system, and that of the Petroleum Council in energy policy.

On the subject of coordinating interests, however, one must ask exactly *whose* interests are reflected in the deliberations of the advisory councils, and, on the other side of the coin, exactly what are the *motives* of the administrative agencies in creating and making use of the councils. One retired civil servant has distinguished between three types of motives behind the solicitation of advice from the councils. First are instances in which the bureaucrats were truly at a loss to decide the direction of policy. Second are instances in which the agency had developed multiple alternative policies to achieve its goals and requested the councils to consider which of them was best. Third are instances in which "the substance of a report had already been prepared by the agency. In order to lend it an air of objectivity and make it more persuasive to third parties, however, it was preferable to present it in the form of a report of the advisory council."[3]

As the above passage makes bluntly clear, an agency's motives for consulting with its advisory councils are hardly unrelated to the interests of the agency itself. Indeed, the third instance is nothing more than the legitimization of agency policy by the council, and the interests represented on the advisory councils (that is, the selection of council members themselves) are hardly independent of this context. Each agency appoints its own advisory councils, and the only selection criteria that are made public involve members' age, terms of appointment, and number of other offices concurrently held. In fact, almost all members are academics and representatives of large interest groups with intimate connections to the administrative agency in question. Moreover, historically speaking, it is extremely rare to find an advisory council with its own staff. All logistical and administrative tasks of the councils are taken care of by the parent administrative agency. In light of this, it is only a slight exaggeration to say that administrative agencies establish advisory councils as their private cheering sections.

In many cases, however, the formulation of national policy requires the coordination of views among multiple governmental agencies. For example, in the establishment of an organization to provide benefits to local public employees, the reports of the Council on Local Government and the Social Security Commission disagreed. This was, in fact, a thinly disguised case of competition between the Ministry of Home Affairs and the Ministry of Health and Welfare. This sort of rivalry and opposition between concerned agencies is a daily administrative occurrence, but in this case the Ministry of Finance was also drawn in. As the official quoted above put it, the Health and Welfare Ministry is involved in all "issues of popular livelihood. So is the Economic Planning Agency. So is the Construction Ministry. [Consequently,] their public statements of principle are very similar. But when it comes to concrete policy they have very different positions. So the Finance Ministry ends up receiving its own council report, which recommends that no budgetary allocation at all be made, and all the other ministries end up with reports from their respective advisory councils, which recommend that their own budgets be increased for the purpose."[4]

When advisory councils serve as tools in these sorts of interagency rivalries, the resolution of interagency disagreements becomes all the more difficult. During the years of rapid economic growth from the mid-1960s to mid-1970s, when everyone could anticipate a comfortable natural annual increase in revenues (and therefore in their own budgets), interagency rivalry did not reach too feverish a level. The acute financial constraints that became endemic after the mid-1970s, and especially in the 1980s, however, made hard choices unavoidable and brought about important changes in the functions of the advisory councils.

CHANGES IN THE POLICY-FORMATION PROCESS AND THE ADVISORY COUNCILS

As noted, in the early postwar period administrative agencies played the leading role in initiating, deciding, and executing public policy. The ruling party, acting rather like an interest group, expanded the national budget annually and provided benefits to a wide variety of constituent groups, thus preserving its electoral base. With the deepening of the financial crisis, however, this pork-barrel method of vote mobilization became less affordable. Amid such conditions, the ruling party, in order to stay in power, found it necessary to strengthen its ties with the most powerful (and well-heeled) interest groups and to assert authority over the bureaucracy. In this process lies the reason why the pathological, corrupt interdependence of the LDP and the business world became so much more obvious during the 1980s.

From the perspective of the advisory council system, the significance of the financial crunch of the 1970s lies in the increase of advisory councils attached to the Prime Minister's Office whose purpose was interagency coordination. "To the extent that this type of advisory council comes to perform coordinating functions, it will become more and more difficult for the bureaucrats to use the councils to enhance their own authority. . . . [Moreover, the consequence of coordination will on] occasion probably be to force major compromises and concessions upon particular ministries."[5]

In fact, the advisory councils in the 1980s dealing with fundamental administrative and financial institutions—such as the Second Ad Hoc Commission on Administration, the Tax Commission, and the Fiscal System Council—have, in conjunction with the business community (which became politically activated in its pursuit of lower taxes) and with the political style of then Prime Minister Nakasone Yasuhiro (who was trying to demonstrate his own independence and political leadership), increased their autonomy vis-à-vis the bureaucratic organs. As can be seen in government budgets of the 1980s, in policy areas such as social welfare, education, construction, transportation, and so forth, the councils have extracted major concessions in the form of expenditure reduction and policy implementation from the ministries concerned. The leading members of these prime ministerial councils—as epitomized by the appointment of business doyen Dokō Toshio, the former chairman of the Federation of Economic Organizations (Keizai Dantai Rengōkai, Keidanren)—are representatives of specific interest groups of extraordinary power. In addition to appointments such as these are people of prestige, learning, and experience with close relationships with the prime minister.

PRIVATE CONSULTATIVE ORGANS

Concomitant with these changes in the functions of the advisory councils during the 1980s was an increase in the number of private consultative organs—"discussion groups," "study groups," and the like—attached personally to the prime minister and certain cabinet ministers. Formerly, such private advisory organs performed the same functions as those of the more politically accountable public advisory councils, but were criticized for existing in the shadows of the law and for blurring administrative responsibility. But the activities of the private advisory organs of the 1980s must be understood within the context of the changes in the policy process described above. That is, they were not simply additional advisory councils dealing with legal regulations; rather, their objective was to actively mobilize expert knowledge for the prime minister or other ministers who could use it, in turn, to manage public opinion on the one hand and the administrative machinery on the other.

Private advisory organs do not require parliamentary approval of their members, and their expenditures do not appear as separate items in the government budget. They are, therefore, extremely valuable as flexible, autonomous tools for the direction of policy. As vehicles for bypassing the bureaucracy, they strengthen the political leadership of the prime minister and the other ministers. At the same time, however—as was seen in the study groups on sensitive policy issues, such as peace and security, as in the case of Prime Minister Nakasone's Peace Issues Study Group and Yasukuni Shrine Discussion Group—the determination of state policies and the legitimation of the actions of political leaders by nonelected councils, however widely drawn from society, is highly problematic from a democratic perspective. And, as the LDP's grip on power was shaken at the end of the 1980s by an enraged public opinion, it indeed began to look as if both public and private advisory groups were being given a less active role. The concentration of decision-making power in these private advisory councils in the 1980s, however, in fact *attest to* the need for a system of advisory councils, in a tense relationship between powerful interest groups and bureaucrats and parliamentary democracy.

NOTES

1. Abe Hitoshi, "Shingikai Seido no Suii" (Changes in the Advisory Council System), *Chiiki Kaihatsu* (January 1978): 10.
2. Muramatsu Michio, *Sengo Nihon no Kanryōsei* (Postwar Japan's Bureaucracy), Tōyō Keizai Shinpōsha, 1981, pp. 124–28.
3. Sakuma Tsutomu, former director, Administrative Bureau, Ministry of Home Affairs, quoted in "Zadankai: Shingikai" (Round Table on Advisory Councils), *Jurisuto* 510 (15 July 1972): 38–39.
4. *Ibid.*, p. 56.
5. Abe, "Shingikai Seido no Suii," p. 14.

CHAPTER 6

INTEREST GROUPS AND THE ADMINISTRATIVE BRANCH

THE "ANOMALOUS ADMINISTRATIVE STATE" AND INTEREST GROUPS

We have already alluded to the role of interest groups vis-à-vis the advisory councils and parliamentary process. Let us look now at the role played by interest groups on the administrative side of contemporary Japanese government. Historically, interest groups emerged in the West as part of the political process during the transition from the "legislative state"—in which parliament dominated government—to the "administrative state," in which civil servants came to rival or surpass the legislature in power. Modern Japan never underwent this transition, however, because at the very beginning of its modern era a system of administrative-bureaucratic control with the emperor at its summit was established. Ideologically, the traditional familial-communitarian order was universalized to the level of the state.[1] Of course, as part of the Westernization of the political system, a parliament (the Imperial Diet) and a judicial system were also established. As the law itself emanated originally from the sovereign emperor at the summit of this familial community, however, the autonomous rule of law could not be established. Moreover, it was impossible to adjust conflicting interests disinterestedly and rationally because the mediating agency between social interests and the supreme sovereign was none other than the administrative bureaucracy, sworn to loyalty to the throne. Thus, modern Japan was an administrative state from the day of its birth. But it was an anomaly as such in that—unlike the Anglo-European democracies—it had no structure capable of controlling the administrative bureaucracy politically and there was no imperative for the bureaucracy to try to persuade the people of the legitimacy of its actions.

46

But, even in this intrinsically anomalous administrative state, in consequence of the growth of capitalism, the 1920s saw an upsurge of increasingly politicized social groups. Additionally, the development of party politics at that time enabled the interests of these social groups to be reflected to a certain extent in the political process. Given the short life of party government and the autocratic wartime state—centered upon the military and the bureaucracy—that followed it, however, it was inevitable that the expression of social interests was severely repressed. In the 1940s most economic and social groups were incorporated into the government-sponsored and -controlled "imperial rule assistance system," in which they were transformed from organizations expressing the interests of specific groups into government tools for mobilizing these same groups in support of the regime.

PARTIES AND INTEREST GROUPS IN POSTWAR POLITICS

The postwar constitutional guarantees of freedom of political activity and association gave rise to a great number of political parties and the eruption of a great number and variety of interest groups. The parties went through a period of merger and fragmentation, schism and unification, which ended in 1955 with the creation of a predominant-party system under the reunified conservatives, who reflected primarily the interests of business, agriculture, and rural areas. They were confronted by a unified Left in opposition, which represented primarily the interests of organized labor, both white- and blue-collar. With rapid economic growth, interest groups grew more influential and more pluralistic. This process is clearly visible in the multiplication of groups representing every sector of the economy—finance, industry, agriculture, labor, and so on—and the efflorescence of smaller interest groups representing regional interests of every hue.

According to political scientist Maruyama Masao, however, the postwar relationship between parties and interest groups became distorted: the parties were consumed with elite-level power politics and had abdicated their usual functions of linking society and government and mobilizing the people for political participation. In consequence, "labor unions and other ostensibly economic organizations, religious groups, [and other interest groups] are filling the vacuum. And, analogously, makeshift, emergency groups organized at the grassroots level, such as neighborhood watch and children's protection groups, have come to perform the functions of pressure groups.

Thus the functions of parties, interest groups, and civic groups have all slipped one notch away from their proper roles."[2]

Postwar politics has indeed developed with parties at its core, but the organizational and financial foundations and policy competence of the parties have been tenuous. In an age of mass society, parties must "massify" their base. Postwar Japanese political parties, however, in their recruitment of candidates, fund raising, and campaigning, have become narrowly dependent on specific, major interest groups. The seduction and incorporation of the parties have taken place among both government and opposition, to such an extent that people ridicule one party or another as the "political arm of group X." Paradoxically, the fact that interest groups try to co-opt the parties in this way is wry testimony to the legitimacy of the postwar political system of "party-centric" parliamentary government.

At the same time that they have developed these sorts of relationships with the parties, interest groups have also brought their pressure-group activities to bear on the administrative branch. As already noted, in the modern state the civil service is influential in the formulation and execution of policy. In Japan, an administrative state from the beginning, this trend is even more striking. For the bureaucracy, too, the utility of particular interest groups as clients is great, and the number and variety of channels through which interest groups pressure the bureaucracy have thus multiplied through mutual consent. Interest groups get their representatives appointed to public consultative organs, such as the advisory councils. They use the parties—in particular, those intraparty groups of special-interest representatives known as *zoku* politicians[3]—to control the bureaucracy. And they provide employment to bureaucrats who retire from the agencies to which their interests are intimately related, and lobby the agencies through them. Of course, none of these methods is mutually exclusive—they are brought to bear simultaneously in combination in pursuit of group goals.

Additionally, interest groups that are weak in political resources can mobilize mass movements. They can also plead the legitimacy of their interests through the mass media. And any new interest group can build groups of supporters within the political parties from scratch by contributing money to them and, through them, communicate its interests to the civil servants.

Amid all this lobbying activity it is unsurprising that, on occasion, corruption surfaces. More serious than specific incidents of corrupt behavior, however, is the incessant, daily flow of vast amounts of money into the coffers of the parties from the major interest groups. The Political Funds Regulation Law sets an upper limit of ¥100 million on political contributions by one corporation, but pressures to raise this limit are increasing. It is probably no exaggeration to say, therefore, that the predominant-party system of the last 30-plus years has produced a government tilted decisively toward the interests of those groups most able to keep the political contributions flowing bountifully. Thus, the interrelationship of politics, administration, and business is described with the word "adhesion"—the sticky fingers of all three groups keep them bonded inseparably together.

THE PLURALISTIC STRUCTURE OF INTEREST GROUPS

It is a political given in contemporary Japan that the influence of the business world prevails over that of both party and bureaucratic elites. When one speaks of the business world, however, one must keep in mind that it is not a monolith—there is no single "Japan, Inc." The Federation of Economic Organizations (Keidanren), which stands at the peak of the business world, shelters under its umbrella a large number of sectoral and industry-specific organizations. But it is rare, and difficult, for Keidanren simply to adjust the views of all these constituent organizations and communicate them to the parties and the administration. Keidanren does articulate to the political and administrative elites the interests of the uppermost echelons of the big-business community, but the interests of all the myriad sectors of the economic world are communicated by their respective representative organizations. In fact, the dramatic changes in Japan's economic structure that have occurred since the period of rapid economic growth have made the adjustment of views between economic organizations increasingly difficult, heightening even more the activism of these smaller organizations. The conflict between the banking and securities industries over the issue of the liberalization of Japanese financial markets is one good recent example of this. Since the late 1960s, the activity of business organizations increased, and the ties between business-related *zoku* politicians within the LDP and their administrative counterparts deepened accordingly.

The same sorts of trends are visible in major interest groups in other areas. Neither agricultural nor medical interests are represented monolithically; conflicts of interest arise between component groups beneath the national peak groups in each field, and the component groups consequently increase in autonomy. The power of peak organizations in labor, ranked right alongside employers' organizations in interest-group power, has also weakened with changes in the economic structure, while the political influence of sectoral federations of enterprise-specific unions has risen. Moreover, these federations have induced the labor movement to change its central strategy from ensuring the interests of labor through negotiations with management to securing the interests of workers in each specific sector through political activity.

Thus, the economic changes that followed the period of high-speed economic growth resulted in the pluralization of interest groups. If one considers the ties between interest groups on the one hand and administrative agencies of the central government and the *zoku* MPs in the LDP on the other to constitute the major nexus of the policy process, then this nexus, too, has become multidimensional.

Along with the pluralization of interest groups, however, there have also grown up in flourishing numbers public-interest groups, organizations of a type quite different from previous types of interest groups. This phenomenon became visible in other advanced industrial democracies in the 1970s, and in Japan, too, movements concerned with environmental conservation, consumer protection, elimination of discrimination on the basis of gender and physical disability, and similar issues of fairness and equality in quality of life have emerged in great numbers. Such groups have called for the reform of both local and national political and administrative structures and practices, and for policy formation reflecting their interests.

CORPORATISM IN JAPAN

The multiplicity of interest groups and the diversity of the policy process may give the impression that an image of American-style pluralist politics applies equally to contemporary Japanese politics. The pluralist structure we have been looking at is, however, not unrelated to the vast volume of financial resources that sustains it. All of the industrial democracies, including Japan, have since the late 1970s encountered long-term economic stagnation and deep financial crisis, and plutocratic pluralism may be a luxury the Japanese interest-group system can no longer afford. By the early 1990s, the system appeared to be spinning out of control. Scandals seemed to surface daily, and revelations of flows of billions of yen—both legal and illegal—from interest groups of all kinds to politicians permeated the mass media.

In this setting, the argument has grown that the form of political integration in these societies is changing from pluralism to corporatism. A pluralist system is one where myriad organized interests all compete freely, and government mediates their competition and allocates benefits in such a way that, over time, all have some say in policy and thus are integrated into the system. Corporatism, which appeared first in northern Europe, is equally consistent with parliamentary democracy. But it attempts to achieve political integration through policies and benefits allocated through agreements made between one or a few giant interest groups in each social or economic sector—such as business, labor, and agriculture—that are formally or informally recognized by government to speak for all the groups in that sector. These agreements, in which the bureaucracy is also a participant, are then ratified by government. Even major policies like economic policy and income policy are reached in fact in concert through labor–management consultation or co-optation of labor organizations.[4]

There are indications that in Japan, too, at least since the 1980s, this type of transformation is occurring. In particular, in November 1989 the two major labor federations of Sōhyō (comprising primarily public-sector unions) and Rengō (a federation of private-sector unions) merged to form the eight-million-strong All-Japan General Federation of Labor Unions (also abbreviated to Rengō). Rengō's public goal is improving worker livelihood through union activity, but it is really a massive, nonelectoral political organization that is, in fact, inching toward electoral status, having established its own political arm (Rengō Sangiin) in the upper house of parliament.

In the 1970s, when the labor movement was fragmented and largely excluded from the political process, Japanese corporatism was referred to as "corporatism without labor." Depending on the course Rengō takes, however, one may expect a more European style of corporatism to emerge in which massive peak groups in both business and labor hammer out major economic policy agreements that are then essentially approved by government.[5] In any case, the question of what influence this form of political integration will have on the plurality of existing interest groups, the rise of public-interest groups, and the relationship between interest groups and parties will constitute one major theme in Japanese politics in the future.

NOTES

1. Fujita Shōzō, *Tennōsei Kokka no Shihai Genri* (Sovereignty in an Emperor-centered State), Miraisha, 1966.

2. Maruyama Masao, *Gendai Seiji no Shisō to Kōdō* (Thought and Behavior in Modern Japanese Politics), Miraisha, 1964, p. 531.

3. I am here following Satō Seizaburō's definition of "*zoku* MPs" as "groups of leading MPs, organized around the interests of specific adminis-

trative agencies, who exert influence on a daily basis on behalf of those interests." Satō Seizaburō and Matsuzaki Tetsuhisa, *Jimintō Seiken* (LDP Rule), Chūō Kōron, 1986, p. 92.

4. Jurg Steiner, *European Democracies*, 2nd ed., New York, Longman, 1991, ch. 14.

5. The term "corporatism without labor" is T.J. Pempel's. See T.J. Pempel and Keiichi Tsunekawa, "Corporatism Without Labor? The Japanese Anomaly," in Philippe Schmitter and Gerhard Lehmbruch, eds., *Trends toward Corporatist Intermediation*, Beverly Hills, Calif., Sage, 1979, p. 231.

PART 2

LOCAL GOVERNMENT AND INTERGOVERNMENTAL RELATIONS

CHAPTER 7

THE HISTORY OF LOCAL GOVERNMENT

LOCAL GOVERNMENT IN MEIJI JAPAN

Given its aim of creating a unified state under the emperor, it is unsurprising that the Meiji government considered the establishment of a comprehensive and consistent system of local government a major political imperative. This undertaking, which began in 1872 with the abolition of the feudal domains and the establishment of a system of prefectures, went through 20 years of trial and error: large and small units of local administration were tried and varieties of municipal and prefectural government and forms of local finance all came and went. It was not until 1890 that a system of regional and local government was decided on and became relatively stabilized.

During the 1880s, under the leadership of Home Minister Yamagata Aritomo, the Meiji government enacted a set of laws determining the structure of local governmental units, establishing a system of municipalities in 1888 and of prefectures and counties in 1890. Subsequently, the structure of local governmental officialdom, established by imperial ordinance in 1885 at the time of the creation of the cabinet system, was revised to accord with this new structure. The laws regulating the structure and staffing of local government were revised repeatedly in later years, but the basis of the legal system remained unchanged until the end of World War II.

The immediate impulse behind the institutionalization of the legal framework of local government was the Freedom and Popular Rights Movement of the 1880s. The Meiji government, an oligarchical, clan-based coalition of elements of the former lower warrior aristocracy, wished to create a stable system of domination over the entire nation. Moreover, it set as a goal the achievement of equality with other foreign powers, which required the modernization of Japan's systems of politics and administration. Toward these goals, in 1881, the emperor proclaimed that parliamentary government would be established in 1890; at the same time, the government began preparing for the promulgation of a constitution. When this political agenda became public, however, groups demanding immediate freedoms and popular rights sprang up in every part of the country among landlords, fallen former nobles, and smaller and poor farmers. These groups, under the influence of Western European political ideas, sought the protection of democratic rights, the prerogative of political participation, and the devolution of political power to regional and local levels. But their arena for action was the previously established prefectural assemblies, which were autocratic in inspiration and weak in practice, and quite incapable of responding meaningfully to these pressures. The political system was in a state of turmoil.

The basic premise that underlay the Meiji system of local government called for the fusion of central bureaucratic control of local government with social control by the stratum of local notables (primarily landlords) whose power base was being consolidated at the base of society. This union promised to achieve both top-down administrative penetration of society and bottom-up political integration of the people into the new state. The system of local government instituted between 1888 and 1890 has been variously described as "an ingenious system of centralized power" and "a dual system under the local government laws and the local officials' system."[1] In response to the political instability created by the Freedom and Popular Rights Movement, it attempted to preempt the movement, give concrete form to the autocratic logic of local government, and yet win the active allegiance of the people.

In any case, the system of 1888–90 endowed the prefectures, counties, and municipalities with the legal status of local governmental entities. Japan's 47 prefectures were subdivided into cities and counties, and counties were subdivided into towns and villages. In each governmental unit a popularly elected assembly was established. On the surface, this amounted to the modernization of local government; however, the municipal assemblies at the base of the polity were elected only by persons paying set amounts of taxes, whose electoral rights varied with the taxes they paid. For example, in city elections, there were three categories of voters according to tax bracket, each of which (regardless of size) elected one-third of the assembly; in village elections, there were two such categories. Thus, the richest group of voters—numbering far fewer than one-third of the electorate—picked one-third of the assemblymen. Government documents of the time expressed frankly the aims of local government: "It is intended as a bulwark against giving free rein to the ignorant, propertyless lesser orders who have no connection with the welfare of the community."[2]

In addition to these restraints on popular participation, the new system of local government included a distinctive prefectural system. As noted above, the prefectures were local governments represented by, and under the control of, the prefectural governor. The governor was, however, an "ordinary agent of local administration" under the administrative laws of the central government, and was appointed by the emperor. That is, he was under the supervision and direction of the home minister in matters of personnel and organization, and performed his other duties under the supervision of whichever ministry had jurisdiction over those particular duties. The governor and other higher prefectural officials were appointed by the national government and were not accountable to the prefecture's assembly, much less its people. Consequently, most of the prefecture's business was the work of the national government—"affairs of state," legally speaking—executed by the prefectural governor. The prefectural assembly had the authority to deliberate and approve the prefectural budget, but, in fact, most of what it did was nothing more than agreeing to the expenditures essential to the work of—and mandated by—the national government. The prefectures were organs of local autonomy in name only; it is probably more accurate, in fact, to call them regional administrative divisions of the state.

The relationship between the prefectures and the municipalities was basically no different from that between the state and the prefectures. Mayors were appointed by the home minister and supervised by him; towns and villages were under the jurisdiction of the county magistrate, himself also a lower-level national government official. In this sense, the prefectural system was, both in itself and as a ministate vis-à-vis the municipalities, the foundation of the Meiji system of local government.

THE INFLUENCE OF URBANIZATION AND INDUSTRIALIZATION

Socioeconomically, the advance of urbanization and industrialization in the 1920s brought a host of problems in housing, health, and transportation to the cities; in the countryside, the unevenness of interregional rates of economic growth brought the problem of poverty to the fore. Politically, these trends gave rise to the movement known as "Taishō democracy,"[3] in which intellectuals, workers, and farmers sought the expansion of political participation and the guarantee of democratic rights. They also gave rise to changes in the system of centralized local government.

First, in response to the movement demanding the broadening of political participation, the government gradually loosened the restraints on participation in both national and local assembly politics: universal male suffrage was introduced in elections for the House of Representatives in 1925 and in elections for prefectural and municipal assemblies the next year. Moreover, the autonomous powers of local government were broadened, if only slightly. Limits were imposed on the authority of the home minister and the prefectural governor over prefectural government, and the governors' supervisory powers vis-à-vis municipalities were also reduced. In this way, pressure from the people, and their integration into politics, brought changes to the foundations of the Meiji system of local government, and the system of bureaucratic control that had excluded the "ignorant, propertyless lesser orders" gradually lost its currency.

During the 1920s, Japan's regions and localities also began to demand the transfer to themselves of the national land and enterprise taxes, but opposition in the House of Peers defeated the campaign. Indeed, in the 1930s, the state, reserving for itself these sources of revenue, adopted a variety of regional transfer grants and subsidies (discussed in chapter 9) as a form of leverage for financing and, at the same time, strengthening its control of local government. This step was a direct response to the deepening, during the Great Depression, of the sorts of urban and rural socioeconomic problems already noted. But at the same time that this policy facilitated a response to these problems by restructuring the fiscal control of local government, it also augmented the centralization of power.

Thus, economic development led to social and economic changes that demanded local and participatory solutions. But the state refused to confront the democratic and decentralized implications of the situation and was unable to respond with anything but schizophrenic, halfway measures hedged about with guarantees of autocratic, centralized authority. Thus, the Meiji system of local government finally reached an impasse. Under the tide of total war and military fascism that gradually engulfed the country after 1931, however, this issue was never properly addressed.

THE POSTWAR REFORMS AND LOCAL SELF-GOVERNMENT

We need not recount here all of the democratic reforms in the areas of politics, administration, economy, and society enacted during the Occupation. The system of local government, as one area of bureaucratic control, was no exception. The basic framework of the postwar system of local government was set by the terms of Chapter 8 of the 1947 Constitution and a new Local Autonomy Act. In the Meiji Constitution, there had been no reference at all to local government; the inclusion in the new Constitution of a whole chapter on the subject was thus in itself of significance. And the treatment of local government did not stop with constitutional guarantees that the organization and operation of local government were to be in the hands of the local people. More positively, the Constitution established two levels of government: a central government responsible for the nation as a whole and local governments responsible for the welfare of their regional populations. The mutually restraining powers of these two levels of government were created on the presumption that they would contribute to the realization of democratic politics.

When one looks back on the postwar reforms, however, the most important point of local government reform appears to have been the provision for direct, popular election of prefectural governors. There was considerable opposition within the Japanese government to this reform but, under the leadership of SCAP (Supreme Commander for the Allied Powers), direct popular election was instituted. By this step, the prefectures became truly autonomous under the directly, popularly elected representative organs of the governor and prefectural assembly; municipalities became the same. And, in December 1947, the Home Ministry, which had exercised preeminent power over all of the organizational and operational affairs of local government, was dissolved. With this, the capability—at least in the formal, legal sense—of local governments to undertake a broad range of autonomous activities was established, including not only the provision of educational and welfare services, but also regulatory and administrative activities based in independently enacted ordinances. Moreover, in the area of taxation, under the terms of the 1949 Shoup Report,[4] the taxation prerogatives of state, prefectures, and municipalities were spelled out, amounting to a wholesale modernization of the regional taxation structure.

BEHIND THE POSTWAR REFORMS:
LOCAL AUTONOMY VS. CENTRAL AUTHORITY

We have already stated that the direct election of prefectural governors constituted a focal point of the postwar reform of local government. This radical reform brought in its train a second defining characteristic of local government in contemporary Japan: central-local tension.

When SCAP began to push hard for direct election of governors, the Japanese government agonized over the question of how tasks delegated by the central government for execution by the prefectural governor, previously a creature of the central government, were going to become accomplished under the new system. One might have thought that the resolution most consistent with the spirit of the reforms would be a reallocation downward of authority and functions among the three levels of government. In fact, however, the government's anxiety over the social turmoil of the time combined with its distrust of the newly elected governors, and it chose to make the utmost effort to keep as many of these tasks as possible under the umbrella of state jurisdiction. Therefore, in law after law and ordinance after ordinance, governors, mayors, and all types of administrative committees were designated as agents of the state, with executive powers delegated to them by Tokyo. The way of getting around this problem, ridden with contradictions as it is, is referred to today as "agent delegation." The execution of agent-delegated duties by prefectural governors as individuals is done under the supervision of the relevant ministry; that carried out by mayors, under the supervision of the governor. Local assemblies, unsurprisingly, have neither legislative nor investigative authority in these areas. In addition, in the case of certain affairs of state, the analogous procedure of "organizational delegation" was used, which refers to the statutory delegation of central government work to local government as a whole for execution. For the execution of this sort of delegated work, local governments are required by law to set up special internal administrative agencies. During the subsequent process of economic development, such tasks—and such agencies, which were effectively beyond the control of the prefecture—multiplied continuously.

HIGH-SPEED ECONOMIC GROWTH AND LOCAL GOVERNMENT

The system of local government instituted after the war was not completely stable during the 1950s. Indeed, abolition of the direct election of governors was even debated within the government. Moreover, the Local Autonomy Act was revised in 1952 and 1954. The ostensible object of these revisions was the simplification of local government organization and operation. In reality, however, it was the recentralization of power, as one can see in the reduction in size of local assemblies; in the differentiation according to population of prefectural legal departments and their reduction in number; in the elimination of direct popular election of the mayors of Tokyo's wards; and in the clarification (read amplification) of the "advisory" authority of ministers and governors. In addition to these reforms, the Municipality Amalgamation Promotion Act of 1953 revealed the government's intention of reducing the number of towns and villages by two-thirds.[5] And, finally, two of the centerpieces of the postwar reforms—the decentralization of education and police organization —were subjected to recentralization through complete rewriting of the laws governing them.

In the background of these reforms, it must be admitted, was the fact that local government had not always been able to respond adequately to the rapid systemic transformations of the postwar era. This was itself, however, the product of the fact that the postwar reform of local government had never been more than pro forma; the governments had always lacked the political—and especially the financially independent—basis of real autonomy. For this reason, the various internal disorders manifest in local government combined with the revision of Occupation policy that began around the outbreak of the Korean War to herald the onset of governmental recentralization.

As Japan entered the high-growth era of the 1960s, the system of local government stabilized. But it was stabilization at a lower level of autonomy, under a new, more centralized system. Specifically, in 1964, the revision of the Highway Act and the enactment of a new Riparian Act took managerial authority of significant public works out of the hands of the governors and placed them in Tokyo. Second was the expansion of actual state operations within prefectural government, as manifest in the establishment and expanded jurisdictions of local bureaus of agricultural affairs and construction. Third was the proliferation of special public corporations—essentially rivals of the local governments—such as the Public Highway Authority and the Water Resources Development Authority. And fourth was the increase in agency-delegated tasks and the development of the local government subsidy system. The state, by means of such measures, aimed to create a solid local basis for industrialization driven by national financial and fiscal policy. And local stability was one of the conditions supporting high-speed economic growth.

In those days, the phrase, "local government with a pipeline to the center," came up in the context of many local elections. At the same time that local governments were threatened by the theft of their authority, given the existing system, they were driven by the need to attract state operations and subsidized activities, and mobilized local politicians to that end. Candidates for local office who could promise a "pipeline" to Tokyo were much in demand. Local government during the era of high growth was in one sense a process that emerged from the pursuit of benefits by local government through the national political process. The policies, administration, and finances of central and local governments were progressively becoming fused.

But at the same time that high-speed economic growth pushed the GNP upward, it gave rise to a multiplicity of urban problems in areas such as pollution, housing, transportation, and social welfare; and movements of citizens seeking solutions to these problems proliferated in response. But solutions were beyond both the means and the will of local politicians who owed allegiance to the very central government whose development-at-any-cost strategy had produced the problems in the first place. Consequently, these sorts of citizens' movements gave rise to a nationwide "local government reform" movement that questioned the contemporary quality of local government overall. This was the popular side of the new quickening of local self-government, symbolized institutionally by the increase of what were called "progressive local governments" in the hands of leftist mayors and governors. These governments, attempting both to resolve urban problems and stimulate popular participation in local government, developed distinctive policy activities. Today, the Left's electoral fortunes have faded and the number of "progressive local governments" has dwindled. The pursuit of regional individuality based on local government has, however, become part of the foundations of Japanese politics. The ideas of local government embodied in the postwar reforms seem at long last to be taking root, and the tense central-local balance of power is tilting more in a local direction.

NOTES

1. The two quotations are from Tsuji Kiyoaki, *Nihon no Chihō Jichi* (Local Government in Japan), Iwanami, 1978, p. 32; and Takagi Shōsaku, "Chiji Kōsensei to Chūō Tōsei" (Central Control and Public Gubernatorial Elections), in Taniuchi Yuzuru et al., eds., *Gendai Gyōsei to Kanryōsei* (Contemporary Administration and Bureaucracy), vol. 1, University of Tokyo Press, 1974, p. 260.

2. Naikaku Kiroku Kyoku, *Hōki Bunrui Taizen, Seitaimon I* (Official Gazette on Legal Affairs, I), Tokyo, April 17, 1888, p. 177.

3. So named for the Taishō emperor, during whose reign (1912–26) it flourished.

4. For the memoirs of Carl Shoup, see his "The Tax Mission to Japan, 1949–1950," unpublished paper prepared for the conference on Lessons from Fundamental Tax Reform in Developing Countries, Washington, D.C., April 1988.

5. In 1950 there were 10,443 municipalities in Japan; in 1955 there were 5,206; in 1960, 3,526; and in 1990, 3,246.

CHAPTER 8

LOCAL GOVERNMENT TODAY

LOCAL GOVERNMENT AND DUAL REPRESENTATION

As of April 1, 1990, there were in Japan 3,293 local governments: 47 prefectures, 633 cities, 23 special wards in Tokyo, 2,003 towns, and 587 villages.[1] Japan's is a two-tier system of local government: the top tier includes the prefectures, the largest local governmental units, which are in turn composed of a lower tier of municipalities: cities, wards, towns, and villages. In principle, prefectural functions include region-wide activities and the coordination of work across municipalities.

With the exception of Tokyo metropolitan prefecture, all prefectures have identical functions; there is considerable variation, however, among the municipalities on the lower tier of the local governmental structure. "City" is a formal administrative category restricted to municipalities that fulfill certain criteria, such as having a population of 50,000 or more. Moreover, there is a separate category of cities, the "specially designated cities," of which there are 13 at present. These have populations of 500,000 or more and are officially designated by government ordinance;[2] as metropolitan administrative units, they are permitted to exercise some prefectural prerogatives and to establish ward systems of internal administration. The functions of the special wards of Tokyo prefecture are essentially the same as those of cities, but such services as fire protection, sanitation, and water and sewers are provided by the prefecture, and fiscal coordination is carried out between the wards and the prefectural government.[3] The criteria for designation as a town are set by prefectural ordinances, and all municipalities too small to be designated towns are classified as villages.

The political and administrative structures of local governments are essentially identical regardless of type, each based on a popularly elected executive and an assembly. This arrangement is referred to structurally as a "presidential" or "dual representation" system. But, substantively, as one might expect, given Japanese history, it has been characterized as a "strong executive, weak assembly" system, without a really balanced duality of power. In such a context, the lack of authority and prestige attaching to local assemblies as organs of representative democracy has been a serious problem. Since the citizens do, however, have these two representative organs—the mayor or governor and the assembly—at their disposal, the common characterization is not necessarily accurate. Indeed, the trend in recent years has been for elected executives not simply to be the domineering heads of an administrative structure; they have enhanced their role as political unifiers of the citizenry and pursued strategies of "intimate government" vis-à-vis the people. This trend, as we shall see, does not slight the significance of the assembly, much less deny it. Rather, it strengthens the meaning of dual representation and casts doubt on the historically based image offered above.

On the other hand, it is a fact that local government is circumscribed by national and regional systems of administration and finance. In this context, the most important component of the work of local governments is the "agent-delegated" activities discussed in chapter 7. It is difficult to define these activities precisely, but the Local Autonomy Act specifies, in no less than 500 separate statutes, the tasks that the state requires prefectural governors and mayors to perform. Since the late 1980s, there has been a trend toward the consolidation of these activities, but the fact is that local governments still expend tremendous amounts of manpower and money on the execution of tasks mandated to them by national law.

The financial relationships of national and local governments are also intertwined to a high degree. In 1990, the combined expenditures of the central government (in its general account budget and 10 special accounts) and local governments (in their ordinary budgets) amounted to ¥123.9 trillion. When one differentiates between local and national spending in this total, national expenditures accounted for ¥46.6 trillion (37.6 percent), and local expenditures for ¥77.3 trillion (62.4 percent); in terms of final allocation, local government is actually Japan's biggest government, especially in the areas of general administrative expenditures, land conservation and development, health, housing, and education (see figure 8.1). As one can see in figure 8.2, however, local tax revenues only amounted to 41.6 percent of local government income. Most of the rest came in the form of transfer payments and subsidies from the central government. If one combines the two types of regional transfer tax grants[4] (which

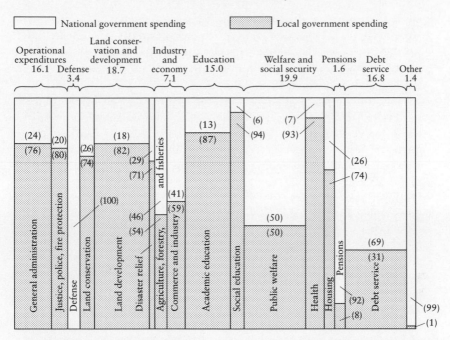

FIGURE 8.1 Total Expenditures of Local and National Governments by Purpose and Share, 1990 (%)
SOURCE: Jichi-shō, ed., *Chihō Zaisei Hakusho, Heisei 4-Nenban* (White Paper on Local Finance, 1992), 1992, p. 40.

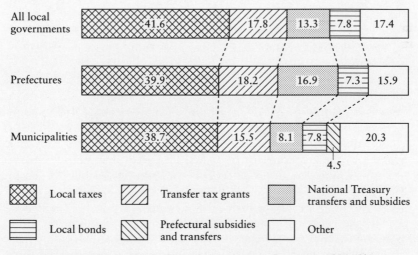

FIGURE 8.2 Sources of Local Government Revenue, 1990 (%)
SOURCE: Same as figure 8.1, p. 8.

are general-purpose fiscal resources for local government) with local taxes (also a general fiscal resource), they amount to almost 60 percent of the general revenues of local government. Most of these transfer payments are one kind of subsidy or another, which come through specified channels (see chapter 9).

Thus, in fact, not all of a local government's general fiscal resources can be spent discretionarily on its own policies. As one can see in the case of agency-delegated operations, a lot of local government spending comes from appropriations made in accord with nationally stipulated spending requirements. In this way, the finances of local and national governments are intimately intertwined. However one evaluates this, the fact that roughly 60 percent of local government revenue comes from the central government in one guise or another imposes a variety of constraints on the administrative operations of local government.

URBANIZED SOCIETY AND LOCAL GOVERNMENT POLICY

The fact that local government is circumscribed by national and regional administrative and fiscal systems hinders the independence of local government in many ways. Since the 1970s, however, local governments, in trying to solidify their links with their citizens, began not simply to give precedence to and supplement national policy but to develop their own policies and programs in response to the diversity of local characteristics. The catalyst for this development, socioeconomically, was the massive urbanization of the 1960s. Popular living conditions and lifestyles—in family structure, consumption, transportation, leisure-time activities, and everything else— in *both* city and countryside underwent a change best described as urbanization.

This change in population distribution and individual lifestyles to urban and metropolitan patterns did not, however, result in a smooth transition to a new, more urban type of social order, comfort, and convenience. Quite the contrary: it gave rise to a host of urban problems. As it became apparent that existing laws were not adapted to these conditions, residents, in search of some framework of norms suitable to an urban type of community structure, began to deepen their ties to their local executives. That is, the political stimulus to this transformation of local government lay in the "rediscovery" by the people of the politically integrative function of the chief executive within the system of dual representation, which in turn facilitated the development of autonomous local policy initiatives under the leadership of the executive.

The foresighted policy inclination of local governments that arose out of this transformation is visible in a variety of administrative areas, one of which was that of regulative activity. The precedent in this movement was the Tokyo Pollution Prevention Ordinance of 1969. This prefectural ordinance required government notification and approval of all factory construction plans. It replaced the prior method of regulating each separate pollution-causing facility with the practice of evaluating factories *in toto* as the object of regulation; as such, it represented a basic rethinking of the legal objects and methods of regulation within the context of local conditions and constituted a new, and more coherent and holistic, method of regulation.

Similar sorts of ordinances were adopted by local governments all over the country, and in the "pollution parliament" of 1970 (so nicknamed for the large volume of environmental legislation it produced), the national government also began to take aim at the adjustment of related statutes and the strengthening of regulations. And one should also take note here, as part of the same movement, of environmental protection ordinances. These ordinances, aimed at protecting the nature being lost amid the wave of rapid urbanization, were adopted by 22 prefectures during 1970 and 1971 and spread to the municipal level also. In March 1972, the national government, too, enacted an Environmental Protection Act.

In this way, local governments, through independently enacted ordinances based on real-life local needs, began to breathe legal life into long-unused formal statutory powers and assumed a policy role in advance of the central government. They are thus seeking to reform the legal system in tune with local social needs in policy areas that have been paralyzed by political and economic conflicts of interest at the national level, taking the initiative with independent policy responses. One can see examples of this in the environmental assessment ordinances originating in Kawasaki City and in the proliferation both of *open* information (of public documents) and personal information *closure* (privacy) ordinances, and political ethics ordinances also. In this way, the regulatory activities of local government have served to ensure the health of the citizenry, to preserve the natural environment, and additionally to enhance the democratic operation of local government.

Nor are initiatives taken by local government limited to regulatory activity. Previously, the social welfare system had been based primarily on a custodial, in-patient model of treatment in public facilities. This practice, however, hindered the intermingling and mutual learning of handicapped and "normal" people in the community.

Gradually, a new system of local welfare service delivery with "residential welfare services" as its theme became seen as necessary. The pioneer in this issue area was, again, local government. The temporary dispatch of homehelpers has already become general practice and, as evidenced by the Musashino City Welfare Public Corporation, there is also a trend toward lifetime at-home services for the elderly. Moreover, the dispersal and integration of such services as day-care centers and short-stay facilities into neighborhood settings is already underway in regions all over the country. Also, along with these sorts of local welfare service delivery systems, new local systems of primary health care are being tried. The national government, too, albeit tardily, revised the Welfare for the Elderly Act in 1990, increasing subsidies for in-home care and encouraging local governments to establish local welfare plans.

Needless to say, with the aging and urbanization of contemporary society, popular values and lifestyles are becoming increasingly pluralistic. The policy developments just noted in local government show how "intimate government" is able to respond flexibly to this kind of contemporary social structure. Partly as a result, municipal policy has overflowed with such things as the "one village, one product" movement promoting the economic distinctiveness of, for example, local folk arts or delicacies, and the construction of distinctive local facilities such as shopping or business complexes, industrial parks, or recreational facilities, in an effort to avoid the drowning of communities in a sea of urban uniformity.

Moreover, many communities are nowadays home to increasing numbers of foreigners with different languages, religions, and cultures. Under the slogan of "internationalization begins at home," local governments are enacting policies for the purpose of accommodating foreign residents. Such policies include the provision of volunteer services to foreign residents and of local centers for intercultural exchange, and the opening of public employment to foreigners. It is only slightly hyperbolic to say that a civic political and administrative culture with a global perspective is emerging from local politics in Japan today.

URBANIZATION AND MULTIPARTY POLITICS

The establishment of local legislative assemblies in Japan was one part of Japan's process of political modernization. Of course, the prewar local assemblies were not founded on the principle of dual representation, or on any other principle of popular sovereignty; on the contrary, they served to join regional domination by the administrative bureaucracy with the local domination of local notables. From this perspective, the significance of the introduction of the principle of dual representation in the postwar reforms is great. Still, this reform did not bring immediate change to the electoral foundations of local politics.

In April 1947, under the terms of the new Constitution and the Local Autonomy Act, two rounds of local elections were held—one for executives and one for assemblies—in prefectures and municipalities nationwide. Electoral conditions at the two levels, and in executive and legislative elections, differed; compared to today, the extent of partisan politics was remarkably low in every case. Most winning candidates were independents, and most of them were local notables; this tendency was especially striking in the municipal assemblies.

The massive wave of urbanization that swept the country after the late 1950s, however, sharply changed this electoral situation. The influx of population into the metropolitan areas, the advance of suburbanization, and the proliferation of urban problems such as pollution, housing, education, welfare, roads, and water and sewers—all of these brought a multiplicity of contentious issues into local politics, and partisan political conflict followed close behind. Then, in the fifth series of unified local elections, held in April 1963, the Democratic Socialist Party and the newly formed Clean Politics League (Kōmei Seiji Renmei, the forerunner of the Kōmeitō) ran candidates for the first time. As a result, the local political arena, like the national, entered the era of multiparty politics.

The advent of multiparty politics in the local assemblies had several implications for local politics and administration. The first involved the modernization of the operations of the local assemblies. Formerly, these assemblies had been run primarily on the basis of behind-the-scenes negotiations among a small number of powerful representatives; "multipartification" brought an end to this situation, and the assemblies were forced to adopt objective, transparent procedural standards and structures. Today, skepticism and criticism about such efforts are once again common, but the drive for such reform of city assemblies actually began during the 1960s, compared to which the current scene is a marked improvement. Moreover, the eclipse of collusive "boss rule" in the local assemblies contributed to the creatively and healthily conflictual relationships between executives and assembly representatives on the local level, of which we have already spoken.

Second, the advance of multipartification brought, for the first time, the reflection in the local political process of the myriad interests and preferences existing among the local populace. As a rule,

issues tend to be polarized by executive elections in which few run
and only one individual—and set of policies—can win. By contrast,
the election of several dozen city assemblymen brings together advo-
cates of many different political agendas and serves to reflect the
natural multiplicity of issues and of viewpoints on each, and the advent of multiparty politics had precisely this effect. Local representatives were, to be sure, criticized for slavishly reflecting local special
interests. There can be no realization of democratic politics, however, without the reflection of manifold interests in the political process. In order to fulfill its mission as a representative organ of the people, in competition with the executive, the assembly must embody
and attempt to aggregate and resolve all of the contending interests
that permeate society. In this sense, one may say that multiparty politics brought local government one step nearer to the intended principles of the dual representation system.

In addition to multiparty politics, one characteristic of local assembly elections in recent years is the increase in women representatives.
In particular, in the local elections of 1987 and 1991 this trend was
striking. The previous high for winning women candidates in prefectural assembly elections was 39 in 1964. In 1983, the total was
only 30, but in 1987 the number jumped to 52 and in 1991 to 81.
Municipal assemblies also witnessed a similar dramatic increase in its
women members: 456 in 1983, 765 in 1987, and 1,042 in 1991. In
metropolitan Yokohama and Kawasaki and in the special ward
assemblies of Tokyo, a large number of women candidates running
as independents were victorious.

In earlier years, most women candidates for local office were put
up by parties, partly as a rather cynical campaign tactic to mobilize
more women voters to their party. In recent years, however, these
sorts of factors have become an insufficient explanation for female
candidacies. Most of the women who have won seats in local
assemblies of late are urban independent candidates who, unlike
most "independent" candidates for local office in Japan, are not even
informally backed by political parties. As citizens well versed in community needs, most of them pursue improvements in environmental
protection, welfare, health, education, and so forth.

On the one hand, this posture has deepened legislative intimacy
with the sorts of populist local executives described above; on the
other, it is a significant protest against local assemblies and representatives who have become entangled with and compromised by
party organizations in Tokyo. For this reason, these sorts of women
representatives, even while struggling to learn and exploit the procedures and customs of local assemblies, are making strenuous efforts

to enhance the openness of the assemblies. Some see this as a battle of "amateurs" against an entrenched, professionalized elite of local assemblymen, but one can also see it as a democratizing transformation of local political culture. It is uncertain how much this trend may accelerate in the future. It *is* certain, however, that it has become part of the foundation of Japanese local politics. The "strong executive, weak assembly" image of local government dominated by Tokyo bureaucrats, autocratic mayors and governors, and powerless assemblies in the hands of exclusive circles of "good old boys" has exhausted its utility as an accurate portrayal of community politics.

NOTES

1. In Japan, unlike the United States, there is no unincorporated land. The entire country is divided into prefectures (*to*, *dō*, *fu*, and *ken*), and each prefecture is divided into counties (*gun*) and cities (*shi*). Counties, which are administrative but not governmental units, are further divided into towns (*machi* or *chō*) and villages (*mura* or *son*).

2. The 1947 Local Autonomy Act provided for a category of "special cities" having powers equivalent to those of prefectures but, as a consequence of the conflict between these cities and the prefectures, it was never put into effect. The "specially designated cities" were created under the revised Local Autonomy Act of 1955 as a compromise between the prefectures and the big cities.

3. The difference between metropolitan prefectures (*to*) and other prefectures (*dō*, *fu*, and *ken*) is that the former act in the capacity of cities vis-à-vis their own wards and in the capacity of prefectures vis-à-vis the municipalities within their administrative jurisdiction.

4. These grants are allocated on the basis of a specified procedure and funded by 32 percent of the revenues from individual income tax, corporation tax, and liquor tax. In accord with the revision of the tax system carried out under Prime Minister Takeshita Noboru in the late 1980s, beginning in 1989, part of the revenue from the new general consumption tax (a form of sales tax) also became part of this fund.

CHAPTER 9

THE POLITICS OF
INTERGOVERNMENTAL TRANSFERS

THE CONCEPT OF SUBSIDIES

The most general purpose of transfer payments from central to local governments—subsidies, revenue sharing, and the like—is to induce society and the economy to move in a certain direction; one can, however, differentiate among types of subsidies according to their specific objectives and functions. In Japan, for example, there are broadly speaking two types of intergovernmental transfers. First, there are subsidies designed to adjust national and local governmental finances. These include unrestricted grants made from the proceeds of two types of regional transfer tax (the *kōfu-zei* and the *jōyo-zei*), which are made by the national government to equalize the disparities in financial capabilities of richer and poorer local governments. The second type of transfer includes subsidies made for the purpose of achieving specific policy objectives. There is a great variety of subsidies in this category. Some are intended to achieve national minimum levels of services in areas like social security and compulsory education, for which the national government also bears significant responsibility. Others are designed to promote certain industries, to meet infrastructural needs like roads, water and sewers, and parks, or to facilitate the execution of some new administrative function of local government. Often these latter types of subsidies are intimately interrelated; conversely, there are also many subsidies that serve more than one of these purposes. For example, subsidies for the construction of primary educational facilities serve to help school systems meet minimum national educational standards, as well as to enrich the social infrastructure of the targeted locality. Similarly, subsidies to agriculture, forestry, and fisheries are a form of industrial assistance, but they also serve to build social infrastructure in rural communities and, in some cases, to underwrite administrative functions.

THE SUBSIDY CONCEPT IN ADMINISTRATIVE PRACTICE

National government subsidies are colloquially known in the administrative world as "National Treasury expenditures" (or NTEs). But this is a very general concept. In the national budget such state expenditures are divided into subsidies (*hojo-kin*), obligations (*futan-kin*), supplementary grants (*hokyū-kin*), delegatory grants (*itaku-kin*), and transfers (*kōfu-kin*). Although the basic statutes governing state expenditures stipulate a state obligation in each instance, in budgetary language, "obligations" are differentiated from "subsidies"; the distinction is somewhat arbitrary, but there are criteria by which they can be distinguished from one another.

Subsidies, strictly speaking, are transfers that constitute state encouragement of a specific administrative activity. *Obligations* are disbursed in order to enable a local government to fulfill its nationally mandated administrative responsibility in areas such as social security and primary and secondary education. *Supplementary grants* are made in order to cover specific deficits and administrative cost overruns, for example, in interest payments on local governments' debts. *Delegated grants* are designed to compensate local governments for expenses incurred in the performance of functions delegated to them by the state, for example, in the administration of national elections. And *transfers* are payments made to local governments for any purpose not covered by the above.

In addition to these five budget categories, however, there are two other categories of NTEs listed in the Finance Ministry's annual publication *Hojokin Sōran* (Subsidy Review): foreign aid (*enjo-kin*) and international contributions (*kokusai buntan-kin*), the first accounted for by economic aid to foreign countries and the second incurred by virtue of Japan's membership in international organizations. Strictly speaking, these international obligations also fit into the category of subsidies, but in customary governmental terminology "subsidy" refers only to domestic allocations to local governments from the National Treasury.

In addition to the categories of subsidy described above, the terms legal subsidies (*hōritsu hojo*) and budgetary subsidies (*yosan hojo*) are also used, according to the criterion of whether or not there is specific legal provision made for a subsidy. Legal subsidies—roughly 85 percent of the total—are those made in accordance with some

statutory prescription. Such subsidies are not limited, however, to instances in which the state's financial obligation is legally stated; in
about one in ten cases they result from the law being interpreted as
permitting state subsidies. Budgetary subsidies, by contrast, are subsidies included in the government's annual budget with no separate
foundation in statute law. In practice, all of these types of transfers
lead to a chaotic, largely unregulated proliferation of subsidies,
which in turn becomes a headache for local and national politicians
and a source of power for the national bureaucracy.

SCOPE AND OBJECT OF SUBSIDIES

Japan's national budget comprises the general account and 38 special
accounts. In the 1991 budget, the subsidy category of the general
account amounted to ¥15,656 billion. This accounted for fully 22.3
percent of the ¥70,347 billion in the entire general account, the
most influential part of the budget vis-à-vis national administration.
Between 1955 and the end of the 1960s this proportion ran to roughly 26 to 27 percent of the general account; in the 1970s it rose to 30
percent and peaked at 33 percent in the 1980s. As a result of the
administrative reforms carried out at the recommendation of the
Second Ad Hoc Commission on Administration, however, this proportion subsequently showed a gradual decline.

The allocation of expenditures, according to purpose, within the
general account budget for 1991 is shown in figure 9.1. The seven
types of subsidies described above are also shown in table 9.1, in
which one can see the predominant role of subsidies and obligations.
It should also be pointed out, however, that ¥12,506 billion—
almost 80 percent of the ¥15,656 billion figure in the subsidy category of the general account—consisted of transfers to local governments (see table 9.2). The composition of the subsidy program, with
roughly 80 percent of the general-account subsidies going to local
governments, is a distinctive aspect of administration and finance in
Japan, with a significant impact on both local and national politics
(as we saw in chapter 8).

Needless to say, in light of this pattern, the allocation and utilization of subsidies has also created a number of political problems. The
subject is so vast and complex, however, that comprehending all its
details and ramifications is nearly impossible, even for specialists.
Therefore, we shall focus here only on relationships between the
national and local governments, and look at the relevant issues surrounding transfers (primarily of the subsidy and obligation types)

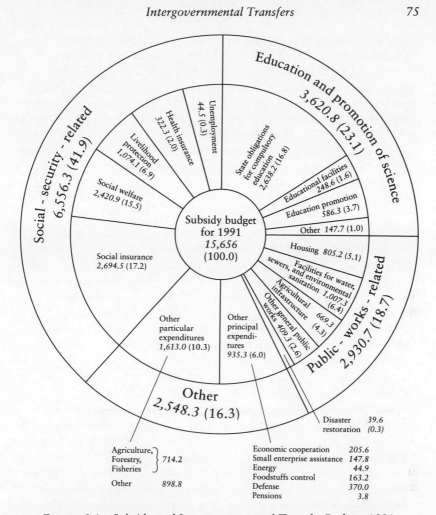

Social - security - related
6,556.3 (41.9)

Unemployment 44.5 (0.3)

Health insurance 322.3 (2.0)

Livelihood protection 1,074.1 (6.9)

Social welfare 2,420.9 (15.5)

Education and promotion of science
3,620.8 (23.1)

State obligations for compulsory education 2,638.2 (16.8)

Educational facilities 248.6 (1.6)

Education promotion 586.3 (3.7)

Other 147.7 (1.0)

Subsidy budget for 1991 15,656 (100.0)

Housing 805.2 (5.1)

Facilities for water, sewers, and environmental sanitation 1,007.3 (6.4)

Agricultural infrastructure 669.3 (4.3)

Other general public works 409.3 (2.6)

Social insurance 2,694.5 (17.2)

Other particular expenditures 1,613.0 (10.3)

Other principal expenditures 935.3 (6.0)

Public - works - related
2,930.7 (18.7)

Other 2,548.3 (16.3)

Disaster restoration 39.6 (0.3)

Agriculture, Forestry, Fisheries ⎫ 714.2

Other 898.8

Economic cooperation 205.6
Small enterprise assistance 147.8
Energy 44.9
Foodstuffs control 163.2
Defense 370.0
Pensions 3.8

FIGURE 9.1 Subsidy and Intergovernmental Transfer Budget, 1991
(¥ billion and as % of total)
SOURCE: Zaisei Chōsakai, ed., *Heisei 3 Nendo Hojokin Sōran* (Subsidy Review, 1991), 1991, p. 6.

allocated for the purpose of realizing particular policy or administrative objectives.

POLITICS AND PROCEDURES OF SUBSIDY DECISION-MAKING

State agencies with jurisdiction over specific subsidy programs determine the general principles of those programs. The basic conditions

TABLE 9.1   Subsidy Budget in the General Account, 1990 and 1991
(¥ billion)

	1990	1991
Subsidies	5,455	5,096
Obligations	8,550	8,698
Transfers	1,005	1,112
Supplementary grants	761	601
Delegated grants	161	147
Total	15,934	15,656
Foreign aid	199	212
International contributions	1,443	153

SOURCE: Same as figure 9.1, pp. 4–5.

TABLE 9.2   Subsidy Budget by Recipient, 1990 and 1991 (¥ billion)

Recipient	1990	1991	Annual increase
Local governments	12,090 (80.5%)	12,506 (79.9%)	416 (3.4%)
Others	2,937 (19.5%)	3,149 (20.1%)	212 (7.2%)
Total	15,028 (100.0%)	15,656 (100.0%)	628 (4.2%)

SOURCE: Same as figure 9.1, p. 6.

of "legal subsidies" are set forth in law; agency guidelines deal with the concrete objects and procedures of the transfers. In the case of "budgetary subsidies," agency regulations still specify the objectives of the subsidies and are as much part of the basic program regulations as is the budget itself. With both types of subsidies the content of program guidelines is a matter of administrative discretion, and it serves as rules for bureaucratic action. Accordingly, the making of decisions on subsidies based on these principles takes place at the bureau and section level of the agencies involved.

To summarize the process of subsidy decision-making, first, extended initial discussions take place between administrators from the subsidy's target government and the subsidy-granting agency. In these talks the representatives of the recipient agency present evidence of the need for the action to be subsidized and their eligibility for subsidization, while the donor agency evaluates their capabilities and qualifications. If on the basis of these negotiations the agency makes an unofficial positive ruling on the subsidy, then the recipient agency submits a formal application in the form and style specified in the program guidelines, and a formal decision to grant the subsidy is then made. Subsequently, there are negotiations on the actual organization of the subsidized work to be done, issuance of permits for necessary activities, provision for reports, and inspection of the finished project, and the exact amount of the subsidy is determined.

Needless to say, the above is a simplified summary of the complex decision-making process involved in subsidies. Moreover, there are variations in every individual case. What is particularly distinctive about the transfer process from the applicants' perspective is that prefectural governments have to coordinate and incorporate applications from all the municipalities within their jurisdictions into the subsidy process. And, from the perspective of disbursement, the state sometimes makes direct transfers to municipalities, but in most instances subsidies are made through the prefectures. In such cases, the prefectural government may add an amount to the subsidy, if provided for by law, or may simply pass the subsidy along to the municipalities. In any case, one cannot ignore the role of prefectural government in the transfer process. This role, as we saw in chapter 8, is one of the ways in which the prefectural governments have taken on some of the character of agencies of the national government.

During the transfer decision-making process—and particularly during the initial discussion stage—there are many opportunities for politics to intervene. Anxious to seize their share of this scarce and coveted fiscal booty, the prefectures mobilize their elected representatives; unsurprisingly, the result is incessant, fiercely competitive overtures to the agencies of the national government. Such political intervention and pressure-group activities do not end here, however. As noted, the prefectures are responsible for aggregating and coordinating applications for subsidies from their municipalities, and for negotiating them with the national government. It is not at all uncommon for municipalities left out of this process to mobilize their own elected officials and try to roll back this process by going around the prefectural government and appealing straight to their representatives in Tokyo. Moreover, powerful politicians carry out similar coordination informally among the municipalities within their districts and lobby the agencies of state personally on their behalf.

The whole subsidy process, in this light, looks disorderly and irrational. Through the transfer process, however, local governments do obtain essential fiscal resources from the state; for the politicians, the return on their exercise of influence is the votes they obtain from the locality. In addition, the ability to offer subsidies is itself a major political resource for the bureaucrats. And finally, by building on the close relationships with interest groups nurtured through the subsidy process, it holds out to civil servants the prospects of an entry into

politics or a comfortable corporate job after retirement. Thus—
disorderly and irrational though it may be—the process is not without benefits for all involved.

LOCAL ADMINISTRATION AND SUBSIDIES

One of the reasons local governments must expend so much time and
energy in the pursuit of subsidies is the weakness of the independent
fiscal base of local government. Moreover, when one examines the
subsidy system from the perspective of the local recipients, one finds
pathological phenomena in addition to those seen from the national
perspective.

If they do not participate in the process of prior negotiations and
petition battles, local governments are at a severe disadvantage in receiving subsidies. Unfortunately, both of these activities are highly
expensive. As one would expect, there are no public data that would
enable one to estimate accurately just how much is spent on these
activities. To cite one example, however, should be instructive. A
study was made of a single highway repair project in one prefecture
in 1972 that involved 7.2 kilometers of road and cost approximately
¥1.7 billion.[1] The initial negotiations with the Construction Ministry
required 2,855 employees and generated 20 boxes of documentation.
In other words, receiving subsidies requires local governments to
spend a great amount of their own financial resources, and one may
assume that the situation is unchanged since the study was conducted.

Moreover, the actual amount of most subsidies is quite small. The
national government does not publish systematic data on the amount
of each and every subsidy. According to estimates made by the Kansai Federation of Economic Organizations, however, in the 1983
national budget, transfers of less than ¥10 million accounted for 13
percent of the total, transfers of between ¥10 and ¥50 million for 18
percent, those of between ¥50 and ¥100 million for 9 percent, and
those of between ¥100 and ¥300 million for 14 percent.[2] In this
case, as in the highway study above, there is little reason to think
that the situation has changed much in the interim. But just because
the amounts are small does not mean that the process is simple. Indeed, one cannot dismiss the frequently heard stories of subsidies
that amounted to less than the cost of applying for them. And what
one must not overlook, in addition to the uneconomic quality of such
subsidies, is that the various agencies of the national government give
many small subsidies for very similar purposes independently of one
another. As a result, even when local governments try to cover a

single project by adding together a number of separate subsidies from different agencies, their efforts are made far more difficult by the rivalries between ministries and even between bureaus in given ministries.

Moreover, subsidies often have a dark underside: they require the recipient to supplement the subsidy with funds of its own. Consequently, to the extent that a local government becomes entangled in the national subsidy game, financial autonomy is lost as the government becomes enmeshed in the vertical compartmentalization of the national bureaucracy, which now penetrates into local government. In addition, even subsidies such as those from the regional transfer tax, which are unrestricted funds intended to achieve interprefectural financial equality, actually go to pay for the "underside" of other subsidies, and thus make the independent development of projects by local governments even more difficult.

NOTES

1. Hirose Michisada, *Hojo-kin to Seiken-tō* (Subsidies and the LDP), Asahi Shinbun, 1981, pp. 192–94.

2. Kansai Keizai Dantai Rengōkai, *Zoku Hojo-kin no Genjō to Mondaiten: Seiri Gōrika no tame no Keizai Bunseki* (Current Issues in Subsidies) (November 1983), p. 22. One should note also that even a subsidy as large as ¥100 million, if split evenly among the 47 prefectures, comes to about only ¥2 million each.

PART 3

GOVERNMENT IN ACTION: POLICY ISSUES AND DILEMMAS

CHAPTER 10

BUDGETARY POLITICS

OUTLINE OF THE BUDGETARY PROCESS

In Japan the cabinet draws up the annual budget for each fiscal year (April 1–March 31) and submits it to parliament for deliberation; following Article 86 of the Constitution, it must be passed by the House of Representatives to be adopted. When people speak of the national budget, it is usually the general account budget that is referred to; the budget submitted by the cabinet, however, consists of more than this. In principle, it would be preferable to have a single budget that governs all state expenditures and revenues. Practically speaking, however, in an age in which state functions have become highly complex and rapidly changeable, it is often more rational to have additional accounts, separate from general revenues and expenditures, in which special revenues are matched with special expenditures. Government accounts are therefore divided into two categories: the general account budget and a set of special account budgets (of which there were 38 in fiscal 1990).

The cabinet is required to draw up and submit to parliament both of these budgets, plus draft budgets for all other government-related agencies whose budgets by law require parliamentary approval. Major state expenditures are required to be covered in principle by regular revenues without borrowing or government bond sales. Public works, government investments, and government loans may, however, be covered by bonds or borrowing within limits approved by parliament (Finance Law, Article 4).

Moreover, both the general and special accounts budgets comprise not only revenue and expenditure as usually conceived of, but an additional five categories: general budget provisions, the revenue and expenditure budget, the continuing budget, carryover expenses, and service of the national debt (Finance Law, Article 16). When analyzing the national budget, one must consider all five of these categories. In any case, the total budget is drafted on the authority of the minister of finance and submitted to parliament after approval by the cabinet. This draft budget prepared by the ministry does not consist only of the budgets of the agencies of the executive branch. It also includes the budgets of parliament, the judiciary, and the Board of Audit—in other words, the budgetary powers of the Finance Ministry and the cabinet are extremely broad.

The Constitution (Article 60) requires that the budget be submitted first to the House of Representatives. Since parliamentary deliberations are centered upon the committee system, the real deliberation of the budget takes place in the 50-member House of Representatives' Budget Committee. Given the extraordinary influence that the budget has on the politics and economy of the nation, it is no surprise that vigorous debate takes place in this arena. Moreover, public hearings are held, with witnesses recommended by the parties or selected from the general public by the committee. After the budget is debated and approved by the Budget Committee, it goes to the full house for debate and approval; then it goes to the House of Councillors. The above process is repeated there. If the upper house renders a different verdict on the budget that cannot be resolved in a joint committee of both houses, or if the upper house reaches no decision on the budget within 30 days, however, then, according to the Constitution (Article 60), the lower house's decision on the budget takes effect.

The parliamentarily approved budget then moves to the implementation stage. Based on the approved budget, the cabinet allocates to the head of each government agency its budget of income and expenditure, its continuing budget, and its debt service budget. Upon receipt of this information, the agency head prepares a planned schedule of obligatory disbursements (including contractual obligations of the state and other agency activities) that is usually submitted to the Finance Ministry in mid-April. Until this schedule is approved by the ministry and the cabinet, no disbursements may be made. Budgetary allocations are rarely made in cash. In principle, they are made by check payable by the Bank of Japan or by a transfer from the National Treasury to the Bank of Japan. In other words, all national funds are brought together under the control of the state's account with the Bank of Japan. And since budgetary disbursements constitute an outflow of currency into the market, the government, through careful coordination of these schedules of disbursement and management of its Bank of Japan account, is able to fine-tune market conditions.

The national budget controls all governmental fiscal inflow and outflow until April 30 of the following year. On that day, the now-terminated budget goes into the stage of settlement of accounts. The head of each agency is responsible for drawing up and submitting to the Finance Ministry by July 31 an accounting of all transactions. Then the ministry is required, by November 30, to submit its own accounting, along with all related materials, to the Board of Audit. The head of the board is required to submit a report, based on the ministerial submissions, to the next regular session of parliament. In Japan, parliament's debate of this report has no legally binding power. Of course, if errors have been made in the execution of the budget, parliament can pursue the question of administrative responsibility, but the fact that there is no legally binding power to hold the government accountable for its spending is one glaring weakness in the budgetary process.

BUDGET COMPILATION: THE FINANCE MINISTRY AND THE EXECUTIVE BRANCH

It is, of course, hardly exhaustive to analyze the politics of the budgetary process solely in terms of budget compilation. In the interest of simplicity, however, we shall limit ourselves here to the compilation process—a scramble for booty in which the interests of every significant political actor are in furious competition.

Work on the next fiscal year's budget begins as soon as the current year's budget takes effect. Work proceeds cumulatively, beginning at the section level in every agency and progressing to bureau, agency, and government-wide levels. On each level there are those who make requests and, locked in struggle with them, those who must assess and pass judgment on those requests. At the government-wide level, the organ of assessment is the Finance Ministry's Budget Bureau; in each agency the analogous organ, which examines and aggregates requests from below, is the accounting or budget section of the minister's secretariat; at the bureau level it is the bureau's general affairs section. Usually, compilation of budgetary requests at the section level begins around May of the previous year. Requests reach the agency level sometime in July. The responsible organ listens to and adjusts the interests of each bureau, and compiles the agency's total budget request. This is compiled in identical form in each agency, showing the items and amounts requested for the coming year, and items, amounts, and changes from the previous year.

Since, for a long time, the cabinet did not provide the agencies with any uniform set of standards for requests, however, there was a temptation for every agency, as a tactic by which to get what it really needed, to present the Finance Ministry initially with outrageously unrealistic requests. In fact, "preliminary estimates of the 1959 budget totaled roughly ¥3 trillion. After all the dust had settled, however, the budget came to about ¥1.4 trillion"[1]—less than half the original amount. In order to avoid this sort of situation, the government began in 1961 to establish ceilings for agency budget requests. (See table 10.1.) During the period of high-speed economic growth, these functioned simply to impose some order on requests; as one can see, they were hardly restrictive. With the deepening of the fiscal crisis of the 1980s, however, they began to serve to control agency requests and indicate the shape and direction of government policy. Toward the end of the 1980s, with greater fiscal stability, the ceilings began again to show some relaxation.

Agency budgetary requests are submitted to the Finance Ministry by August 31. Beginning in mid-September, the ministry's Budget

TABLE 10.1   Trends in Budget Request Ceilings, 1962–90

1962–64	Maximum allowable request	50% increase over previous year
1965–67	Maximum allowable request	30% increase
1968–75	Maximum allowable request	25% increase
1976	Maximum allowable request	15% increase
1977	General administrative expenditures	10% increase
	Other expenditures	15% increase
1978–79	General administrative expenditures	
	(a) Operating expenditures	0
	(b) Other general administrative expenditures	5% increase
	Other expenditures	13.5 increase
1980	General administrative expenditures	0
	Other expenditures	10% increase
1981	General administrative expenditures	0
	Other expenditures	7.5% increase
1982	General administrative expenditures	0
	Other expenditures	0
1983	Ordinary expenditures	5% decrease over previous year
	Investment	0
1984–87	Ordinary expenditures	10% decrease
	Investment	5% decrease
1988–90	Ordinary expenditures	10% decrease
	Investment	0

SOURCE: Based on figures from Zaisei Chōsakai, ed., *Kuni no Yosan* (The National Budget), Hase Shobō, various years.

Bureau holds hearings on each agency's request, attended by the chief investigators from the budget bureaus of those agencies.[2] At the same time, the head of the general affairs section of each bureau in each agency is explaining the major features of the bureau's request to the staff of the Finance Ministry's Budget Bureau. The Budget Bureau considers all the information thus obtained and, after a series of internal conferences, compiles the Finance Ministry's draft of the budget. Sometime after December 20 this draft is submitted by the minister to the cabinet, and presented unofficially to the agencies.

The above is the public side of the process. There is, however, another side of freewheeling stratagems on the part of both the Finance Ministry and the other executive-branch agencies. Early on, the agencies make contact with those members of parliament with whom they have deep relationships (the *zoku* politicians, organized around the committees of the LDP's PARC and other organs), and begin to firm up their support groups in order to fight for the more important items in their requests. Moreover, they leak information about new programs to the mass media in the hope of generating public support, and issue white papers and other publications as part of their PR campaigns. In addition, both budget officers and investigators make full use of personal contacts (through fellow alumni of their universities, among others).[3] At the same time, however, these sorts of strategies for realizing agency requests serve to provide the assessors and Finance Ministry staff with information that reveals the real priorities of the agencies and helps measure their public support. The assessors have ample criteria for judging requests, but in the last analysis they are all rules of thumb. Thus, when ten public works projects are proposed and there is money enough for only five, for example, it is easy to understand why the ones to be cut are often selected in reverse order of the political outcry the cut is likely to provoke, and this calculation is facilitated by the publicity process noted above.

BUDGET COMPILATION: NEGOTIATION AND RESURRECTION

Ordinarily, the Finance Ministry's draft budget shown informally to the various executive agencies makes major cuts in their requests—especially in their big-ticket projects. The agencies, as soon as they have the draft, report on it to their allies in the parties. At these meetings, the heads of the ministerial secretariats and the directors general of the bureaus explain their positions to the politicians, and strategies of negotiation to resurrect the agencies' pet projects are polished. It is usually from about this stage in the compilation process that the process begins to attract major media coverage, and interest groups of all stripes begin to mobilize nationally and, along with the *zoku* MPs, to pepper the Finance Ministry and the party leadership with appeals. The negotiations begin at the general affairs section chief level and climb the administrative hierarchy to the bureau director general, the administrative vice-ministerial,[4] and the ministerial level before reaching a resolution. Issues of a strongly political nature that are still unresolved at this stage are entrusted to conferences between the government and the party, or even to a decision by the prime minister. Then, the compilation process moves toward a conclusion amid a final flurry of arithmetic adjustments.

In fact, however, there is almost no difference between the size of the Finance Ministry's draft budget and that of the total budget finally arrived at. "This is because there are, hidden in the ministry's original draft, a number of revenue sources placed there for the precise purpose of compensating for items resurrected. They are referred to as 'closet resources.' The draft of the assessors' version of the general account budget shown to the executive agencies is broken down not by agency but by major expenditure type. This device allows room to create and hide closet resources. Because the various agencies see the assessors' draft in bits and pieces, and cannot add up their respective totals, they cannot tell how much revenue is really hidden there."[5]

During the era of high-speed economic growth, this pool of "closet resources" added up to a considerable amount. With the annual stage thus set, both demands and resources for program resurrection entered from the wings and a furious competition between major interest groups unfolded in short order. In fact, this conflict between interests brought all the interest groups openly onto the stage and satisfied their supporters' demands for action. Thus the process satisfied the major actors and facilitated the reaching of agreements acceptable to all. And, in turn, this movement was mediated during the period of LDP rule by groups within the ruling party and more recently by the members of the ruling coalition. It is in this party-mediated interest group competition that one finds part of the reason that the LDP itself developed a behavioral style resembling that of an interest group; whether its successors will follow a similar path it is too soon to tell. Thus, although it is generally conceded that the ability of the parliament to control the budgetary process is weak, this is not necessarily an example of some universal tendency for the legislative function to atrophy in a modern administrative state. Because the interests of the ruling party have long permeated the budgetary process and have been resolved before the budget gets to parliament, there has simply been no need for parliament to make a major issue of it.

BUDGETARY POLITICS IN A TIME OF FISCAL RECONSTRUCTION

As the government's fiscal crisis deepened during the 1980s the room for creating "closet resources" narrowed. On the contrary, as we saw in table 10.1, there were years in which the budget process was characterized by "minus ceilings," or absolute cuts. In such a situation, the ruling party's ability to spread benefits evenly in response to all the different interests represented within the party disappeared. The determination of budget priorities came to reflect clearly the priorities of those who held real power. Figure 10.1 shows the rates of change in the general account budget overall and in its major areas of expenditure between 1980 and 1990. During this decade, although the general account budget increased 1.56 times, expenditures for social security (1.41) and education (1.14) increased much less. By contrast, the rate of increase of defense expenditures (1.86) and foreign aid (2.05) surpassed that of the budget overall. Such figures reveal starkly just what administrative reform means in the Japanese political context (see chapter 11). In particular, a rapid increase in the military budget in any given year is not an isolated problem. In addition to defense expenditures for that year, the military budget determines the content and size of the following year's obligations. Subsequent years' obligations are referred to as expenses carried over and service of the national debt, but they are for the most part expenses inflicted on later budgets by long-term arms purchases. The total of such prior obligations in 1990 was ¥2.93 trillion, amounting to 70 percent of the 1990 military budget; obviously, this figure severely constrained the budget in 1991 and subsequent years, and makes state finances increasingly inflexible. There is an extremely problematic quality to budgetary politics that represses expenditures directly associated with the welfare and quality of life of the people and reduces fiscal flexibility, all for the sake of enhancing the nation's military power.

Rising rapidly, along with defense expenditures, is the servicing of the national debt. The sale of deficit bonds began in earnest in 1975; along with the construction bonds authorized under Article 4 of the Finance Law, they totaled ¥164 trillion by 1989. In 1984 the government committed itself publicly to the objective of financial reconstruction and reduction of the sale of deficit bonds to zero by the time of the 1990 budget. And the government did in fact precisely

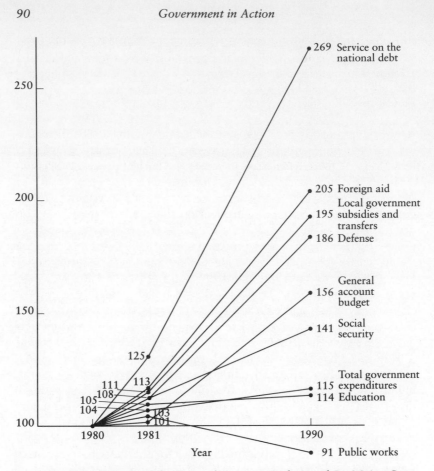

FIGURE 10.1   Growth in the General Account Budget and Its Major Components, 1980–90 (1980 = 100)
SOURCE: Based on figures from Zaisei Chōsakai, ed., *Kuni no Yosan* (The National Budget), Hase Shobō, various years.

this. The reality of ¥164 trillion of bonds that had to be repaid still existed, however, and the sale of construction bonds continued. Moreover, one may anticipate that the sale of construction bonds will increase, in light of the fact that in July 1990 the government promised to invest another ¥340 trillion in public works over the next decade in order to stimulate the economy and, hopefully, demand for imported goods and services.

Given this reality, plus a desire to fine-tune the economy and an unrelenting foreign pressure for budgetary stimulation, the government must endeavor to maintain budgetary flexibility and restraint.

Moreover, the corruption that surfaced in the late 1980s and early 1990s clearly calls for highly transparent policy priorities and financial controls in order that those who compile, deliberate, and implement the budget can be held accountable for their actions.

NOTES

1. Katō Yoshitarō, "Zaisei no Shikumi" (How Public Finance Works), in Higo Kazuo, ed., *Zaiseigaku Yōron* (Essentials of Public Finance), Yūhikaku, 1985, p. 78.
2. The agency representatives attending the Finance Ministry's hearings are not personnel of the budget section of the ministry's secretariat but are the heads of the budget sections of each bureau. Together with their assistants and members of each bureau's general affairs section, between 10 and 20 representatives typically attend such hearings.
3. On this process, see John Campbell, *Contemporary Japanese Budget Politics*, Berkeley, Calif., University of California Press, 1977.
4. One of the characteristics of these negotiations is that they do not take place between appellants and assessors of equal rank, but between superior appellants and subordinate assessors. That is, a general affairs section chief will meet with a Budget Bureau assessor, a bureau chief with a lesser Budget Bureau official, and an administrative vice-minister with the vice-chief of the Budget Bureau—although "pulling rank" may be too strong a word to infer from this tactic.
5. Katō, "Zaisei no Shikumi," p. 79.

CHAPTER 11

ADMINISTRATIVE REFORM

THE FIRST AD HOC COMMISSION ON ADMINISTRATION

One attempt to achieve fiscal flexibility and restraint has been the practice of administrative reform. Such governmental restructuring has long been a part of the administrative picture in Japan. Before World War II, the process of abolition and amalgamation of government agencies was known as administrative adjustment. Moreover, the Occupation reforms also included a massive reorganization of the basic system of administration. In 1949, 1951, and 1954, abolition of the wartime system of economic controls and a series of personnel retrenchments were, similarly, carried out under the old label of administrative adjustment. The now-popular term "administrative reform" came into common usage around 1962, when the cabinet of Prime Minister Ikeda Hayato institutionalized the review of administrative structures and practices by creating the First Ad Hoc Commission on Administration, commonly known by its abbreviated name, Rinchō (Rinji Gyōsei Chōsakai).

The First Rinchō, established by a unanimous vote of parliament, was an advisory council composed of seven prominent members (the first chair was Satō Kiichirō, president of Mitsui Bank), with a number of technical experts and investigators under them. In 1964, after two years of deliberations, the First Rinchō submitted a set of 16 recommendations dealing, among other things, with the functions of the cabinet, the ministerial system, the coordination of interministerial activities, regional administration, and budgetary accounting. As stated in its introduction, the report of the First Rinchō did not involve itself directly in evaluation or prescription of politics and policy. The report was limited in scope to reform of administrative structures and managerial functions.

This report subsequently became known as the bible of adminis-

92

trative reform, so highly was it regarded. But, as a result of its can-onization, the principle that administrative reform should not involve normative evaluation of policy and politics became established dog-ma. In fact, from today's vantage point, it is clear that the function of the First Rinchō was to coordinate administrative structures in re-sponse to, and in order to promote, high-speed economic growth. In this sense, perhaps it was unnecessary for it to concern itself explicit-ly with the content of policy. But whether or not it was appropriate for administrative reform to limit itself to adjustment of administra-tive structures and improved managerial practice, it is clear that the apolitical concept of reform that became rooted at that time was the product of the specific conditions of that time.

SUBSEQUENT ADMINISTRATIVE REFORM

It is difficult to evaluate the exact extent to which the report of the First Rinchō was actually put into effect. But the government, enthu-siastic over the general process, followed up the First Rinchō with an Administrative Supervision Commission, an Administrative Reform Headquarters, and an Administrative Management Agency, under which it carried out, among other things, reductions in the number of public employees and in the number of agency subdivisions. In the area of personnel, in particular, a program of reduction of public em-ployees was initiated in 1967. The result of this, as can be seen in figure 11.1, was a stabilization after the mid-1960s of the number of national public employees. Moreover, in relation to the number of agency subdivisions, after a policy of reduction of one bureau per agency was adopted by the Satō cabinet in 1968, the increase in their numbers also came under control (see figure 11.2). But apart from these slimming-down outcomes, even the government has recognized that in the area of the management of administrative organizations it is difficult to say that the report of the First Rinchō has borne much fruit.

RISE OF THE "SMALL GOVERNMENT" ARGUMENT

With the first oil crisis of 1973, Japan's economy went suddenly from rapid growth to much slower growth. Japan, along with all the other advanced industrial nations to varying degrees, entered a very difficult economic situation in which inflation and unemploy-ment increased simultaneously. Naturally, these dramatic economic changes had an impact upon each nation's finances. Each responded differently, but many, to keep their economies solvent and vigorous,

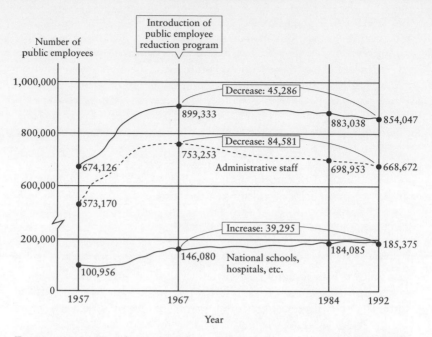

FIGURE 11.1 Trends in Number of National Government Employees, 1957–89

SOURCE: Somu-chō data; Gyōsei Kanri Kenkyū Senta, *Dēta Bukku Nihon no Gyōsei 1992* (1992 Data Book for Japanese Public Administration), 1992, p. 32.

NOTE: Figure excludes public employees in Okinawa and Self-Defense-Force personnel.

chose to issue deficit bonds either for public works or to make up the deficiency in ordinary spending. In many cases, the cumulative amount of their national debts snowballed rapidly, bringing them to the verge of fiscal disaster. In Japan, too, even though the numbers of employees and administrative bureaus had already been cut back, government expenditures rose steadily. In a supplement to the fiscal 1975 budget, the government issued ¥2.9 trillion worth of deficit bonds; these issues continued annually until 1989, although they peaked in 1980 at ¥7.22 trillion. By 1989, the national debt—the total of outstanding deficit and construction bonds—had risen to a total of over ¥164 trillion.

Under these conditions of fiscal near-disaster, arguments in favor of "small government" gradually came to the fore. The most extreme versions of this position can be seen in the political philosophy of Britain's Thatcher government and the U.S. presidency under Reagan, but it also became influential in Japan. It did *not* signify a

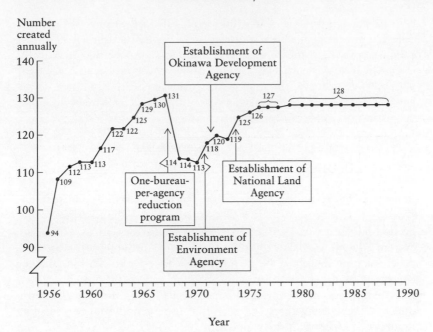

FIGURE 11.2   Trends in the Creation of New Intraministerial Secretariats and Bureaus, 1956–88

SOURCE: Sōmu-chō, *Sōmu-chō Nenji Hōkoku* (Management and Coordination Agency Annual Report), 1990, p. 28.

NOTES:

1. Data refer to secretariats and bureaus as defined under Article 25 of the National Administrative Organization Law.
2. The increase of 15 bureaus in 1957 (including 4 in the Local Autonomy Agency, 3 in the Administrative Management Agency, and 4 in the Economic Planning Agency) resulted from a revision of the National Administrative Organization Law that permitted non-ministerial agencies to establish bureaus in place of departments.

contraction of the overall realm of government responsibilities. Indeed, there is no universally accepted criterion for differentiation of the spheres of the public and private sectors, and Japan did not attempt to define one. Contemporary "big government" was, however, seen as having clearly gone overboard: by intervening excessively in the economy and the economic activities of private individuals, it was considered as sapping the creativity and individualism of society. In line with this assumption, the "small government" position argued that the framework of government responsibility should be streamlined, focusing on the fundamental governmental functions of defense and foreign relations, and its regulation of and intervention in society and the economy should be ameliorated or reduced. Of course, few proposed that this political philosophy should be reflected simplistically in national policy. In a situation of financial collapse, in which the reduction of public spending was politically imperative, however, it was a philosophy with considerable political appeal. Accordingly, in the 1980s, administrative reform went beyond the orthodox vision of structural reform and involved itself deeply in the content of government policy.

THE SECOND AD HOC COMMISSION ON ADMINISTRATION

In March 1981, amid the economic and fiscal conditions just described, the Second Ad Hoc Commission on Administration (the Second Rinchō) was established. The organizational structure of the Second Rinchō was basically the same as that of the first: it was composed of nine members (with business leader Dokō Toshio, former chairman of the Federation of Economic Organizations, as chair), with a number of technical experts, consultants, and investigators under them. During the two years that the Second Rinchō met, five reports were filed with the prime minister.

Overall, the reports of the Second Rinchō and the use made of them differed clearly from those of the first commission. It set forth as the basic objectives of administrative reform the "construction of a vigorous welfare society" and "positive contributions to international society," to be achieved through (1) reconsideration of an administrative structure that has become bloated since the period of high-speed economic growth and (2) fiscal reconstruction without tax increases. And, indeed, the Second Rinchō proposed reforms across a multiplicity of policy and institutional arenas.

As the commission's occasional reference to administrative *and fiscal* reform implies, however, the distinctive character of the Second Rinchō's proposals lay in the question of how to reduce the mounting national debt. The pursuit of this goal within the constraints of fiscal reconstruction without increased taxes directed the attention of the commission toward the specifics of policy and government operations. Despite its name, the Second Rinchō resembled an advisory council on budget reduction; the theoretical viewpoint that informed its deliberations was that of "small government" and "vitality of the private sector." It saw the reduction of governmental regulation and assistance and the invigoration of the private sector as being intimately tied to a reduction in government spending and to socioeconomic development. Accordingly, it sought a specific and concrete reversal of government policy and operations in every policy sphere—

including social security, social welfare, and education—that had expanded along with the welfare state, beginning with the privatization of two huge public corporations, the Japan National Railways and Nippon Telegraph and Telephone.

The recommendations of the Second Rinchō were incorporated in each of the budgets of the fiscal years during its operations, and enabling legislation was passed. After the commission was dissolved, a "mini-Rinchō"—the Advisory Council for the Promotion of Administrative Reform (Gyōkakushin, from Rinji Gyōsei Kaikaku Suishin Shingikai), also chaired by Dokō Toshio—was established. This council submitted periodic "opinions" to the prime minister regarding implementation of the reports of the Second Rinchō through the budget process. Thus, from the outset, the Second Rinchō and its successor pursued a policy turnabout in accord with the concepts of "vitality of the private sector" and "small government," though in doing so they sparked criticism that their budgetary recommendations amounted in fact to the proliferation of defense spending and the evisceration of welfare.

ADMINISTRATIVE REFORM AS POLITICAL REFORM

Administrative reform centered upon fiscal reconstruction was marvelously compatible both with the strong, "presidential" political style advocated by then Prime Minister Nakasone and with a period of heightened foreign pressures brought about by economic friction, and it promoted the strengthening of prime ministerial leadership and organizational reform for the purpose of crisis management. In July 1985, the Gyōkakushin submitted a report in which, among other things, it called for (1) a strengthened coordinating role for the cabinet secretariat, for the purpose of dealing with international issues such as trade friction as they pertained to every executive agency, and (2) the reorganization of the Defense Council into a National Security Council capable of responding to international emergencies.

Upon receipt of this report, the government revised the ordinance on cabinet secretariat organization and submitted a proposal for the establishment of a national security council to parliament. On July 1, 1986, the National Security Council (NSC) and a new cabinet secretariat came into being. The NSC was chaired by the prime minister and included the foreign minister, finance minister, chief of the cabinet secretariat, chair of the National Public Safety Commission, director of the Defense Agency, and director of the Economic Planning Agency, with the participation as necessary of other ministers and the chair of the Self-Defense Forces Joint Chiefs of Staff.

Moreover, to the cabinet secretariat was added, in addition to offices of foreign affairs, domestic affairs, intelligence and research, counselors, and public information, an office of national security incorporating the former general affairs bureau of the Defense Council. The head of each held the rank of director of bureau. Thus, at least structurally, the foundation was laid for the consolidation of functional integration under the prime minister.

Viewed in this light, the administrative reforms that began with the Second Rinchō did not amount simply to fiscal reconstruction. It is hardly an exaggeration to say that, together, they amounted to a neoconservative turnabout in economic policy, as symbolized by the "invigoration of the private sector" argument, and a political reform with a strong nationalistic tone.

THE "BUBBLE ECONOMY" AND "POLITICAL REFORM FROM WASHINGTON"

Unfortunately, these administrative reforms emphasizing the invigoration of the private sector also comported quite well with the excessive circulation of the yen, and promoted speculation in stocks and land. This speculative "bubble economy"—ever expanding, but with nothing solid inside it—fed on itself and, swelling beyond the nation's borders, led to takeovers of foreign corporations and speculation in artworks, land, and national bonds abroad as well. The explosive rise in the 1980s of land prices became a major social problem, and overseas Japanese investment also generated foreign criticism.

Moreover, the relaxation of governmental regulation epitomized by the breakup and privatization of public corporations gave rise to the sort of massive political corruption seen in, for example, the Recruit scandal of 1988. The Recruit scandal, which also embroiled Nippon Telegraph and Telephone in a tangle of bribery and shady political favors and payoffs, is probably the best example of the more outrageous byproducts of administrative reform. The privatization of the telecommunications industry certainly made possible the entry into that field of new enterprises. It was by no means the case, however, that anybody at all could freely enter the field. Bureaucratic permissions and permits of various kinds were necessary, and those most able to play the political game either legally or illegally found entry easiest. Despite the rhetoric of privatization and deregulation, as of the end of December 1985, the number of governmental approvals was 10,054; by the end of March 1989 it had risen to 10,278. Under such conditions, in order to prevail over their competitors, it was natural for new enterprises like the Recruit Company to seek—and reward—political and administrative patrons. And, of course, in exchange for their patronage, politicians sought political contributions.

Thus, not only did administrative reform, while trumpeting invigoration of the private sector and governmental deregulation, not fundamentally attack the interwoven, collusive structure of business, administration, and politics; rather, one may even say that it simply opened up new territory to be carved up, exploited, and traded on by entrepreneurs and their political cronies. In January 1987, the government convened the Ad Hoc Advisory Council for the Promotion of Administrative Reform (the Second Gyōkakushin), chaired by former Mitsubishi Cement President Ōtsuki Bunpei, to study, among other issues, the land problem. With the malign consequences of the administrative reforms carried out since the Second Rinchō becoming clearer and clearer, however, the Second Gyōkakushin was dissolved in April 1990, having exerted hardly any influence at all. Nevertheless, in October 1990, a Third Gyōkakushin, with former Mitsubishi Chemical President Suzuki Eiji as its chair, was convoked.

It was at this time that the United States, as part of the Structural Impediments Initiative (SII) talks that had begun in the autumn of 1989, presented to the Japanese government a "Policy Action Reform Proposal" running to over 200 items. The talks themselves represented a new, bilateral attempt to go beyond specific, contentious trade issues and address basic features of American and Japanese society, economy, and politics that gave rise to economic friction, misunderstanding, and conflict. The 1990 proposal called for fundamental reform of the structure of Japanese business, administration, and politics nurtured since the era of high-speed economic growth, which the United States contended had produced a Japanese political economy based on fundamentally unfair trade practices. The proposal emphasized such things as the development of social capital, the strengthening of the Anti-Monopoly Law in order to eliminate such things as rigged bidding and exclusionary business practices, the consolidation of authority over land-use regulation, and the strengthening of consumer protection administration. And, specifically because many of the elements of this proposal were part of the vision of administrative reform that the Japanese public had sought for so long, it came as quite a shock to Japan.

The government, in the SII talks, promised to accommodate many of the American demands, in effect adopting an American plan for administrative reform. Based on this commitment, the Third Gyōkakushin began to consider concrete reform measures, and, in December 1991, the council submitted a report calling, among other things, for the enactment of an administrative procedures law that would standardize the procedures involved in the obtaining of government permits and in administrative guidance, thus creating an administrative process transparent to foreign observers as well as to the Japanese public.

CHAPTER 12

SECURITY POLICY AND DEFENSE SPENDING

NATIONAL SECURITY IN POSTWAR JAPAN

Defense and national security have been ever-present components of politics since the emergence of the modern nation-state. Domestically, modern nation-states have commonly promoted a polity and economy based on liberalism; at the same time, externally, they have repeatedly generated military confrontations and instigated numerous wars, revolving most often around the maintenance and expansion of economic interests. Such international confrontations and conflicts became increasingly numerous and intense with the progress of capitalist economic development in the nineteenth century. And, as one can see in World Wars I and II, the great powers have repeatedly formed alliances and initiated all-out wars that put the very survival of their nations at stake.

After World War II, international conflict ceased to be a matter of rivalry between capitalist states and was transformed into one based on differences in ideologies and political and economic systems, epitomized by the Cold War polarization between the two camps centered upon the United States and the Soviet Union. Under Stalin's leadership, the postwar Soviet Union, with the aid of the Red Army and the "proletarian democratic" revolutions that occurred in Eastern Europe and Asia, established a number of communist dictatorships and succeeded in building a bloc of socialist countries with itself at the head of the alliance. At the same time, the United States, drawing on its immense economic power, established the political, economic, and military leadership structure known as the Pax Americana among the capitalist democracies. Thus arose in Europe the intense military confrontation between the North Atlantic Treaty Organization (NATO) and the Warsaw Pact; in Asia there was not

only cold but hot war as well—in China, Korea, and Indochina—
and the tragedy of war swept the region time and again.

In its essence, national security refers to the peaceful pursuit by nations of their respective independence and coexistence; it does not
imply the building of the independence of one's own nation upon the
sacrifices of others through economic or military hegemony. Nevertheless, in the intense postwar rivalry between the United States and
the Soviet Union the concept of national security, in fact, took on
overwhelmingly, if not exclusively, military overtones.

Subsequently, the Cold War structure that had determined the
shape and tone of the postwar world came to an end with the democratic revolutions in Eastern Europe in the late 1980s and the collapse in 1991 of the Soviet Union. On one level it appeared that the
international community had been presented with a golden opportunity to redefine national security radically and pursue coexistence
free from the threat of global war. On another level, however, local
military conflicts continued to occur without interruption, just as before. And Japan, too—which had built its military strength within
the context of the U.S.–Soviet bipolar rivalry—faced a major turning
point revolving around the question of how to respond to the conditions of this new era.

THE U.S.–JAPAN MUTUAL SECURITY TREATY
AND REARMAMENT

In the words of Article 9 of the new postwar Constitution:

> Aspiring sincerely to an international peace based on justice and
> order, the Japanese people forever renounce war as a sovereign
> right of the nation and the threat or use of force as a means of
> settling international disputes.
>
> In order to accomplish the aim of the preceding paragraph,
> land, sea, and air forces, as well as other war potential, will nev-
> er be maintained. The right of belligerency of the state will not
> be recognized.

It is because of this article that the Japanese Constitution is frequently referred to as the peace constitution. But, alas, it presumed a
world without big-power rivalry, already a vain hope in the late
1940s. Even as the Constitution was being promulgated, the U.S.–
Soviet Cold War was intensifying, and in June 1950 war broke out
in Korea. In his 1950 New Year's Day message, Supreme Commander for the Allied Forces in Japan General Douglas MacArthur had
praised the significance of Japan's new Constitution, but his posture

changed abruptly with the outbreak of the Korean War, and he instructed the Japanese government to initiate the process of rearmament, beginning with the creation of a National Police Reserve. The purpose of this force was to meet the "threat from the north"—that is, the Soviet Union—in place of the U.S. forces that had been hurriedly transferred from Japan to the Korean peninsula. And, indeed, most of the National Police Reserve created by the Yoshida cabinet in response to MacArthur's order was deployed in Hokkaido.

Then, on September 8, 1951, the same day as the signing of the San Francisco Peace Treaty between Japan and its erstwhile enemies, a Treaty of Mutual Security was signed between the United States and Japan. According to the provisions of this treaty, the Japanese government would—even after the end of the Occupation and the restoration of full independence—continue to guarantee to the United States the right to station military forces in Japan; the United States for its part, promised to protect Japan militarily from the threat of both domestic insurrection and foreign attack. Moreover, the Japanese government agreed that it would not allow any third country the use of Japanese territory for the deployment of military forces without the consent of the United States. In sum, what this treaty meant was that Japan was going to become a permanent American military base in East Asia.

Three years later, in July 1954, the Japanese government completely reorganized the National Police Reserve into the Self-Defense Forces (SDF), a tripartite air-land-sea military with an authorized strength of 146,000 men. At the same time, it established the Defense Agency, the director of which held cabinet status. This new defense establishment centered upon the Defense Agency comprised, below the director, a vice director, a group of counselors, a series of internal administrative bureaus, the joint chiefs of staff, and the general staffs of the three service branches. The internal bureaus, which were in charge of such major matters as generating proposals for defense policy, organization and strength of the SDF, personnel management, and administering the budget, were composed of civilian officials. By contrast, the joint chiefs and service commanders were composed of uniformed personnel and were in charge of strategic and tactical planning and operations. In this way, the Japanese defense establishment clearly established a military apparatus—albeit civilian-controlled—with its own administrative structure. On the face of it, it seems hard to deny that this was in clear contradiction of the renunciation of both war and military capability set forth in the Constitution.

As Japan initiated this process of rearmament and subsequently,

in the 1960s, launched a program of high-speed economic development, the United States pressed Japan to build a military capability
appropriate to an ally with whom the United States could build a
truly mutual security arrangement. Accordingly, in January 1960, an
entirely new U.S.–Japan Mutual Security Treaty was signed, replacing
the 1951 treaty. The new treaty obligated both Japan and the United
States to increase their military forces for the purposes of self-defense
and mutual assistance. Moreover, Japan and the United States were
both committed to responding to an attack on the other by a third
country, if the attack occurred within Japan's territory, and the
United States was given the right to maintain bases on Japanese territory for the purpose of maintaining security in East Asia. Thus, the
new treaty had strong overtones of a U.S.–Japan military *alliance*
rather than just a passive defense agreement. For this reason, it provoked massive opposition, which rocked the entire nation, from
those who saw its potential for entangling Japan in American military adventures and endangering Japanese democracy and peace.
Nevertheless, articles of ratification were exchanged on June 23,
1960. The treaty was automatically extended in 1970, 1980, and
1990, and remains in force today.

GROWTH OF MILITARY POWER AND TRENDS IN MILITARY SPENDING

Since the establishment of the Defense Agency, Japan has carried out
a series of five-year National Defense Buildup Plans, gradually enhancing its military capability. Between 1958 and 1976, it drew up
and executed four such plans. The equipping of military forces carried out under the first plan consisted primarily of the supply to
Japan of older American weapons. Beginning with the second plan,
however, Japan has equipped itself with the most up-to-date equipment currently available, most of it either wholly domestic or manu-
factured in Japan under license from foreign arms producers. It was
only with the third plan, however, that the most likely actual targets
of military response have been specified and appropriate buildup
objectives and costs accordingly assigned.

In November 1976, prior to the end of the fourth National
Defense Buildup Plan, the government elaborated its thinking on
national security, presenting in lieu of another concrete buildup plan
a set of *General Principles* of defense planning. This document, as is
clear from terms such as "maintenance of the status quo in basic defense capability" and "response to situations up to limited and small-
scale invasion," was designed to impose constraints on the further

growth of military power. The *General Principles* also established the principle that military spending should not exceed 1 percent of the GNP. The *General Principles*, in contrast to previous plans, did not, however, specify time frames or costs of fulfillment of their objectives or the quantity or quality of equipment necessary. Consequently, it was inevitable that the budget for weapons procurement and maintenance of the military establishment became the subject of variously influenced political decisions in the annual budget compilation process more than had previously been the case. Thus, whatever may have been the intentions of Prime Minister Miki Takeo and Defense Agency Director-General Sakata Michita, authors of the new approach to defense planning, the shift to the *General Principles* type of defense planning, from the very beginning, actually concealed within itself the possibility of *weakening* governmental control over military power.

In November 1978, two years after the adoption of the *General Principles* process, the American and Japanese governments agreed to a de facto transformation of the mutual security arrangement in the form of a set of *Guidelines for U.S.–Japan Defense Cooperation*. These *Guidelines* had three features.

First, consistent with the objective of "a defense posture for preventing invasion before the fact," they established nuclear deterrence as the foundation of security cooperation. As shown by the passage, "The American forces will maintain a [strategic] nuclear deterrent force and, at the same time, develop a [tactical] response force in a frontline position," the Japanese government was in this document clearly recognizing the nuclear deterrent role of the American forces in Japan.

Second, the *Guidelines* called for "coordinated, cooperative action" between Japanese and American forces.

Third, the *Guidelines* called for U.S.–Japanese military cooperation in the event of a situation in East Aisa *outside* of Japan if it bore serious implications for Japan's own security. By the terms of these guidelines, the geographical limits of U.S.–Japanese security cooperation spread far beyond the horizon—and beyond all previous Japanese military obligations as well.

The cabinet of Prime Minister Nakasone cemented its agreement with the activist principles behind the *Guidelines* by incorporating them into defense policy. Nakasone was already well known for espousing revision of the postwar Constitution and a more independent national defense posture. He nevertheless jolted the public immediately after taking office with sweeping statements that, in the case of an international crisis, Japan would close off the four straits enclosing the Sea of Japan, thus blocking egress of the Soviet fleet into the Pacific and that, with its many U.S. air bases, Japan would become an "unsinkable aircraft carrier" in the defense of East Asia. The popular impression, unsurprisingly, was that it was his firm intention to turn Japan into a major military power.

In 1983, Nakasone set up a personal advisory council, the Peace Issues Study Group, initiating a debate over Japanese military strategy. In its report submitted the next year, the study group recommended that the basis of Japanese military strategy should be a shift from a "destroy the invader on the beach" to a "destroy the invader on the high seas" concept of defense, an emphasis on mastery of offshore air space and submarine capability, and on a strong and effective air defense system built around aircraft and missiles. Following receipt of this report, the Nakasone cabinet in 1985 decided to put its resources into a major military buildup, drawing up another medium-term National Defense Buildup Plan for the period 1986 to 1990, entailing the expenditure of ¥18.4 trillion.

Japan's defense budgets since 1980 are presented in table 12.1; what is noteworthy about them is that, although the 1980s were a time of drastically reduced public expenditure rates (column C), the annual rate of increase of military spending (column E) regularly exceeded that of the general account budget overall. Moreover, from 1987 to 1989 spending broke through the 1-percent-of-GNP barrier, albeit by only a small margin. And, building upon this military growth, in 1990 the 1991–95 Medium-Range National Defense Buildup Plan—with a total estimated expenditure of ¥22.8 trillion—was compiled and moved toward implementation.

EVAPORATION OF THE "NORTHERN THREAT" AND THE RAISON D'ETRE OF THE SELF-DEFENSE FORCES

Although interpretation of Article 9 of the Constitution has always been a problematic issue, the growth of the SDF was long supported by the "northern threat" argument, which postulated the Soviet Union as Japan's major hypothetical military adversary. With the collapse of the Soviet Union, however, this argument, repeated interminably by the government in parliamentary debate and annual Defense White Papers, is no longer persuasive. To be sure, there is in some circles a movement to emphasize that a Russian or North Korean threat has succeeded the Soviet threat, but in light of current trends in international politics, combined with the internal economic and fiscal condition of Russia, there is no likelihood that Russia could achieve a dominant, superpower role like that of the

TABLE 12.1 Trends in Defense Expenditures, 1980–92 (Initial Budget) (¥ billion)

Year	GNP (A)	General account expenditures (B)	Increase over previous year (C)	Defense expenditures (D)	Increase over previous year (E)	Defense spending as % of GNP (D/A)	Defense spending as % of govt. spending (D/B)
1980	247,800	42,600	10.3%	2,200	6.5%	0.900%	5.3%
1981	264,800	46,800	9.9	2,400	7.6	0.910	5.1
1982	277,200	49,700	6.2	2,600	7.8	0.930	5.2
1983	281,700	50,400	1.4	2,800	6.5	0.980	5.5
1984	296,000	50,600	0.5	2,900	6.6	0.990	5.8
1985	314,600	52,500	3.7	3,100	6.9	0.997	6.0
1986	336,700	54,100	3.0	3,300	6.6	0.993	6.2
1987	350,400	54,100	0.0	3,500	5.2	1.004	6.5
1988	365,200	56,700	4.8	3,700	5.2	1.013	6.5
1989	389,700	60,400	6.6	3,900	5.9	1.006	6.5
1990	417,200	66,200	9.6	4,200	6.1	0.997	6.3
1991	459,600	70,300	6.2	4,400	5.5	0.950	6.2
1992	483,700	72,200	2.7	4,600	3.8	0.940	6.3

SOURCE: Bōei-chō, ed., *Bōei Hakusho 1992-nen-ban* (1992 Defense White Paper), 1992, p. 306.

TABLE 12.2   Top Ten Countries in Military Expenditures, 1990

Rank	Country	Defense spending (in billions of 1985 U.S.$)	Per capita defense spending (in 1985 U.S.$)	Defense spending as % of GNP/GDP
1	United States	249.1	1,001	5.4 %
2	Soviet Union	91.6	318	11.1
3	Saudi Arabia	33.5	2,386	36.2
4	United Kingdom	19.6	346	3.7
5	France	18.1	321	2.8
6	Germany	16.9	281	2.2
7	Japan	16.3	132	1.0
8	Kuwait	11.8	5,816	51.7
9	Italy	9.3	163	1.8
10	India	8.5	10	3.2

SOURCE: Same as table 12.1, p. 142.
NOTES:
1. Defense spending in NATO member states are aggregate estimates in accordance with NATO definitions.
2. Soviet defense spending is an estimate based on revised data published by the Soviet Union.
3. Data for Germany are from the pre-unification Federal Republic of Germany.
4. Defense spending for Saudi Arabia and Kuwait includes estimated spending incurred during the Gulf War.
5. In calculating defense as a percentage of GNP/GDP, GDP was used for those states for which it was available; for others, GNP was used.
6. The exact definition of what constitutes defense spending is not identical for all countries.

former Soviet Union, and simultaneous pressures from the United States, Japan, China, and Russia for North Korea to restrain itself diminish that threat also.

Using NATO criteria, Japan in 1991 ranked third in the world in military spending; even on the basis of the Defense Agency's more modest figures, it ranked seventh. (See table 12.2.) Japan's military spending as a proportion of GNP or GDP, however, is smaller than that of the other leading powers. At the same time, Japan is an economic superpower with a GNP equal to 15 percent of the world's total. Obviously, Japan still has the reserve capacity to significantly further increase its military strength. And its present force levels, as shown in figure 12.1, are hardly minimal. Even if one does not call into question once again the intrinsic validity of the government's northern threat argument, given the frequency with which this argument is presently disputed, the development and implementation of

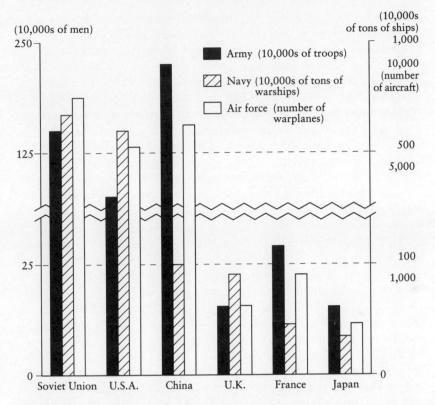

FIGURE 12.1 Force Levels of Major Military Powers, 1991
SOURCE: Same as table 12.1, p. 143.
NOTES:
1. Japanese data are as of the end of 1991. Air force strength includes warplanes in both Air (transport aircraft excluded) and Maritime (fixed-wing warplanes only) Self-Defense Forces.
2. Warplane data from countries other than Japan include air force, navy, and marine aircraft.

a clear program of arms reduction by Japan will no doubt be de-manded before long.

Paradoxically, with the collapse of the northern threat, it was not the opposition political parties (which denied the very constitutional legitimacy of the SDF) that agonized the most over the present and future raison d'être of the SDF; rather, it was the ruling LDP itself. According to the 1992 Defense White Paper, the military situation in the Asia-Pacific region is determined by

a complex interweaving of continents, peninsulas, islands, and other geographical forms, and a rich variety of races, histories, cultures, and religions. Traditionally, these nations have embraced a variety of perceptions of national interest and security and there has been very little regional unity; consequently, these perceptions have been complex and heterogeneous. It is within this context that China, Korea, the ASEAN states, and others have striven to fulfill their respective defense needs. Moreover, the region contains unresolved issues such as the divided Korean peninsula, the islands to the south of Japan [claimed by both Japan and China], and our northern islands [seized from Japan by the Soviet Union after World War II]. Consequently, the security environment of the Asia-Pacific region differs markedly from that of Europe, and has not yet witnessed major change.[1]

This perception is repeated frequently in subsequent portions of the White Paper; in short, instead of a northern threat, it cites the military instability of the Asia-Pacific region as a whole, and asserts that this constitutes a new justification for a militarily powerful Self-Defense Force. What is ignored is that, should Japan aim to maintain or raise its military capabilities in accord with this perception, it would be Japan itself that would be seen by its neighbors as a source of military instability in the Asia–Pacific region. The success or failure of Japanese arms reduction will probably be determined by the willingness of the major military powers to boldly initiate gestures of unilateral disarmament and thus put an end to competitive military expansion.

It will also be determined by the balance of power within the Japanese government between those who define national security in military terms and those who define it more broadly. In fact, there are in Japan those who have for over a decade espoused the notion of "comprehensive national security," which includes the political and social stability and economic growth of Japan *and its neighbors* as components of Japan's own national security. Accordingly, Japan has argued that its own economic growth and its aid to the countries of Southeast Asia are contributions to the security of itself and of the region as a whole. There are, to be sure, those who suspect that comprehensive national security is a Japanese rationalization for single-minded economic diplomacy and avoidance of rearmament. To others, however, this broad and not exclusively military definition of national security seems positively prescient in a post-Cold War world where military power promises to be a less valuable currency in international affairs than it was before. But even in Japan the comprehensive national security view is not dominant. Given this, the prospect for a Japanese arms-reduction program is as yet unclear.

UN PEACEKEEPING OPERATIONS AND OVERSEAS DEPLOYMENT OF THE SELF-DEFENSE FORCES

After the Gulf Crisis of 1990, voices rose within the ruling LDP and some intellectual circles over the need for Japanese international military cooperation in addition to the economic and financial contributions mentioned above. Accordingly, in 1992 parliament passed the Peacekeeping Operations (PKO) Cooperation Act and in October of that year an SDF engineering battalion was dispatched to Cambodia as part of the UN peacekeeping program there. Officially, this was a UN-sponsored peacekeeping mission; in substance, it was also the first instance since World War II of Japanese military personnel being sent to serve in a foreign country. Given this, during parliamentary debate of the PKO Cooperation Act, public opinion was polarized and vehement in regard to the prescriptions, proscriptions, and implications of Article 9. Moreover, such Southeast Asian political leaders as Singapore's former Prime Minister Lee Kuan Yew criticized the step harshly: "Call it a PKO if you like—the overseas dispatch of the Self-Defense Forces is still like offering whiskey bonbons to an alcoholic." As his comment suggests, the peoples of Asia—who still bear the scars of Japanese aggression—were hardly unanimous in welcoming the overseas dispatch of the SDF PKO unit.

Few will deny that Japan, notwithstanding its extraordinary economic power, should also be making a positive commitment of its own human resources in the area of international cooperation. Nevertheless, as one could see, as the SDF overseas dispatch issue wound its way through constitutional and parliamentary debate and into implementation, the matter is mired in complexity. The SDF is, in terms of international comparison, a very highly equipped military, and the Japanese government is seeking a new raison d'être for it in the military instability of the Asia–Pacific region. One may view the participation of the SDF in UN peacekeeping operations, too, as an attempt to invest the SDF with a raison d'être in a world from which the northern threat has evaporated, but it is also necessary to consider dispassionately the significance of the dispatch of the SDF to regions where instability is manifest. It is also a fact that, within Japan, reflection upon the enormity of war responsibility has been, by comparison with Germany, reluctant and weak. This is one reason why the nations of Asia raise a distrustful eyebrow when Japan takes an active international role.

Under its previous constitutional structure, Japan inflicted incalculable suffering upon both international society and its own people. With the dawning of the post-Cold War era, it is imperative that Japan develop leadership intent upon peaceful coexistence with these countries. The conscious pursuit of this goal is without a doubt one of the major tasks of contemporary Japanese politics.

NOTE

1. Bōei-chō, ed., *Bōei Hakusho 1992-nen-ban*, (1992 Defense White Paper), 1992, p. 6.

PART 4

POLITICAL PARTICIPATION

CHAPTER 13

POLITICAL PARTIES

THE 1955 SYSTEM

In October 1955, the previously divided right and left wings of the Japanese socialist movement were unified, creating the Japan Socialist Party (JSP),[1] and, in November, the conservative Liberal and Democratic parties combined to form the Liberal Democratic Party (LDP). The influence of these events—the emergence of the two major actors in the postwar party system—on the course of Japanese politics between 1955 and 1993 was of such moment that the political system thus created is still commonly referred to as the "1955 system." The characteristics of this system included the following: first, between them, the JSP and the LDP won over 80 percent of the vote and held over 90 percent of the seats in parliament. What evolved, however, was not a two-party system in which the two major parties alternate in power, but a "predominant party" system in which the LDP held power continuously. The parliamentary strength of the JSP was never more than about half that of the LDP; consequently, some described the situation as a "one-and-a-half-party" system. Without alternation in power, the best that can be said is that there were "pseudo-turnovers" of ruling power among the coalitions of factions within the LDP that controlled the cabinet. The battles for power previously fought among the multiple conservative parties were now carried on within the ruling LDP. The result was intense competition and rivalry among factions within the LDP. The exercise of political power within the government was as much a reflection of the factional dynamics within the LDP as it was the will of the people, the press of issues, or any desire for good government.

Second, the leitmotif of domestic Japanese politics between the 1950s and 1990s was the opposition between the Right and Left. The Right and Left fought it out on the following ground:

In *foreign policy* and *defense*, the conservatives supported a role for Japan as a member of the Western camp of industrial democracies, while the Left unceasingly advocated unarmed neutrality.

In *public security*, *policing*, and *justice*, the conservatives had had a strong interest in social control and domestic public order, while the Left attacked this as an invasion of the rights and freedoms of the people.

The conservatives stressed tradition and the status quo of the structure of *society*, while the Left attacked those traditions that were putatively connected to prewar militarism, viewing LDP support for tradition as an attempt to re-create the repressive political climate of the 1930s.[2] These cleavages set the tone for political debate and constituted the fundamental political battleground of Japanese politics. What was missing was mutual trust and any common ground that would make compromise between ruling and opposition parties possible. The LDP saw the Left as desiring to create some sort of totalitarian socialism, while the Left feared that the LDP wanted to re-create a totalitarian fascism.

Third, separate conflicts over each of these issues converged in parliament. The 1955 system emerged just as the social chaos that accompanied defeat and occupation had come to an end and parliament and the political parties were beginning to assert their leading role in the political system.[3] The LDP was able to monopolize governmental power, but it was not able to enact all of its policies into law. The LDP was never able to win the two-thirds majority in parliament necessary for constitutional revision, and vehement opposition, both in parliament and in the streets, deterred the LDP from pushing other measures. In this sense, the JSP and the other parties of the Left, which supported and defended the postwar Constitution, were able to perform the role of an effective opposition by frustrating the aims of the LDP to enhance the position of the emperor, rearm Japan, and strengthen the central government by revising the Constitution.

In other words, although "the Opposition does not initiate or carry through major policy decisions," nevertheless "the Opposition parties do affect decisions in certain ways by their very presence."[4] The opposition freely used intraparliamentary tactics of obstruction and boycott, and extraparliamentary tactics of street demonstrations, in challenging government policy. The ruling party, ever mindful of the need to keep the legislative process moving, was on many occasions forced willy-nilly to compromise with the opposition, although it held only a minority in parliament.

THE EROSION OF THE 1955 SYSTEM

Since 1955 there were numerous minor changes of actors, tactics, and ideas in the party system, but no major realignments. In subsequent years, however, the basic framework of the party system began slowly to dissolve, and collapsed amid the major realignment of the party system in 1993. One can divide the erosion of the 1955 system into two stages: the 1960s and early 1970s, and the early 1970s to the present.

During the first period, the LDP declined, with its vote diminishing gradually from election to election. The major cause of this erosion was the decline of the LDP vote in the big cities. While the LDP vote declined only 6.7 percent between 1958 and 1969 in the most rural regions, it fell 15.2 percent in the metropolitan regions. High-speed economic growth produced a flood of job-seeking migrants from the country to the cities. These migrants, who had been integrated into traditional, conservative vote-mobilizing social networks in the country, were not absorbed into similar networks after moving to the big cities, and many of them lost their party loyalties or even stopped voting entirely. In this way, cityward migration led to the long-term decline of the LDP's vote.

Simultaneous with the decline of the LDP a fragmentation of the opposition, which can be seen in table 13.1, occurred. The vote of the JSP, like that of the LDP, dwindled. The JSP's electoral foundation was centered upon the unions of the Sōhyō labor federation, and it made no effort to expand this foundation beyond the limits of organized labor. In 1960, the right wing of the JSP split off in a doctrinal dispute and formed the Democratic Socialist Party; the intra-party influence of the left wing grew, and the party's woes continued. In 1967, the Kōmeitō ran candidates for the House of Representatives for the first time and, capitalizing on the power of the Sōka Gakkai religious organization, gathered the votes of social elements hitherto unrepresented in politics and won 25 seats. The Japan Communist Party (JCP) had adopted a policy of armed struggle during the 1950s and had, as a consequence, lost almost all of its seats in parliament; in the 1960s, however, it switched to a parliamentarian party line. Party relations with both the Soviet Union and China worsened at this time and the JCP, under Secretary Miyamoto Kenji, proclaimed its independence from foreign influence and began to put its efforts into building the party organization. As a result, during the 1960s, the party's vote gradually rose; in the 1972 general election it won 38 seats and leaped into the second spot among the opposition

Political Participation

TABLE 13.1 Seats Won by Each Party in the House of Representatives Elections, 1958–93

Party	Year												
	58	60	63	67	69	72	76	79	80	83	86	90	93
LDP	287	296	283	277	288	271	249	248	284	250	300	275	223
JSP	166	145	144	140	90	118	123	107	107	112	85	136	70
Kōmeitō	—	—	—	25	47	29	55	57	33	58	56	45	51
DSP	—	17	23	30	31	19	29	35	32	38	26	14	15
JCP	1	3	5	5	14	38	17	39	29	26	26	16	15
NLC	—	—	—	—	—	—	17	4	12	8	6	—	—
SDL	—	—	—	—	—	—	—	2	3	3	4	4	4
Shinsei	—	—	—	—	—	—	—	—	—	—	—	—	55
JNP	—	—	—	—	—	—	—	—	—	—	—	—	35
Sakigake	—	—	—	—	—	—	—	—	—	—	—	—	13
Other parties	1	1	—	—	—	2	—	—	—	—	—	1	—
Independents	12	5	12	9	16	14	21	19	11	16	9	21	30
Total	467	467	467	486	486	491	511	511	511	511	512	512	511

NOTES: LDP = Liberal Democratic Party; JSP = Japan Socialist Party; DSP = Democratic Socialist Party; JCP = Japan Communist Party; NLC = New Liberal Club; SDL = Social Democratic League; JNP = Japan New Party parties. In this way, the overall strength of the opposition grew, and the gap between it and the LDP narrowed.

The high-speed economic growth of the 1960s succeeded in raising people's incomes; at the same time, however, environmental degradation in urban areas, the shortage of social capital such as housing, and the backwardness of the welfare system became issues. The fact that neither of the two major parties could resolve these problems was one cause behind the growth of the smaller parties, and also led many voters to turn their backs on the existing parties altogether. These issues were in many cases regional in nature; rising popular concern regarding them was the force behind a wave of leftist prefectural and municipal governments that came to power all across the country between the 1960s and the mid-1970s. In most instances, leftist governors and mayors won office running as independents in localities where conservatives still held a majority of the seats in the local assembly. With leftist administrations emerging in such politically and economically important places as Tokyo, Kyoto, and Osaka prefectures and the cities of Yokohama, Kawasaki, Nagoya, Kyoto, Osaka, and Kobe, however, a dual political structure—conservative on the national level, progressive on the local—had emerged. At its high-water mark in 1975, leftist governors held power in prefectures that were home to 39 percent of Japan's population; thereafter, however, a period of slow economic growth set in and a number of these administrations—whose welfarist policies outstripped their fiscal bases—failed financially; there were several prominent incidents of corruption, and the image of progressive local government began to fade. As a consequence, many of the leftist local administrations gave way to conservative ones.

A completely different set of qualities came clearly to characterize the later 1970s from those characteristic of the first half of the decade. This transformation had four aspects: First, since the 1970s, because the number of parliamentary seats held by the various parties fluctuated more, a cycle developed between periods in which the LDP held a stable majority and periods in which the Left and Right were in close competition. Even though each party's share of the vote did not fluctuate greatly, slight shifts in the vote were translated into significant changes in the distribution of parliamentary seats.

In the 1976, 1979, and 1983 general elections, LDP candidates did not win even a majority of the seats in the House of Representatives;[5] in 1980 and 1986 they won sweeping victories, and in 1990 they at least won a stable majority. A stable majority, in the House of Representatives, means that one party or coalition of parties holds enough seats to take for itself the chairs of all 20 of the house's

standing committees and still hold a majority on each committee
—today, this means 271 seats or more. When the LDP had a narrower
majority, it could not maintain a one-seat LDP majority on every
committee. On any committee on which the LDP and the opposition
were equally represented, if the LDP chose to select one of its own
as chair and thus control debate and the agenda, it then became the
minority on the committee; if it wanted to be in the majority, it
had to allow an opposition MP to take the chair.

Second, the increased volatility of the seat distribution led to a
second cycle, within the opposition, between euphoric visions of im-
minent coalition government and states of dark despair and interne-
cine quarreling. The coalition vision, unfortunately, was diffracted:
the JCP had clearly articulated plans for a multiparty coalition government, but the DSP and the Kōmeitō envisioned a DSP-Kōmeitō-
JSP coalition that excluded the JCP. The JSP vacillated between a
DSP-JSP-Kōmeitō coalition and a grand coalition of all the opposition parties, but in 1980 the Kōmeitō engineered agreements with the
DSP on one side and the JSP on the other, and the JSP-DSP-Kōmeitō
line thus became clear. In 1980, however, the LDP swept the general
election and the enthusiasm of the opposition parties for a coalition
cooled; each turned its attention to strengthening its own party organization and discussions came to a halt. From then until the early
1990s, interparty efforts at coalition and cooperation alternated between progress and collapse. The Kōmeitō and DSP reacted negative-
ly to the strong advance of the JSP in the 1990 election (which came
largely at their own expense), and until 1993 interparty talks made
no progress.

The third characteristic of the post-1970s period was the emergence of national issues. The electoral shakeup of the 1970s, brought
about by slight changes in the parties' votes but sharp changes in the
distribution of parliamentary seats, was accompanied by the emergence of a nationwide swing in the vote. The causes of this national
swing were the expanding political horizons and increased sophis-
tication of voters and, linking this change with the vote, the emergence of a series of nationally salient issues. These included the Lockheed scandal of 1976, the proposal of a consumption tax in 1979,
and the 1983 conviction of former Prime Minister Tanaka for his
role in the Lockheed scandal; consumption tax legislation was passed
in 1988 amid further uproar, and in 1989 the Recruit scandal swept
the headlines, followed by additional scandals between 1991 and
1993. Each of these issues hurt the LDP, leading to failures to win
solid majorities in the House of Representatives and to disastrous
defeats in the 1989 House of Councillors election and the general

election of 1993. Whenever there was no such issue in the public eye, however, the LDP won at the polls.

The fourth characteristic of more recent years is the gradual, increasing conservatism of Japanese society. This is not exactly a rightward *political* trend, but rather a *social* preference for the status quo, for stability, which finds its natural political home under the LDP umbrella. But such support can quickly turn away when the party demonstrates outrageous behavior or compromises the status quo, as it did in 1993. If one looks at the monthly surveys of popular support for the parties, the LDP's support fell gradually from the 1960s until 1974, when it bottomed out; since then it has rebounded and, since 1980, it has held relatively steady at a high level. From such indicators it seems only natural that the LDP has won most recent elections. As noted, however, the fluctuations of votes and seats have been violent. In the 1986 general election, LDP candidates won an unprecedented 300 seats, and the JSP, DSP, and the rest of the opposition were soundly whipped. The results were a shock to both ruling and opposition parties, and pundits were quick to come up with sweeping generalizations about a new "1986 system" and a "deepening conservatism." The very next year, however, a proposed sales tax ran into furious popular opposition and was dropped. In 1989, a 3 percent consumption tax *was* introduced, despite popular outrage; in combination with the Recruit scandal, it brought a precipitous drop in the LDP's support rate and a crushing defeat for the LDP in the 1989 House of Councillors election.

In the 1990 general election, the LDP did manage to win a stable majority of 275 seats, but at the same time the JSP also scored a major victory, winning 136 seats, while the rest of the opposition parties took a pounding. Votes cast in protest against the LDP seem to have flowed to the largest of the opposition parties and accounted for its great strides; the LDP for its part had spent the previous six months in a furious resort to its tried-and-true pork-barrel campaign strategy, which in the end won it a stable majority. The result was an anomalous situation in which the LDP held a majority in the lower house and the opposition a majority in the upper house. Thus, it became clear that the long-term conservative trend, in concert with recurring issues of national import, can push voters either toward or away from the LDP, and is in fact a cause of instability in the party system.

THE REALIGNMENT OF 1993

In the fall of 1992 it was disclosed that Kanemaru Shin, the leader of the Takeshita faction (the largest in the LDP) and the LDP vice

president, had received more than $4 million from the Tokyo
Sagawa Express Company, thus violating the Political Funds Regulation Law, which sets limits to the amounts of political donations.
Faced with a furious public response, he was forced to resign all his
party posts as well as his parliamentary membership. A conflict took
place over who should succeed Kanemaru as leader of the Takeshita
faction, eventually leading to a breakaway from the faction of a group
of 44 MPs led by Hata Tsutomu and Ozawa Ichirō. They formed
a group called "Reform Forum 21" within the LDP. Although
they were closely connected with Kanemaru and thus somewhat
tainted by his scandal, they claimed to be intent upon political reform and the elimination of corrupt political practices.

Additional revelations of dubious political contributions to the
LDP, and of outright bribery of a number of its local leaders, forced
the reluctant Miyazawa cabinet to initiate another round of political
reform proposals similar to those originally undertaken by the Kaifu
cabinet after the revelations of the Recruit scandal (see chapter 14).
The LDP decided that the key reform would be a new electoral system based on single-member districts. The opposition vehemently rejected such a system because, among all the systems being proposed,
it was the most advantageous to the biggest party—in this case, the
LDP. Since the LDP was perfectly aware of this hostility, and since
the opposition controlled the House of Councillors, it is doubtful
that the LDP was really serious about trying to pass the reform at all.

In June 1993 the LDP's political reform bills were debated by a
special committee of the House of Representatives. But although
Prime Minister Miyazawa made a public pledge to accomplish political reform, the LDP leadership refused to make any concessions to
the opposition parties in regard to a new electoral system. Ultimately,
with defeat of its own proposals certain, it simply did not submit
them to a vote in the lower house. The opposition parties submitted
a motion of no confidence in the Miyazawa cabinet, accusing it of
failure to fulfill its public pledge, and the Hata-Ozawa group defected
from the LDP and cast the decisive votes in favor of the motion.
Prime Minister Miyazawa thereupon dissolved the House of Representatives and called for a general election. A group of ten disillu-
sioned reform-minded LDP members left the party and formed the
Sakigake (Harbinger) Party, and the Hata-Ozawa group left also,
forming the Shinsei (New Life) Party.

In the July 1993 election, as seen in table 13.1, the LDP lost its
majority in the lower house, although it remained the largest party.
In fact, the 223 seats won by the LDP amounted to a net gain of one
seat over the LDP's pre-election strength, since all the defections had
left it with only 222. The Japan New (Nihon Shin) Party, a group

formed in 1992 by reformist conservatives led by Hosokawa Mori-hiro, won 35 seats in this, its first electoral test. The Shinsei Party won 55 seats and the Sakigake Party 13, while the Kōmeitō and Democratic Socialists improved their positions marginally. The JSP, on the other hand, took a severe beating, losing almost half of its parliamentary strength.

It was not certain from these results whether the voters really wanted the LDP out of power or not. It does seem clear, however, that the electorate was more disenchanted with parties and elections than desirous of real political change: the voting turnout was 67.3 percent, the lowest in Japanese electoral history, but the total vote won by all of the conservative parties together was higher than in 1990. The conservative social trend noted above was clearly confirmed: once provided with a conservative alternative to the LDP, protest voters moved toward it, away from the JSP (for whom they seem to have voted in 1990). And the alternative Japan New Party, Shinsei Party, and Sakigake Party, together with the middle-of-the-road Democratic Socialists, the Social Democratic League, and Kōmeitō, and the chastened and conciliatory Socialists, successfully crafted a seven-party coalition cabinet headed by the Japan New Party's Hosokawa, which brought to an end the uninterrupted rule of the LDP. Thus, though the voice of the people was ambiguous, the politicians' was not; indeed, it was not the electorate which brought about the realignment and change of government of 1993 so much as it was the politicians, especially those who formed the Shinsei Party.

The new cabinet set political reform as its primary agenda and began immediately to prepare a set of reform bills (see chapter 14). But beyond political reform, the degree of consensus of the coalition government is unclear, and the new political situation is still unstable at the time of this writing. The multi-party system consisting of the LDP in opposition and the seven-party coalition government may not last for long. There is much room for disagreement over policy, and even if political reform succeeds, that will in itself bring change, because a new electoral system may restructure the rural-urban balance of political power and will certainly reward the larger parties and penalize the smaller ones. Thus there is a prospect for another major realignment: unless the governing parties manage to form a successful coalition in the next election campaign, or merge into a few large parties, the new Hosokawa cabinet will not survive the next election intact.

THE LIBERAL DEMOCRATIC PARTY

The free-enterprise, conservative LDP, from the day of its founding until today, has been a coalition of factions. The origins of the factions can be attributed to the following four factors:

(1) The president of the LDP (who, when the LDP had a majority in the House of Representatives, then became prime minister) is elected by vote of all the LDP members of parliament. Candidates for the presidency organize factions in order to mobilize support among the LDP MPs who are the electors.

(2) LDP MPs join factions—that is, attach themselves to influential figures within the party—in order to win positions in the cabinet, party, and parliament. The factions are the basic units on the basis of which these posts are allocated.

(3) In the postwar period, political funds have become dispersed. With the dissolution of the *zaibatsu*, the few large sums of money once gathered by party presidents became myriad small sums, and they are gathered not only by the party but also by a large number of faction leaders.[6] As a result, the development of factions, which perform the fund-raising tasks of LDP politicians, was facilitated.

(4) The medium-sized electoral district system in effect from the formation of the LDP in 1955 to 1993 inevitably pitted LDP candidates against one another. Rivalries between such politicians within single constituencies strengthened the ties of each to different power-holders within the party. The intensification of campaign conflict further enhanced the need to mobilize electoral support through such activities as fund-raising, local pork-barreling, and high-profile activity on the national level. By joining a faction, one can obtain financial help and promises of "pork for the folks back home" from the faction leader. Moreover, as internally reciprocal organizations, the factions function as vehicles for mutual assistance, with MPs who are members of the same faction supporting each other's campaigns and making appeals to the voters.

The LDP's factions appeared in 1956, in the very first contested presidential election after its founding. At first there were eight; subsequently, weaker factions were weeded out and leadership succession problems caused the demise of others. And, by the 1980s, the functions of the factions had significantly changed. In the first place, the factions came to resemble corporations, evolving from collectivities of individual politicians centered upon prime minister hopefuls into highly structured and institutionalized organizations. Each faction established a managerial council and a secretary-general, and factional operations and fund-raising were carried out by these executives and their faction staff.

Second, the role of factions in political finance changed. Today, backbenchers do not rely on factional leaders for most of their campaign finances. The function of the faction is less to provide direct assistance by raising and disbursing money than it is to sponsor, or provide a seal of approval for, its members. The faction serves as promoter when a politician holds a fund-raising party, giving him access to its network of financial sources by circulating a subscription book to wealthy individual and corporate contributors.[7]

Third, as Prime Minister Tanaka put it—and did, at least with his own faction—a faction is like a general hospital: it acquires leading experts in every specialty and provides superlative facilities, thus enabling it to cope with any political disease or injury that may befall a constituent. This is not a bad metaphor for the structural machinery of the faction. The member politicians, who between them possess expertise in every administrative area, provide information, knowledge, and influence to each other and are thus able to respond to almost any grassroots' request or appeal that might arise. The quickening of this cooperative, reciprocal activity among factional members is an important aspect of the evolution of the factions.

The fourth way in which the factions have evolved involves their intervention in personnel matters. Personnel practices within the LDP are organized around three principles: (1) factional balance: governmental positions (ministerial portfolios, etc.) were, during the period of LDP hegemony, distributed among the factions in accord with the number of MPs in each; (2) factional representation: each faction is entitled to nominate one member for party positions such as vice secretaries-general and associate chairs of PARC, Executive Council, and upper house party caucus; and (3) universal participation: every MP gets a chance to serve in a party or government post such as parliamentary vice-minister, PARC committee chair, or House of Representatives committee chair, usually in chronological order based on the first year in which they were elected to parliament. The factions have become essential to this personnel process.

Fifth, the factions have grown in size. It used to be said that the optimum size for a faction was between 30 and 50 members. With fewer than 20 members, it was difficult to win government and party posts; going over 50 members gave rise to competition within the faction between members wanting to run for parliament from the same constituency, and exceeded the capacity of the faction leader to gather enough money to support all his underlings. The refinement of factional fund-raising techniques and the avoidance of intrafactional rivalry through careful candidate selection, however, made the maintenance of larger factions not only possible but advantageous. The introduction in 1977 of a primary election for party president further narrowed the clout of smaller factions, and the advantages of factional scale grew. At present, the LDP has five factions, led by Obuchi Keizō, Mitsuzuka Hiroshi, Miyazawa Kiichi, Watanabe Michio, and Kōmoto Toshio. With the exception of the Kōmoto faction, all exceed what was previously thought to be the maximum faction size.

The LDP's party organization is comprised of the party headquarters, 47 prefectural federations of party chapters, and the local party chapters themselves. The headquarters' party machinery includes the party's chief executive officer, the party president, who is empowered to carry out all party affairs. The secretary-general assists the president, and actually administers party business on a day-to-day basis. Formerly, it was the custom that the secretary-general, who possesses the authority to manage party affairs on behalf of the president, was a powerful politician and a close and trusted confidant of the president, but recently it has become the practice to separate the factions of the two.

The LDP's highest decisionmaking body is the annual party convention, which debates and decides broad party policies, political goals, and action plans. The convention is composed of all the LDP MPs plus four representatives from each prefectural party federation. In between its sessions, the party caucus in parliament meets to make decisions on policy, party administration, and parliamentary activities. Final decisions regarding party administration and parliamentary activities are made by the Executive Council. Specific party policy and legislative proposals are deliberated and decided upon by PARC, under the guidance—some would say the domination—of its chair. PARC comprises 17 committees that correspond approximately to the standing committees of the lower house (indeed, many LDP MPs are on both); they discuss and approve all legislation to be submitted to parliament and important policy questions facing the administrative agencies and ministries. PARC also has over 30 consultative committees covering such topics as the tax system, national security, and foreign affairs, and special committees are created on an ad hoc basis to deal with specific questions. The intraparty policy process involves, first, deliberation and approval of proposals in a PARC committee, followed by approval by the PARC plenary session and then the Executive Council. The whole process is overseen by the *tō san'yaku*, or "three party executives": the secretary-general, the chair of the Executive Council, and the chair of PARC.

PARC was a key part of the government's policymaking process when the LDP was in power. The committees of PARC: (1) carried out intraparty discussion and generated party approval of proposed legislation before it was presented to the cabinet; (2) provided opportunities for MPs to study legislative proposals and build relationships with civil servants; and (3) ironed out disagreements among branches of the bureaucracy regarding legislative proposals. It is generally conceded that, since the 1970s, the influence of civil servants vis-à-vis the policy process has diminished, while that of party politicians has grown. Some see this development as a victory of politics over administration or, more narrowly, victory of the LDP over the bureaucrats. And the vehicle for this change was the party's *zoku* politicians, MPs who acquired expertise and consequently influence in particular legislative areas and who exerted their influence primarily in PARC. The *zoku* MP phenomenon appeared as a way for the ruling party to control the bureaucracy despite the fact that the parliamentary committee system did not originally provide it with sufficient power. Parliament has always had the power to make law, but, in the absence of knowledge and expertise, the party was at the mercy of highly trained and experienced civil servants. Over the years, LDP MPs acquired both experience and expertise and, acting collectively, were able to assert a degree of power over the bureaucracy. But what evolved is less a rivalry than a process in which the respective powers and policy competences of the bureaucrats and the politicians are intertwined in every sphere of policy, resulting in a mutual infiltration and manipulation of civil service and ruling party.

The regional organization of the LDP includes the local party chapters and their prefectural federations. On the constituency level, each MP has organized his supporters into a personal support group, or *kōenkai* (see chapter 16). As a result, the party organization carries out almost no independent activities whatsoever on this level. Efforts to strengthen local party organization, caught up in the "swirling torrents of individual antagonism and factional conflict among MPs"[8] in the prefectural federations, have been uniformly unsuccessful. The introduction in 1977 of a primary election into the party presidential selection process opened the way at last for participation by rank-and-file party members in the process. But what it really brought was competition among the factions to mobilize party members, with the result that factional politics penetrated right to the local level. The result: party membership exploded—to 1.4 million members in 1978, 2.5 million in 1986, and 3.8 million in 1992. But this membership fluctuates wildly, because the desire to pay dues (most party members' dues are paid by the MPs of the faction they support) depends in any given year on whether there is a party presidential primary and whether the factions are recruiting members in order to boost the position of their respective MPs on the proportional representation constituency ballot for a House of Councillors election.

THE JAPAN SOCIALIST PARTY

The history of the JSP is a tale of ideologically based conflict and schism. Beginning from its establishment after the war, the party has been a coalition of three factions: a right wing based on moderate unionism, a Marxist left wing, and an ideologically centrist faction. The Right aspires to be a popular, national party, while the Left wants to be a class-based party; together they comprise a "united front" papering over a dissonant mixture of socialist forces. The party factions are rooted in ideological differences, but there are also intense power struggles and quarrels over the allocation of party posts.

After the right wing seceded from the JSP in 1960 to establish the Democratic Socialist Party, power passed into the hands of the left wing. In an earlier attempt to construct a moderate party line, Secretary-General Eda Saburō had introduced the concept of "structural reform," arguing that capitalism could be reformed by parliamentary action, and by its own natural evolution, toward a more just society. Revolution, therefore, was unnecessary. He proposed a number of policy stands regarding equalization of wealth and enhanced living standards for all that were realizable within the framework of a capitalist economy. These positions had originally passed the party convention with almost no debate, but, in 1962, the Marxist theoreticians of the Left counterattacked, condemning structural reform as a mere palliative and a de facto approval of capitalism. Eda's policies were repudiated at the party's national convention; Eda, backed into a corner, resigned.

During the 1960s and 1970s, the left wing held sway within the JSP. In 1966, the party issued its program, "The Road to Socialism in Japan," establishing a party line that called for a socialist but peaceful revolution. In the early 1970s, the intraparty strength of the extreme left-wing Socialist Association (Shakaishugi Kyōkai) faction expanded; by the middle of the decade its radical adherents made up nearly half of the delegates to the party's annual convention. Critics of the Association and moderate elements in the party were alarmed by this advance, and intraparty politics became little more than contention between pro- and anti-Association groups. As a consequence of this conflict, Eda left the party in 1977; the party, sobered, embarked on a program of party reform. The Association retreated, redefining itself as a "theoretical study group." Party procedures were also changed so as to reduce the role of radical union activists and guarantee the influence of more moderate party MPs in the party convention. Overall, the balance of power within the party shifted to the Right.

This is not to say that reassessments had not been made earlier. In 1963, the then secretary-general, Narita Tomomi, issued a critique of the party that came to be known as the "Three Narita Principles." He cited as party weaknesses (1) failure to provide organization and independent leadership for daily party activities, mobilization of popular support, and mass movements; (2) domination of the party by its elected assemblymen and MPs; and (3) excessive dependence on labor unions. His critique is as valid today as it was 30 years ago: party membership in 1992 was only 152,000 and, with the exception of local assemblymen and unionists, the party has hardly any activists. The only reason the party is able to muster more than 10 million votes in national elections is that pro-JSP labor unions, surrogates for the party, mobilize the electorate. The unions, acting as support organizations for the JSP, send their own union officers to work in election headquarters on behalf of candidates from their own unions, and then back them comprehensively in their campaigns. Each union decides which candidates it will support, and mobilizes votes for them. It is a very rare JSP candidate who wins a parliamentary seat without union support. But during the 1980s, union membership declined. This phenomenon, together with the JSP's continued organizational dependence on organized labor and its inability to build any base beyond this constituency, goes far to explain the long-term decline of the JSP.

Beginning in 1983, under the leadership of Central Committee Chair Ishibashi Masashi, the party launched a drive to revive the party under the banner of the "New Socialist Party Line." This new line signified the party's intention to cease simply sniping from the opposition benches and trumpeting ideological rhetoric, and to emerge as a party intent on seizing power. Toward this goal, the party put a new emphasis on popularly appealing policies and on demonstrating an ability to deal sensibly and competently with current issues. It also signified the abandonment of the party's earlier line of "peaceful revolution." In order to give this program additional impetus, the party at its 1986 convention adopted a new, moderate, and realistic party platform, the "New Manifesto."

Unfortunately, the JSP took a merciless beating in the 1986 general election, winning only 85 seats; Chairman Ishibashi assumed responsibility for the debacle and resigned. His successor was Doi Takako. Despite Doi's great personal popularity—she was the first woman ever to lead a major Japanese political party—it remained to be seen whether she would display the ability to realize the New Manifesto and push through party reform. Moreover, the party's environment at that time was becoming increasingly threatening. Under the Nakasone cabinet, the splitting up and privatization of the Japanese National Railways (JNR) was proceeding apace, which augured disaster for the militant (and pro-JSP) JNR unions that opposed privatization. Moreover, the Japan Teachers Union—one of the pillars of the pro-JSP Sōhyō labor federation—was embroiled in internal conflict.

The clouds began to part in the summer of 1988 as the Recruit scandal came to light, with a sequence of ruling party politicians being revealed as beneficiaries of the Recruit company's unethical largesse, and a wave of public outrage and criticism sank the Takeshita cabinet. Then, at the end of 1988, the LDP pushed a consumption tax through parliament over vehement opposition, and popular support for the LDP took an unprecedented nosedive. By contrast, popular support for Doi and the JSP rose. Doi's bracing and genial personality and her straightforward, no-holds-barred attack on the consumption tax won further supporters. In the 1989 House of Councillors election, the JSP actually won more seats than the LDP; for at least the next six years it is unlikely that the LDP will be able to regain the majority. Then, in the 1990 general election, the JSP again took a leap forward, winning 136 seats. At the party's 1990 convention, the term "the achievement of socialist revolution" was deleted from the preface to the party rules and replaced by "social democracy by choice." Moreover, the party moved toward the appointment of its own shadow cabinet, in order to strengthen the party's policy planning capability.

Clear moves were thus afoot to transform the JSP into a potential ruling party. But, as has happened so often in the party's history, the euphoria was shortlived. As noted, the JSP's general election performance came at the expense of the other opposition parties, not of the resurging LDP. In the spring of 1991, a series of elections for local assemblies, mayoralties, and governorships was held nationwide; the JSP was unable to maintain its electoral momentum in the face of this LDP offensive, and the total number of offices it held declined. Doi took responsibility for this loss and resigned, followed as Central Committee chair by Tanabe Makoto.

Thereafter, the pace of change became almost dizzying. When Kanemaru Shin of the LDP was accused of receiving an illegal political contribution from the Sagawa Express Company in 1992, Chairman Tanabe's position was jeopardized by his longstanding, close relationship with Kanemaru. Tanabe did not take a strong stance against Kanemaru's wrongdoing, and he was forced to resign. Yamahana Sadao assumed leadership of the JSP, just in time for the 1993 general election. The election was at best a mixed blessing for the party: in seats won, the party was devastated; nevertheless, it still entered the cabinet as the largest party in the coalition. Yamahana was appointed minister without portfolio in charge of political reform was but forced to resign as party chief over the election debacle; Murayama Tomiichi was elected the new chair. Doi Takako reclaimed a share of the spotlight as speaker of the House of Representatives. And the waning months of 1993 saw ongoing squabbling between the right and left wings of the party over its concurrence with the policies of the new coalition government.

THE KŌMEITŌ

The Kōmeitō, or Clean Government Party, formed in 1964, is a religious-affiliated party connected to Sōka Gakkai, a lay organization of believers of the Nichiren Shō Sect of Buddhism. In a proclamation accompanying the establishment of the party, the Kōmeitō explicitly adopted the principle of *ōbutsu myōgō*, or the goal of building an ideal society through the fusion of religion and politics. Its concrete program, however, emphasized middle-of-the-road, welfare-state policies. In the 1969 general election, the party's parliamentary strength jumped to 47 seats, up from the 25 won in 1967. In the same year, however, it came to light that the Kōmeitō had brought pressure to bear in an attempt to prevent publication of a book critical of the Sōka Gakkai; in the aftermath of the election, the Kōmeitō was the target of harsh criticism by the other parties in parliament for violating freedom of expression and publication. Reform was forced upon the party: Kōmeitō executives resigned their leadership positions in the Sōka Gakkai, all organizational links between the Sōka Gakkai and the party were formally severed, and the party adopted a new, more secular platform. In its words, the Kōmeitō was now a "popular party devoted to respect for humanity and middle-of-the-road politics," with no religious coloration whatsoever.

During the 1980s, the Kōmeitō moved toward a more realistic posture, recognizing, for example, the constitutionality—because it is exclusively defensive—of Japan's postwar military. Additionally, with the creation of an LDP–New Liberal Club coalition cabinet in late 1983, the Kōmeitō's concept of coalition government also shifted, from emphasis on cooperation with the JSP and the DSP toward collaboration with the LDP or some part of the conservative camp. With the LDP victory in the 1986 general election, however, everybody's visions of coalition government evaporated, and the party action plan adopted at the Kōmeitō's 1986 convention placed emphasis on strengthening the party's autonomy and cooperating with the JSP and the DSP. Moreover, it was at this time that Takeiri Yoshikatsu, Executive Committee chair for the last 20 years, passed the party leadership to a new generation led by Chairman Yano Jun'ya.

The Kōmeitō had long adhered to a policy of not accepting money from corporations; hence, it came as a shock when, in 1988, one Kōmeitō MP after another appeared on the list of those on the take from the Recruit company. Chairman Yano himself was connected to a stock manipulation scheme involving the Meidenkō Corporation, and in May 1989 he resigned to take responsibility, succeeded by Ishida Kōshirō. The party tried to regain its stature under this new leadership, but in the 1990 general election won only 45 seats, as opposed to 56 in the previous election. The Kōmeitō, fearing polarization of the political system between the LDP and the JSP, advocated a tripolar system in which the parties of the center have a significant role to play. Consequently, they have opened up some distance between themselves and the JSP by, among other things, beginning to consider seriously a comprehensive agricultural policy in which the opening of Japan's markets to imported rice—to which the JSP is rigidly opposed—is a possibility.

But even if its policy and leadership problems are solved, the party has an image problem that must be overcome if it is to recover from its 1990 setback. In 1991, a long-simmering conflict between the Sōka Gakkai and the parent Nichiren Shō Sect burst into the open, with the clerics accusing the lay tail of trying to wag the religious dog, and the Sōka Gakkai suggesting that the priests mind their own spiritual business. The Kōmeitō seems to have escaped this mudslinging largely unstained, in light of its recovery—to 51 seats—in the 1993 election. But it remains a strong advocate for the partisan realignment of the present political scene. Instead of its prior tripolar position, it now supports an electoral system that would promote the emergence of a two-party system. It proclaims that it does not care if the party name of Kōmeitō should disappear after the new electoral system is enacted and a realignment takes place. In such circumstances it is possible that the Kōmeitō would merge with the Shinsei Party to form a new party.

THE DEMOCRATIC SOCIALIST PARTY

The Democratic Socialist Party (DSP) was formed by right-wing elements of the JSP which left the party in 1960. Ideologically, it advocated the creation of a democratic socialist welfare state. But in that its electoral base was organized labor—specifically, the Dōmei labor federation—it resembles the JSP. The chronic problem of the DSP, ever since its inception, has been an inability to expand its power; from an initial strength of 41 seats, it fell to 17 in the general election of 1960. In 1967, it rose to 30 seats and in 1969 to 31, but in 1972 it fell again to 19; since that time it held relatively steady at around 30 seats. The DSP occupies a political position between the LDP and the JSP; consequently, it sometimes gets overlooked by the public. There have also been occasions, however, when it was able to exert influence beyond what the number of seats it holds would suggest. In the latter half of the 1960s, it sponsored a number of candidates for local office jointly with the LDP; after the appearance of the Kōmeitō, it has pushed the idea of a government based on a coalition of the centrist parties and, again, co-sponsored a number of successful candidates.

In 1983, the LDP entered a coalition government with the New Liberal Club. At its 1985 convention, the DSP adopted an action plan that allowed for entering such a coalition, thus demonstrating its own intention—or hope—to seek an active role in government. The party leadership of Committee Chairman Tsukamoto Saburō pinned its hopes on the 1986 election; in the election, the DSP lost 12 seats, however, falling from 38 to 26. In the face of the LDP landslide, the DSP, like the Kōmeitō, abandoned its visions of coalition government and adopted a program emphasizing its own autonomy and its opposition status.

But the party's environment was volatile: in the fall of 1987, organized labor began a historic transition as the Dōmei labor federation, which had been the pillar of DSP support, dissolved itself and a new federation, Zenmin Rōren, was formed. In the fall of 1989, this new organization was replaced by another union federation, Rengō, and the other major labor union federation, Sōhyō, was absorbed by Rengō, further complicating party-labor ties.

The DSP also had internal problems: Chairman Tsukamoto, like so many other politicians, was discovered to have received some of the Recruit company's pre-flotation stock, and in February 1989 he turned the chair over to Nagasue Eiichi. In the House of Councillors election of 1989, it was the JSP that rode the wave of anti-LDP popular sentiment to victory—the DSP gained almost nothing. And, in the 1990 general election, the parties of the center, caught between the JSP's own victory and the LDP's vigorous campaign efforts, all stagnated—the DSP fell to 14 seats, the lowest since the founding of the party. The next scene of the drama was predictable: Nagasue resigned and Ōuchi Keigo became party chair. The party's 1990 convention was a time for reflection: there were debates over changing the party's name and adopting a new party program, and a Committee for Party Renewal was mandated to examine both. Chairman Ōuchi called for a realignment of the major forces of the Right and the center to create a political structure that would facilitate the alternation of parties in power, and stressed that the DSP should play a leading role in this movement. But, as before, the opposition, with no leverage vis-à-vis the LDP whatsoever, was whistling in the dark. For the DSP, in particular, with matters as basic as the party's name and program in question, the real problem for the future was not how to inveigle the LDP into sharing power but how to survive. And the problem is still unresolved: The 1993 election saw a proliferation of parties with which the DSP had to compete. It at least held its own, winning 15 seats, and entered the cabinet for the first time ever. But it is one of the two smallest partners in the coalition, and commensurately weak. Moreover, it must contemplate a new electoral system which, at least in its single-member districts, will be heavily biased against the smaller parties. At the very moment that it has come to share power, its future is still cloudy.

THE JAPAN COMMUNIST PARTY

Until the middle of the 1960s, the Japan Communist Party (JCP) was under the influence of China and the Soviet Union. In 1963, however, a quarrel between the Soviets and the Chinese broke out over the Partial Nuclear Test Ban Treaty; the JCP supported China, which opposed the treaty, and the communist parties of Japan and the Soviet Union became estranged. Then, in 1966, a JCP delegation to Beijing was pressured to join in a declaration calling for an international united front against both the United States *and* the Soviet Union; the JCP refused, and its relationship with Beijing also became chilly. Party Secretary Miyamoto Kenji took the opportunity to establish a new, autonomous, and independent party line and launched a party-building drive featuring expansion of the circulation of the party's newspaper, *Akahata* (Red Flag), and increasing party membership. At the Eleventh Party Congress in 1970, a moderate Eurocommunist party line entitled "Revolution in Advanced Industrial States" was adopted. Simultaneously, Miyamoto was appointed chair of the party's Executive Committee, with Fuwa Tetsuzō as party secretary.

Moderation and independence worked, and, during the 1960s, party membership grew steadily. In 1958, the party had claimed "300,000 subscribers to *Akahata* and 80,000 party members"; in

1964, this was revised upward to "800,000 readers and over 100,000 party members" and, in 1970, to "2 million readers and 300,000 party members." At the Twelfth Party Congress in 1973, the JCP demonstrated its own desire to seize political power by adopting an Outline of Democratic Coalition Government. Moreover, the term "dictatorship of the proletariat" was deleted from the party program, replaced by "proletarian authority." The party continued to moderate its image and actions, as epitomized by its ten-year declaration of reconciliation with the hitherto hostile Sōka Gakkai in 1974. In 1976, even the term "proletarian authority" was expunged from the party program, and "Marxism-Leninism" was changed to "scientific socialism."

This strategy seemed to pay off in the 1972 general election, in which the JCP leaped into the second spot among the opposition parties by winning 38 seats; but in the 1976 election, they fell by half, to 17. The JCP rebounded in 1979, winning an all-time-record 39 seats, but thereafter party strength stagnated. In the 1980s, the party goal of "500,000 members and 4 million readers" proved incapable of realization; on the contrary, membership declined. At the 1982 Party Congress, Miyamoto was elevated to party chairman; Fuwa became Central Committee chair and Kaneko Mitsuhiro was named secretary-general. This leadership lineup has continued essentially unchanged into the 1990s. Among the reasons given for the party's recent stagnation are the media publicity in the late 1970s surrounding Chairman Miyamoto's involvement in the prewar slaying of a police spy, the conservative current among the electorate in general, and intense anti-Soviet popular sentiment.[9] In addition, the massacre at Tiananmen in 1989 and the collapse of communism in Eastern Europe struck hard blows at the party. At the JCP's 1990 Congress the atmosphere of crisis and beleaguered defensiveness was palpable, with good reason: the party went from 26 to 16 seats in the general election of that year.

In parliament, the centrist parties such as the DSP and the Kōmeitō have since the 1980s worked toward cooperating among themselves to the exclusion of the JCP; consequently, isolation has become its normal state of affairs. Stung by this rejection, the JCP has vehemently criticized even the fellow-Marxist JSP for its flirtation with the DSP and the Kōmeitō, calling this a betrayal of the working class and the progressive forces. Even the JCP was not completely oblivious to the futility of its carping, however, and when Prime Minister Uno resigned in 1989 and parliament elected a new prime minister, the JCP's MPs for the first time ever voted for another party's candidate—Doi Takako of the JSP. And in 1990 the party began to participate in discussion groups from both houses of parliament on the tax system and other issues. The JCP seemed to be groping its way toward some new sort of relationship with the other parties. But there were clearly limits to this movement: in the wake of the 1993 election (in which the JCP held its own, winning 15 seats), the JCP was the only party in the lower house which did not join the new non-LDP coalition government.

NEW PARTIES IN THE 1990s

The Japan New Party was formed in May 1992 by Hosokawa Morihiro, the former LDP governor of Kumamoto prefecture. Drawing discontented conservatives to its banner, it made a successful debut by winning four seats in the 1992 House of Councillors election. Riding the crest of popular desire for change, it won 35 seats in the 1993 general election and Hosokawa—the cleanest and most exciting new face in the winning coalition—became the first non-LDP prime minister in 38 years. All of the Japan New Party's MPs, however, are in their first terms, and they are therefore far less experienced than their allies in the coalition. The Japan New Party criticizes political corruption and proposes clean and participatory politics, and aims to work for replacing the long-standing producer-oriented policies of the LDP with consumer-oriented ones.

The Sakigake Party was formed by 10 dissident LDP MPs immediately after the Miyazawa cabinet lost the vote of no confidence of June 1993. Its leader is Takemura Masayoshi, former governor of Shiga prefecture and a former member of the LDP's Mitsuzuka faction. The party increased its strength to 13 in the 1993 election, and Takemura was appointed chief secretary of the Hosokawa cabinet. But Sakigake is one of those small parties most threatened in the single-member districts of the new electoral system, and may well merge with another party, most probably the politically compatible Japan New Party.

The Shinsei Party played a decisive role in the realignment of 1993. Thirty-six representatives and 8 councillors from the Takeshita faction had already set up their own intraparty faction, Reform Forum 21, but in June they broke ranks completely, casting the crucial votes of no confidence in the Miyazawa cabinet. The Shinsei Party won 55 seats in the subsequent election, a net gain of 19. Ozawa Ichirō, secretary-general of the party, himself largely crafted the new seven-party coalition cabinet by persuading the hesitant Socialists, who had lost almost half of their strength. Early in the coalition-building negotiations party chief Hata Tsutomu was a top candidate for prime minister, but Ozawa proposed that Hosokawa be prime minister in order to bind the seven parties together more effectively in the new government. Because the Shinsei Party used to be part of the most powerful faction in the LDP, its members could be tarred with the same brush of corruption as were former LDP strongmen Kanemaru and Takeshita, and Ozawa therefore kept a low profile. And his calculation seems to have paid off: in late 1993 the Hosokawa cabinet enjoyed higher public popularity than any other government in the entire postwar period. But these same LDP origins meant that Shinsei Party members had more government experience than anyone else in the coalition; hence, they received several important cabinet portfolios. They also have long had close ties with the Kōmeitō, and once the new electoral system is installed many expect them to merge into a new party.

It should be noted that all of the three parties described above are conservative. Nevertheless, they advanced in the 1993 election at the expense of the JSP, not the LDP, drawing moderate voters who wanted party competition, not policy change. Thus, the most distinct characteristic of the 1955 system, opposition between Right and Left, is on the verge of extinction. The end of the Cold War caused the decline of public support for the Left, combined with the sclerosis of the JSP and the sudden appearance of moderate alternatives to the LDP. Politicians, pundits, and citizens are all presently trying to envision the future of the Japanese party system. Prime Minister Hosokawa has stated that a moderate multiparty system will emerge from the realignment in the near future; the Kōmeitō and the Shinsei Party expect a two-party system facilitating the sort of regular government turnover seen in the United States and the U.K. In any case, at least one more general election will be necessary before a new alignment becomes apparent, and one can confidently anticipate only that the process will involve partisan twists and turns as yet unforeseen.

NOTES

1. In 1991, the party changed its English name to the Social Democratic Party of Japan; however, the Japanese name, Nihon Shakai Tō, remained unchanged. For this reason—and to avoid confusion with the Democratic Socialist Party and the Social Democratic League—we shall refer to the party as the Japan Socialist Party, or JSP.

2. Kyōgoku Jun-ichi, *Gendai Minshusei to Seijigaku* (Contemporary Democracy and Political Science), Iwanami, 1969, pp. 225–26.

3. Takabatake Michitoshi, "Taishū Undō no Tayōka to Henshitsu" (Diversification and Deterioration of Mass Movements), in Nihon Seiji Gakkai, ed., *Gojūgonen Taisei no Keisei to Hōkai* (The Formation and Breakdown of the 1955 System), Iwanami, 1979, p. 323.

4. J.A.A. Stockwin, *Japan: Divided Politics in a Growth Economy*, London, Weidenfeld and Nicolson, 1982, p. 167.

5. They did, however, end up with a majority of seats, since in any given election the majority of the independent candidates are in fact staunch conservatives, and after the election those who win immediately join the LDP.

6. Uchida Mitsuru, "Senkyo Jiban" (Electoral Base), in Sōma Masao, ed., *Kokusei Senkyo to Seitō Seiji* (National Elections and Party Politics), Seiji Kōhō Sentā, 1977, pp. 251–52.

7. Satō Seizaburō and Matsuzaki Tetsuhisa, *Jimintō Seiken* (The LDP Government), Chūō Kōron, 1986, p. 61.

8. Masumi Junnosuke, *Gendai Seiji* (Contemporary Politics), vol. 2, University of Tokyo Press, 1985, p. 384.

9. Stockwin, *Japan: Divided Politics in a Growth Economy*, p. 186.

CHAPTER 14

THE ELECTORAL SYSTEM

POLITICAL DISTRUST AND ELECTORAL SYSTEM REFORM

In the summer of 1988 the Recruit scandal broke, when it was revealed that an information services company called Recruit had sold
as-yet-unlisted shares of its stock widely to members of both the LDP
and the opposition parties and to top civil servants as well. The company had even provided financing to cover the purchases. When the
stock was publicly listed and its price rose, the favored few sold,
reaping handsome profits. Recruit had also bought tickets to politicians' fund-raising parties and made other political contributions
running into the millions of dollars. This criminal interweaving of
politics and money provoked a wave of popular anger and political
revulsion. In early 1989, Prime Minister Takeshita Noboru and his
cabinet resigned to take responsibility and defuse the situation. But
the stratagem failed: the successor cabinet under Prime Minister Uno
Sōsuke took the LDP into the 1989 House of Councillors election,
where the party suffered a pounding at the hands of an enraged
electorate, and the Uno cabinet, too, resigned.

There were calls for political reform to assuage the popular distrust of politics, and in the summer of 1989, the Eighth Election System Council convened to consider fundamental reform of both the
electoral system and the system of financing of parties and elections.
In the background of this examination lay a recognition that the
"medium-sized-district" system under which the House of Representatives is elected had contributed to the LDP's long-term monop-
oly of political authority, which in turn had given rise to a variety of
abuses and invited political stagnation and corruption. This chapter
will first consider the electoral system and its attendant problems,
and then turn to the actions of the Election System Council and subsequent efforts at electoral system reforms.

THE MEDIUM-SIZED-DISTRICT ELECTORAL SYSTEM

Under the electoral system that was used until 1993 the 511 members of the House of Representatives were elected from 129 constituencies. The district magnitude ranged from two to six, with most districts having between three to five seats. Voters cast a single ballot regardless of the number of seats in their district. The ballots were counted in each district and in, for example, a four-seat district, the top four vote-getters were elected. It was not necessary to get a majority of the vote, or even a plurality, to be elected—just to finish in the top four.[1] In contrast to the small-, or "single-member-district," election system used in U.S. House of Representatives elections— in which one representative is elected from each district—this is a variant of the "large-district, single-vote" system, in which multiple representatives are returned from each constituency, but it is commonly referred to as the "medium-sized-district," or MSD, electoral system.

A comparison of the characteristics of the MSD system with those of the small-, single-member-district (or SM) system and the large-district, proportional representation (or PR) system used in most of the countries of Western Europe and North America is instructive. First, in the Japanese MSD system, each candidate's victory or defeat is crucially influenced by the pattern of competition within the district. In an SM system, only the top vote-getter is elected. All one has to do is get more votes than any of the other candidates. Since the prospects of victory are practically zero for all candidates below the top two, and the very meaning of minor candidacies (and minor parties) questionable, SM systems frequently tend, as is the case in both the United States and Britain, to result in battles between candidates of two big parties. In such cases, 50 percent of the vote becomes the cutoff between winning and losing.

In PR systems, there are multiple seats in each district, and seats are won in proportion to each party's share of the vote in the district. For example, if party X receives 40 percent of the vote in a 10-seat district, it wins 4 seats. Therefore, each party is assured that the number of seats it wins will accurately reflect its popular electoral appeal, however small. By contrast, the requirement for victory in an MSD system is not to win a majority, or simply to win any particular share, however small, of the vote, but to push one's share of the vote high enough to finish somewhere among the winners. Where several candidates with closely similar shares of the vote run in one district, very small differences in vote share decide victory or defeat. And where one overwhelmingly popular candidate wins the lion's share of the vote, quite small shares may be sufficient to win one of the remaining seats. Thus, in MSD systems, the proportion of the vote that one needs to win a seat is not fixed but varies with the competitive situation in the constituency, and thus varies from constituency to constituency. This fact has two other consequences: it heightens the anxieties of MPs, and it leads to extraordinarily intense competition in elections.

Second, since the 511 members of the House of Representatives were elected from 129 districts, any party seeking to win a majority of 256 seats and thus take power was forced to run two or more candidates in every district. The result—candidates of the same party running against each other—was a unique consequence of the MSD system. In a PR system, more than one candidate from a given party run in each district, but, one will recall, the number of seats the party wins is determined by the *party's total* vote; thus, all candidates are campaigning not against each other but together, in order to maximize their party's vote and, thus, their own chances to be among the victors. In the general election of 1990, the LDP ran 338 candidates, more than enough to win a majority in the House of Representatives. The Japan Socialist Party (JSP) and Japan Communist Party (JCP) ran 149 and 131 candidates respectively, neither one enough—even if every single candidate won—to win a majority. The other parties ran even fewer candidates, entering the fray only in constitutencies where they had a chance of success. In other words, only the LDP had any real intention of winning sole control of the lower house and thus taking over the government.

The fact that the LDP ran multiple candidates in most districts has important implications for party organization. Campaigns are centered upon individual candidates rather than the party (one LDP candidate cannot gain any advantage over the others if all run on the party platform), and the local party organization is weakened because candidates need not rely on it to win—indeed, they cannot, since the local party organization can hardly favor one LDP candidate over another. At the same time, the position of the candidates themselves is insecure: at times battles between rival LDP candidates lead to a division of the LDP electorate in the district such that neither gets enough votes to win and both go down to defeat; at other times, such rivalries lead to intense battles to get out the party faithful, and the resulting tide of LDP voters going to the polls swamps the opposition.

As for the opposition itself, this electoral system complicates the relationship between candidates at the grassroots and their parties' efforts at concerted action and coalition-formation on the national level and in parliament. Even when coordination and cooperation are major goals at the level of parliament and the top party leadership, competition is inevitably fierce at the constituency level. The postwar opposition parties have always been resource-poor relative to the LDP, and, in the minds of many, they should have been attempting to coordinate rather than dissipating their campaign activities fratricidally at the constituency level, in order more effectively to attack, and perhaps defeat, the LDP.

Third, the MSD system creates a unique relationship between the share of the *votes* a party receives and the number of parliamentary *seats* it wins. The relationship is not necessarily close—in a U.S. congressional race, a party that gets 49 percent of the vote in a district gets no seat at all—as we can illustrate with national election data from Japan and Western Europe. In general, the discrepancy between votes and seats is small in PR systems and large in SM systems; Japan's MSD system falls between the two, and is therefore sometimes referred to as a "semi-PR" system. The relationship between votes and seats in the different systems is revealed in the following regression equations:[2]

in single-member-district systems: $S = 1.20V - 6.3$
in Japan's medium-sized-district system: $S = 1.17V - 2.4$
in proportional representation systems: $S = 1.07V - 0.8$

where S is the percentage of seats won by any given party and V is that party's percentage of the vote.

As the equations show, in SM systems, when a party's share of the vote goes up or down by 1 percent, its share of the parliamentary seats won goes up or down by 1.2 percent. By contrast, under PR, a similar 1 percent change in votes won results in a change of only 1.07 percent in seats won. Thus, it is possible, under SM, for a slight change in voter preferences to be translated into a significantly larger change in the number of seats held by each party. Japan's MSD system is closer to SM, bringing a 1.17 percent change in seats won for every 1 percent change in a party's vote. But, under every system, a party's share of seats (S) increases by more than the proportion of votes it wins (V); that is, in every system, when seats are allocated, there is a mathematical bias in favor of large parties. This advantage is greatest under SM, but the largest party is also relatively advantaged under MSD. The advantage accruing to party size is minimized—but not eliminated—under PR.

Now, if small parties are disadvantaged and big ones rewarded, what is the cutoff point above which disadvantage ends and the "reward" sets in; that is, where does S = V under each system? According to our statistical analysis, in SM systems, the threshold is 31.5

percent of the vote; in Japan's MSD system, 14.1 percent; and under PR, 12 percent. "Big" parties (those that win *more* than these proportions of the vote) begin to win seats—so-called bonus seats—in the disproportionate ratios shown above. The threshold after which a party begins to win bonus seats is highest in a SM system and lowest under PR. In other words, any party unable to command 31.5 percent of the vote in an SM system is disproportionately penalized, while, under PR, only those unable to muster 12 percent are penalized. Since, under SM systems, third and smaller parties can never win shares of legislative seats equal to their share of the vote, they tend to decay; this trend is far less likely to occur under PR. This seat bonus, caused by the mechanics of the electoral system, is one of the reasons why it is most common to find two large parties in SM systems, and multiparty systems under PR. Under Japan's MSD system, any party that can win more than 14.1 percent of the vote gets bonus seats, and in this sense the MSD system is closer to PR. In contemporary Japan, the only parties able to win 14 percent or more of the vote are the LDP and the JSP; consequently, the electoral status quo works to their benefit.

HOUSE OF COUNCILLORS ELECTIONS

Members of the House of Councillors serve six-year staggered terms, with half of the 252 seats up for election every three years. In each election, 76 seats are filled from prefectural constituencies, each with between 1 and 4 seats, and 50 are filled from a single, national constituency operating under proportional representation. When voters go to the polls, they cast two ballots: one vote for a *candidate* in their *local* constituency and another vote for a *party* in the *national* constituency. Winners in the local constituencies are decided as in the House of Representatives; in the national constituency, all votes are tallied and each party wins a share of the 50 seats equal to its share of the national vote.

The prefectural constituencies are a combination of both small, single-member,[3] and large, multi-member districts. When one adds them together to get a national total, the relationship between votes and seats more resembles an SM system than is the case in the House of Representatives. This is offset, of course, by the PR constituency, which was instituted in 1983. The particular PR system used (the "d'Hondt formula") is considered to be one of the fairest of all PR systems, in that the allocation of parliamentary seats parallels most closely each party's share of the vote. The requirements of size and organization that a party must meet, however, before it is permitted to nominate lists of candidates, and the share of the vote that must be won in order to avoid forfeiting the deposit put up to register before the election, are rigorous, and work to the advantage of the larger parties.

After the adoption of the upper house PR system, the LDP proved unable to work out a procedure by which to decide the rank of each candidate on its list. (This is crucial, and much fought over, because, in this system, winning candidates are selected starting from the one ranked first on the candidate list, and continuing down until all of the seats to which a party's vote entitles it are filled. If a party gets 40 percent of the vote, that party's 20th-ranked candidate wins but its 21st candidate loses.) Thus, the LDP took the number of party members each candidate had recruited into consideration in ranking candidates on their list. The result was a furious competition among LDP politicians to recruit new party members. This, one need hardly note, defeated the whole purpose of the PR system, which was to make House of Councillors elections more party-centered. Along with reform of the House of Representatives electoral system, the Election System Council reconsidered the House of Councillors system, but it is too soon to tell how the PR system is going to articulate with the Japanese political system, and with what results.

ELECTORAL INEQUALITY

A number of problems thus accompany the electoral system; nevertheless, it does not grossly discriminate against any particular party, and, in general, the distribution of seats in parliament reflects the will of the people as expressed at the polls. The most serious problem is malapportionment of seats in the House of Representatives relative to population across constituencies. If one accepts the basic assumption of democratic elections—one person, one vote, one value—then gross discrepancies in the value of a vote across constituencies are unconstitutional.

Indeed, the Public Office Election Law states, in its discussion of the number and apportionment of seats in, and the boundaries of, electoral districts, that "every five years after the promulgation of this law electoral districts shall be rectified in accord with the results of the national census taken closest to that date." The law specifies no concrete procedures for this purpose, however, entrusting the task to parliament. Reapportionment is directly connected to the fate of MPs; revision of the Public Office Election Law threatens the most intimate interests of each member (who owes his or her position to the electoral status quo) and party, and, unsurprisingly, makes little headway.

Since the original apportionment of 1947, explosive urban population growth and an accompanying increase in the number of depopulated rural areas have resulted in gross disparities in the value of a vote across constituencies. Although the lower house was expanded before the general elections of 1967 and 1976, with additional seats allocated to metropolitan constituencies, Japan is still a long way from eliminating cross-district inequalities in the value of a vote. In the general election of 1983, this disparity reached a high of 1:4.4— in other words, it took 4.4 times as many votes to elect an MP in the most underrepresented metropolitan constituency as it did in the most overrepresented rural one. Thus, 1 rural vote was worth 4.4 urban ones. On the not unreasonable grounds that such a discrepancy violated the constitutional guarantee of equality under the law, citizen groups throughout the country sued, and on July 16, 1985, the Supreme Court decreed that the current regulations for the apportionment of seats were unconstitutional. This implied that, until the Public Office Election Law was revised, no election would be valid; thus, the prime minister's constitutional power to dissolve parliament and hold new elections was also suspended. An emergency revision of the law, which reapportioned seats in 15 of the most grossly gerrymandered districts (7 districts lost one seat apiece and 8 districts gained one each), enabled a general election to be held in 1986. At that time, parliament passed a resolution to "undertake as quickly as possible a thoroughgoing revision of the Public Office Election Law on the basis of the results of the 1985 census," but neither the ruling party nor the opposition ever followed through on it until 1992, when 19 districts were reapportioned, with 10 districts losing one seat apiece and 9 districts gaining one each.

Let us look at the implications of malapportionment for each party. Table 14.1 (based on data from all general elections from 1958 to 1993) presents the correlations between the number of voters per seat in a constituency and the proportion of the vote won there by the LDP, the JSP, and the JCP.[4] In districts with many voters per seat, each vote is devalued and the voters are underrepresented; where there are few voters per seat, each vote's value is enhanced and voters are overrepresented. The correlation coefficients for the LDP in each of the last 13 general elections are negative, and the strength of the relationship has grown over time: the LDP's electoral base has always been, and is increasingly, in the most overrepresented, rural areas. But the recent reversal of the trend probably reflects the volatile nature of LDP support. The JCP shows a diametrically opposite pattern, being strongest in those districts (mostly metropolitan) with large numbers of voters per seat.

The coefficients for the JSP are interesting. In the first years after

TABLE 14.1 Correlations Between Voters per Seat and Share of Vote for Major Parties in House of Representatives Electoral Districts

Year	LDP	JSP	JCP
1958	−.46	.49	.51
1960	−.44	.27	.39
1963	−.56	.33	.42
1967	−.62	.04	.47
1969	−.57	−.11	.62
1972	−.58	−.05	.62
1976	−.61	−.15	.56
1979	−.61	−.16	.53
1980	−.61	−.20	.45
1983	−.63	−.23	.40
1986	−.61	−.14	.46
1990	−.54	.10	.40
1993	−.50	−.17	.33

the creation of the 1955 system, the JSP, like the JCP, drew its strength from underrepresented urban constituencies. This condition gradually changed and, beginning in 1969, it began to evince a pattern similar to that of the LDP, becoming stronger in the overrepresented rural areas. Thus, it has recently come to some extent to resemble the LDP in its electoral foundations. The result for 1990 represents a one-time reversal, and its closeness to zero shows the more broad-based, national appeal of the JSP in that election but which did not last in 1993. In general, overrepresented constituencies are in regions of the country with low population density and underrepresented ones are found where densities are high. The similarity of the electoral structure of both the LDP and the JSP—weak in the big cities—is visible in table 14.1, and suggests that the current malapportionment works to the detriment of the JCP and to the benefit of *both* the LDP and (except in 1990) the JSP, which helps to explain why, until 1993, even the opposition was never united against the electoral status quo.

CAMPAIGN ACTIVITIES

A further characteristic of the electoral system is the regulation of election campaigns as set out in the Public Office Election Law.[5] The law, in the interest of clean elections, sets forth highly detailed limits and proscriptions regarding the length, subjects, and methods of campaigns. It is clearly impossible for any candidate with any hope of success to adhere to them all; thus, in the words of J.A.A. Stock-win, the "restrictions are so stringent as to be self-defeating."[6] The length of campaigns is specified by law; in the case of the House of Representatives, it is only 12 days from the official registration of candidates and legal beginning of the campaign to election day. Prior "campaigning" is banned; activities involved in arranging for one's candidacy or designed to cultivate one's constituency (apart from a specific election), social intercourse with constituents, and other such "political activities" are, however, all legal. "Political activities" also include the dissemination of the policies of a party or political organization, party publicity, activities designed to expand party membership, and political "education," such as politicians giving speeches on "current political issues" to citizen groups.

"Campaigning," by contrast, is activity designed to solicit votes for the election of a specific candidate in a specific election. Restrictions on campaign methods, in principle, limit a candidate to a single campaign office, which may not be located close to a polling place. Regarding campaign speeches, only individual speeches or appearances together with all other candidates in a race are permitted, and street-corner speechmaking is strictly limited. A candidate may use one campaign vehicle and public address system. As for campaign literature, there are strict and detailed regulations governing number, size, location, and postelection removal of officially approved brochures and postcards, posters, notice boards, and signs of all sorts. Election announcements containing all candidates' biographical sketches and political views are published at public expense and distributed to voters. The freedom of information and of expression of newspapers and magazines is, for the duration of the campaign, effectively restricted.

Additionally, the door-to-door canvassing so common in other countries is illegal in Japan. Moreover, there are bans on signature drives, publication of poll data on the relative popularity of candidates, distribution of food and drink to voters, and activities "designed to excite popular fervor." Criminal penalties are specified for all of the above, and for vote-buying, providing refreshments, and infringing on the electoral freedom of others. In cases of violation of electoral laws by candidates, campaign officials, or individuals with close ties to a candidate, the law specifies collective culpability and election victory is nullified.

All of these prohibitions—despite the fact that they are routinely violated—have a considerable influence on political activities. In the first place, they amount to a high threshold that is much easier for incumbents to cross than new candidates having neither high name recognition nor campaign skills and resources. This makes it difficult for newcomers to win office and leads to low legislative turnover. Second, all these restrictions prevent candidates from making an appeal to the voters on the basis of a political platform. A candidate's legal campaign activities are effectively limited to riding around the district in a sound truck, repeating his or her name over and over and asking the people for their votes.[7] Third, given these restrictions, the voters are relegated to the passive role of judges in a beauty contest—direct participation in campaigns is practically impossible.[8] Voters who seek the election of some candidate in a particular election and who wish to take some individual initiative are basically limited to telephoning their friends, soliciting votes from customers or co-workers in the course of business, or chatting up those who pass by their homes.

THE ELECTION SYSTEM COUNCIL

The Eighth Election System Council, which was convened in 1989, submitted two reports to then Prime Minister Kaifu Toshiki in 1990. The first report called for reform of the House of Representatives electoral system and of campaign financing, with the aim of remedying popular distrust of politics; the second dealt with reform of the House of Councillors electoral system, public financing of political parties, and the laws governing political parties. In regard to the House of Representatives electoral system, the Council pointed out that, under the current MSD system, election campaigns were candidate-centered and, since turnover of the party in power did not occur, all the suspense went out of politics and corruption set in. The Council called for reform of the electoral system that would enhance the salience of parties and issues and increase the probability of turnover of the party in power. To these ends, the Council proposed the creation of a dual electoral system for the House of Representatives, with 301 seats to be filled from 301 SM districts and another 200 from a small number of multimember PR districts. As with the House of Councillors, each voter would cast two ballots in an election, one for a local candidate and one for a party and its list of candidates. This plan aimed to ameliorate the tendency of the SM system to reward (or punish) small changes in the vote with disproportionate changes in a party's legislative strength, since PR would give even small parties the chance to win seats, but was all the same an SM-centered system, a source of no little anxiety to the smaller parties.

In regard to campaign finance reform, the Council proposed that corporate and other contributions could in the future be made only to political parties, not to candidates or their personal support organizations, consistent with the goal of making parties the primary actors in election campaigns. It focused also on political fund-raising receptions, a currently legal vehicle for the collection of extraordinary sums of money, recommending that only political organizations be permitted to stage such fund-raisers, that they be obliged to report their receipts and expenses, and that limits be placed on the number of tickets to such receptions that any one supporter could buy. Moreover, political organizations would have to report exactly which politician(s) they supported, and each politician would be limited to two support organizations of the type that, under the current Political Funds Regulation Law, may receive contributions of up to ¥1 million without being required to report them; other political organizations would be required to report all contributions over ¥10,000. This measure was designed to put an end to the present situation, in which an individual or group could contribute small amounts to a large number of political organizations and not report any of them. Additionally, as a deterrence to illegal campaign activity, relatives and personal assistants of candidates and intended candidates would be subsumed under the umbrella of collective culpability. Penalties would include, in addition to nullification of electoral victory, a five-year ban on the candidacy of anyone convicted.

Public political financing, it was proposed, would strengthen the financial base essential to a party's activities and obviate the mad scramble for private and corporate contributions. And, in order that the parties' freedom of action not be restricted, there would be no restrictions on the uses to which public funds were put—only the requirement of a public financial statement. Finally, to enable MPs to better carry out their parliamentary activities, the Council proposed an increase in the number of publicly funded secretaries available to MPs as policy staff and the construction of a parliamentary office building so that they would have sufficient space to perform their official duties.

As for the laws regulating political parties, only parties fulfilling certain size and vote-getting conditions would be allowed to nominate candidates in the House of Representatives' SM constituencies. Parties wishing to contest elections on the national level would have to fulfill these conditions through their results in elections other than those for the SM districts. In the House of Representatives' PR constituencies, parties would be allowed to nominate lists of candidates if they fulfilled the conditions for running candidates in the SM constituencies, *or* if they could present a list with candidates equal to

20 percent or more of the total seats in the constituency. Moreover, parties would be required by law to announce publicly the procedures by which they selected their candidates for the SM districts. Criminal penalties were provided to guarantee that parties would follow their own procedures faithfully.

Based on these proposals, in late May of 1991, the LDP drew up a package of political reform bills. It included revisions of the Public Office Election Law and the Political Funds Regulation Law, and a new Public Assistance for Political Parties Law. The Election Law revision incorporated the dual SM-PR electoral system for the House of Representatives (300 seats for SM and 171 seats for PR), but no attempt was made to change the electoral system for the House of Councillors. This revision and that of the Public Assistance for Political Parties Law marginally relaxed the restrictions on party finance and tightened the definition of a political party somewhat but, otherwise, generally followed the recommendations of the Council.

Unfortunately, the LDP was unable to generate universal support for the legislative package, even among its own members. In particular, opposition to the introduction of SM constituencies—gerrymandered though they were—erupted in the party's Executive Council among junior MPs who had not yet consolidated their electoral bases and feared defeat under a new electoral system. It was not until July 9 that the bills were approved.

The three bills were introduced in the Diet session that opened in August 1991. It was at this time, however, that yet another scandal erupted. This one stemmed from the stock market fall of 1989, during which a number of major stockbrokers had secretly compensated their biggest clients for losses suffered in the market. In the Diet, debates over the Finance Ministry's oversight and responsibility and preventive measures for the future dominated the agenda, and the issue of political reform was pushed aside. We have already noted opposition to the bills within the LDP. The opposition parties were also opposed to an SM district system that would benefit the LDP, and ultimately the three bills died in committee. But it was not only the bills that died: Prime Minister Kaifu had staked his political career on the three bills, and when they expired, despite his utmost efforts, he lost the confidence of the Takeshita faction, the largest in the party at the time and a crucial component of his coalition. Without this support, he was forced to give up his hope of running for another term as party president in the fall of 1991.

In the fall 1991 party election, Miyazawa Kiichi was elected party president, thus becoming prime minister. When he named his cabinet, it was heavily populated by politicians tainted—like Miyazawa himself—by the Recruit scandal, right back in their old positions of authority. Three years after the Recruit scandal, both the party's sense of crisis over popular political disgust and its enthusiasm for political reform had faded.

THE HOSOKAWA CABINET AND POLITICAL REFORM

The LDP's enthusiasm for irregular political finance, however, did not fade, and the years 1992 and 1993 saw a series of additional scandals involving astronomical sums, climaxing in the seizure from LDP leader Kanemaru Shin's home of tens of millions of dollars' worth of gold bullion and bearer bonds. These scandals, combined with the inability of the Miyazawa cabinet to fulfill its public pledge to pass political reform legislation in the 1992–93 session of parliament, triggered the realignment of 1993. A vote of no confidence in the Miyazawa cabinet passed due to the defection of the Hata faction, and Miyazawa countered by dissolving the House of Representatives. A group of ten reform-minded politicians left the LDP and formed the Sakigake Party, as did the former Hata faction, which then formed the Shinsei Party. In the general election one month later, these two parties and the Japan New Party increased their shares of seats. The LDP could not garner a majority of the seats, although it remained the largest party in parliament.

With this result, one possibility was that the LDP might form a coalition government with the JNP and/or the Sakigake Party. These two parties proposed that the next government should place highest priority on the achievement of political reform with the introduction of a dual SM-PR electoral system for the House of Representatives, with 250 seats to be chosen from 250 SM districts and 250 from a single, national PR constituency, and that the government should be formed by a coalition of those parties formally committed to this plan. Within a week, all parties, including even the LDP but excluding the JCP, had reached formal party decisions to this effect, thereby qualifying as coalition partners. The JNP and the Sakigake Party chose to form a coalition with the non-LDP parties, and new Prime Minister Hosokawa Morihiro made a public pledge to pass political reform legislation by the end of 1993.

In September the Hosokawa cabinet introduced into parliament four political reform bills, which resembled in many respects the unsuccessful reform bills pushed by Prime Minister Kaifu. A revision of the Public Office Election Law proposed the introduction of a dual SM-PR system for the House of Representatives. Voters would cast one ballot for a candidate in one of 250 single-member districts, where they live, and another ballot for a party in the single national constituency whose 250 seats would be filled by PR. In the SM system, parties having five or more MPs or having won 3 percent or more of the vote in the most recent national election would be entitled to nominate candidates, although independent candidacies would not be prohibited. In the PR system, parties had to fulfill the above qualifications or otherwise nominate lists of 30 or more candidates. The method of voting would also be simplified from the current writing in of the name of a candidate or party on the ballot to the marking of one from a list of candidates or parties. Other important revisions included the abolition of the ban on door-to-door canvassing, the broadening of the collective culpability of candidates' relatives and personal secretaries in violations of election law, and a five-year suspension of the civil rights of campaign law violators.

Redistricting was to be postponed until the political reform bills had passed. A proposed bill on the Commission on House of Representatives Districting stated that redistricting would be conducted by the Commission within six months of the enactment of electoral system reform, and that the ratio of the values of the votes in any two SM constituencies should not exceed 2 : 1, a ratio which would move significant numbers of parliamentary seats from rural to urban districts.

The proposed revision of the Political Funds Regulation Law stipulated that contributions by corporations and organizations to individual politicians were to be immediately prohibited, and those to parties and political fundraising organizations reconsidered for restriction or prohibition five years following this legislation. Parties, political fund-raising organizations, and political organizations would be required to report names and addresses of those making contribution over ¥50,000.

Finally, the reduction of private contributions to political parties would be compensated for by a new law providing for the public financing of parties, which specified that government would contribute ¥335 per capita, or a total of about ¥41.4 billion, to political parties to cover their campaign and other activities. The fund would be allocated to parties having five or more MPs, or earning 3 percent or more of the vote in the most recent national election, in proportion to their number of MPs and shares of the vote previously won. Parties would be required to report any expenses over ¥10,000 together with audit reports prepared by certified public accountants.

The LDP made a counterproposal for the electoral reform which, unsurprisingly, was more to its own advantage, calling for more seats to be filled from SM districts and fewer by PR. It also proposed a smaller amount for public financing of parties. Still, there was no basic disagreement on the government bills among parties, including the opposition LDP. Reform was the main plank of every party's platform, and it had been the issue of major interest to the electorate in the 1993 election. The government negotiated with the LDP on the revision of the bills and conceded that SM seats be 274 and PR seats 226 and that the per capita amount of public financing be ¥250, totalling about ¥3.09 million. Although this proposal did not satisfy the LDP, the LDP agreed to submitting the political reform bills to a vote in the House of Representatives. Thus the bills with the above revisions were passed by the majority support of the coalition MPs in the lower house in November 1993.

But when the bills were put up for a vote in the House of Councillors, there was unexpectedly strong opposition. Adamant LDP Councillors were joined by 17 JSP Councillors who defected from the party to vote down the bills. Subsequently, a joint committee of both houses was formed to hash out the differences between the opposing decisions, but it could not reach a compromise. Finally, Prime Minister Hosokawa and LDP President Kōno Yōhei held a meeting to settle the six-year-old political reform issue. They agreed that SM seats would be 300 and PR seats 200 and that PR seats would be elected from 11 regional blocs. (Ironically, these points were almost identical to those in the original proposal of the Election System Council and closer to those in the defeated LDP bills than those in the government bills.) They also agreed that each politician would be allowed to have one fund-raising organization to receive political contributions from corporations and organizations; thus the proposed ban on contributions by corporations and organizations to individual politicians was effectively suspended. The abolition of the ban on door-to-door canvassing was also suspended. Based on these agreements, the revised reform bills were passed by the overwhelming majority support of the coalition MPs and LDP MPs in both the houses in February 1994.

NOTES

1. In order to be elected, one must win at least the legally defined minimum number of votes (*hōtei tokuhyōsū*): one-fourth of the total valid votes divided by the number of seats in one district. For example in a four-seat district, the legally defined minimum vote share is one-sixteenth of the total valid votes, not difficult to secure for any serious candidate.

2. The statistical technique used here is that of simple regression with $0 < S$, $V < 100$. See Douglas Rae, *The Political Consequences of Electoral Laws*, New Haven, Yale University Press, 1967, p. 89. The data for SM and

PR systems are composite measures from several political systems in postwar Europe; the coefficients for Japan's MSD system were calculated by Kawato using vote and seat statistics for all parties in all general elections between 1947 and 1986.

   3. Recall that only one of the seats in a two-seat district is contested in each upper house election.

   4. These correlation coefficients are measures of the strength and direction of the relationship. They can vary between +1.00 (a perfect, positive relationship) and −1.00 (a perfect, inverse relationship). Zero represents no relationship whatsoever. Thus, the bigger the coefficient in either a positive or negative direction, the stronger the relationship. Analysis of this relationship for the Democratic Socialist Party, the Kōmeitō, the Social Democratic League, and the New Liberal Club is impossible because they ran candidates in too few constituencies.

   5. For a related discussion on campaigning, see Kawato Sadafumi, "Elections and Electioneering," in Richard Bowring and Peter Kornicki, eds., *The Cambridge Encyclopedia of Japan*, Cambridge, Cambridge University Press, 1993.

   6. J.A.A. Stockwin, *Japan: Divided Politics in a Growth Economy*, London, Weidenfeld and Nicolson, 1982, p. 104.

   7. *Ibid.*, p. 105.

   8. Gerald Curtis, *Election Campaigning Japanese Style*, New York, Columbia University Press, 1971, pp. 211–21.

CHAPTER 15

VOTING BEHAVIOR

POLITICAL PARTICIPATION

There are many ways in which citizens participate in politics in democratic societies. Table 15.1, showing the results of a 1983 survey, indicates some of the ways in which the Japanese people participate politically. The type of political participation that people chose far more than any other was to vote. Next in frequency came attendance at political meetings and participation in election campaigns, after which came participation in neighborhood associations and other local political activities and personal contacts with public officials and other locals with political influence. Behavior that required a great deal of energy or resources, such as contributing money or raising funds for candidates or parties and participating in citizens' movements, petitioning government offices, and demonstrating, was chosen by far fewer people.

Political participation can be divided into three independent dimensions in Japan—voting, election campaigning, and local and neighborhood political activities and movements—and people involve themselves with each to varying degrees.[1] Some prefer one or another, some do all three, and some—as in every democracy—participate seldom or not at all. Voting differs from the other two in that it requires very little initiative; indeed, in Japan, the government registers all citizens automatically when they turn 20 and sends each one a postcard before every election informing them of the date and the location of their polling place. Unsurprisingly, voting is the most common form of participation, and voting rates are considerably higher than is the case in the United States. In fact, for most Japanese voting is the *only* way in which they participate politically. Thus, it deserves special attention; in this chapter we shall examine Japanese

TABLE 15.1   Patterns of Political Participation (%)

Type of participation	Respondents reporting each type of participation
1. Voted in 1983 House of Representatives election	86.8
2. Voted in 1983 House of Councillors election	75.4
3. Attended political meeting or rally in last 5 years	28.7
4. Made contact with local public official or assemblyman	17.5
5. Participated in some campaign activity in last 5 years	17.4
6. Participated in local problem-solving activity, e.g., through neighborhood association	16.3
7. Made contact with influential local figure	13.6
8. Participated in citizens' or residents' movement	8.3
9. Joined in petition or request to assembly or public office	6.9
10. Contributed money to or raised funds for party or candidate in last 5 years	6.8
11. Made contact with member of parliament	5.8
12. Participated in demonstration	4.4

SOURCE: Miyake Ichirō et al., *Nihonjin no Senkyo Kōdō* (Japanese Electoral Behavior), University of Tokyo Press, 1986, p. 176.

voting behavior in three ways: statistically (using election data), sociologically, and psychologically.

ANALYSIS OF AGGREGATE ELECTORAL RESULTS

First, let us look at the trends in the outcomes of Japanese elections. Figure 15.1 depicts the proportion of the total electorate voting for each party, and the proportion of nonvoters, in all of the general elections for the House of Representatives. The figure may be divided into three periods. Period 1 extends from the first postwar election in 1946 until 1955, when the two major conservative parties merged to form the Liberal Democratic Party. This was the period during which the postwar party system took root, as both conservative and leftist parties enlarged their strength. On the Right, the Liberal and Democratic parties competed, while the Left witnessed a similar competition between right and left socialists and communists. As the chaos of the immediate postwar period passed, the proportion of nonvoters gradually declined.

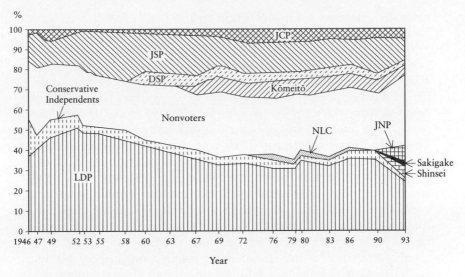

FIGURE 15.1 Election Results: Each Party's Share of the Electorate in General Elections, 1946–93

NOTES: LDP = Liberal Democratic Party; NLC = New Liberal Club; DSP = Democratic Socialist Party; JSP = Japan Socialist Party; JCP = Japan Communist Party; JNP = Japan New Party.

The LDP and JSP figures for the pre-1955 period are the sum of the votes won by the parties that merged to form the LDP and JSP in 1955.

The second period runs from the establishment of the 1955 system until the early 1970s. The most striking characteristic of this period is the gradual but consistent decline in the LDP's share of the vote. When one looks at the opposition, on the other hand, the growth of the Japan Communist Party and the emergence of the Democratic Socialist Party and the Kōmeitō signify the onset of a multiparty system. The JSP's share of the vote, like that of the LDP, shrank. Thus, although overall the opposition increased its power during this period, its fragmentation meant that its power vis-à-vis the LDP did not increase commensurately.

The third period encompasses the years from the 1970s to 1993. The opposition's share of the vote stabilized at 30 to 35 percent of the total. (See in figure 15.1, the area above the stratum labeled "Nonvoters.") The decline of the LDP vote leveled off in about 1970 after which it fluctuated up and down rather sharply between 30 and 36 percent of the electorate. Moreover, the magnitude of these fluctuations increased. The years of the LDP's decline also saw a growth in the number of nonvoters, but in fact it looks as if the LDP vote was riding on a wave of voter turnout: the more people who went to the polls, the better the LDP did.

The general election of 1993 ushered in a new stage, the full outline of which will not be clear for another year or two. At the end of a seemingly nonstop series of scandals, followed by yet another abortive LDP attempt at reform, some 50 LDP members of parliament defected from the party in the summer of 1993, forming two new parties: the Shinsei Party and the Sakigake Party. Along with the Japan New Party, created in 1992 from conservative elements opposed to LDP hegemony, this development meant that the long-suffering Japanese voter—caught between the corruption of the LDP and the manifest ineptitude of the Socialists—finally had an option: a credibly critical mass of conservative strength outside the LDP. And, as figure 15.1 shows, some 14 percent of the electorate turned to this option in the 1993 election. The LDP support fell from roughly one-third of the electorate to roughly one-fourth, but the Socialists were hit even harder, losing almost half of their support.

As seen in chapter 13, the party system has been completely transformed: the LDP is in the opposition, the Socialists are threatened with eclipse, and the other parties have doubled in number. But in terms of voting behavior the change is less impressive, although no less instructive. Conservative strength at the polls has in fact increased: the total vote garnered by the LDP, the Japan New Party, the Sakigake Party, and the Shinsei Party in the 1993 election was greater than that won by all conservative candidates in previous elections. It seems rather clear that the electorate is more conservative than the party system previously allowed it to be. Given a conservative alternative to the LDP, voters have embraced it. How the new system will channel voting behavior one cannot tell: some of the new parties will quite probably merge, and the new electoral system established in 1994 will provide voters with different options than the old system. But it does seem likely that Japanese voting behavior will from now on more closely reflect the true preferences of the people than was hitherto the case.

Urbanization and the Vote

Table 15.2 presents the LDP's share of the vote (as a portion of the total electorate) in constituencies of different degrees of urbanization between 1958 and 1993.[2] In the 1958 election—the first after the conservative merger of 1955—the LDP took votes of 34 percent of the electorate in the metropolitan areas, 43 percent in urban areas, 49 percent in semiurban areas, and 53 percent in rural areas. Ever since its founding, the LDP has been strongest in the traditional rural

TABLE 15.2   Degree of Urbanization and the LDP Vote, 1958–93 (%)

| Year | Type of constituency | | | |
	Metropolitan	Urban	Semi-urban	Rural
1958	33.61	43.45	49.19	53.34
1960	30.03	41.79	48.02	51.19
1963	25.84	39.18	46.12	48.58
1967	21.85	37.00	44.76	49.25
1969	18.46	35.51	40.66	46.65
1972	18.94	36.45	42.57	47.90
1976	17.47	31.86	38.41	44.89
1979	15.30	31.10	39.55	46.97
1980	21.97	34.99	43.69	50.61
1983	17.96	31.48	39.15	46.83
1986	20.88	35.54	43.84	50.37
1990	22.22	35.48	40.97	45.92
1993	14.87	22.95	32.76	35.64

areas, a trend that continues even today. During the 1960s, one can see, as the LDP's strength waned, how it dropped most markedly in the metropolitan areas: from 1958 to 1972 the LDP's vote dropped only 5.4 percent in the rural areas, but it dropped 14.7 percent in the metropolitan areas.

Why should this difference have been so great? High-speed economic growth in the 1960s brought about massive migration from the country to the cities. The newcomers to the cities were uprooted from the human networks that interwove traditional village society and were incorporated into new types of social relationships in the cities. These relationships differed from those in the countryside, which were susceptible to manipulation and mobilization by conservative politicians who used them to build their electoral bases. Many cityward migrants were not recruited into conservative vote-mobilization organizations, and it is likely that many of them became independent and "floating voters," those with weak and volatile party loyalties and inconsistent voting behavior. One element of this stratum of independents and floaters became supporters of the newly established Kōmeitō, but they served to expand the strength of the parties of the Left as well.

In the elections since 1972, there were up-and-down fluctuations of the LDP vote in all types of constituencies. As the period of rapid economic growth drew to a close, both the LDP's decline and the opposition's expansion halted. Looking at regional differences, the difference between the LDP's share of the vote in the metropolitan and rural areas in 1958 was about 20 percent; in 1963 it was 23 percent, in 1967 it was 27 percent, and in 1972 it was 29 percent. After 1972 it fluctuated between 27 and 32 percent. In other words, between 1958 and 1972 the urban-rural gap grew, and the LDP's relative dependence on the rural vote increased. Since 1972, the gap and the relative dependence of the LDP on the countryside have stabilized. At the same time that the urban-rural gap crystallized, the LDP's nationwide vote became more volatile; what we see now as an electoral trend is an up-and-down fluctuation of the LDP vote all across the nation, in all types of constituencies.

Nationalization of the Electoral Swing

If we look at the results of a series of elections during a particular period, we can estimate this "nationalization" of the electoral change statistically. This involves separating and calculating the separate effects of the extent to which the difference in a party's share of the vote in each constituency from one election to another (the "swing") is due to uniform national influences or to specific characteristics of the constituency. When a party's share of the vote changes almost identically from one election to the next in all constituencies nationwide, we can speak of a "national swing." For example, if we look at figure 15.1 and table 15.2 together, we can see that the LDP's decline—a negative swing—occurred disproportionately in metropolitan districts; an analysis of the decline should thus focus on these constituencies. By contrast, the fluctuations or swings of the 1980s occurred in all types of constituencies; hence, our attempts to explain them focus on national political phenomena.[3]

Figure 15.2 analyzes this swing during a series of such periods, based on the vote share (as a proportion of the total electorate) of the LDP and (before 1955) its conservative predecessors. Here we can see a national swing in the early postwar years, but after the creation of the 1955 system, it was eclipsed by constituency-specific swings and vanished almost completely, although a small, localized swing due to urbanization continued throughout the 1960s. National factors reappeared in the 1970s at the end of the high-speed economic growth period and increased through 1986, diminishing slightly in 1990. As causes of this national swing, one can cite the increasing fluidity of popular political attitudes nationwide, and certain specific phenomena (such as issues that draw national attention) that operate so as to affect voters nationwide simultaneously. By contrast, as the actions of parties and the support groups of individual politicians develop differentially in one constituency or another, the national element in electoral swings declines. In the 1990 election, amid a gener-

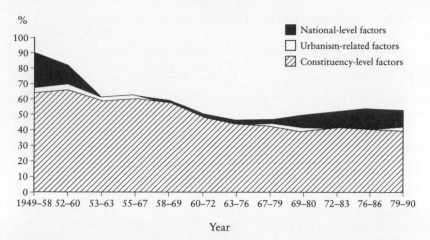

FIGURE 15.2   National- and Constituency-level Swing in Conservative Voting

al tendency toward the Socialists, LDP candidates adopted campaign strategies focusing on local issues and interests, and the influence of the national swing declined slightly.

THE SOCIOLOGICAL APPROACH

The sociological approach to voting behavior presupposes the existence of social differences, or "cleavages," between groups in society, and bases its analysis on the assumption that these cleavages influence voting behavior. For example, in North America and Western Europe, social class and religion give rise to social cleavages, and class-based and religious groups are linked to particular parties. Let us examine one sociological factor of importance—occupation—and assess its role using public opinion survey data. Table 15.3 presents such data, showing the relationship between occupation and voting for the LDP and the JSP.

If one compares votes for the two parties in the 1963 general election, an occupational cleavage is clear: those in the primary sector (farming, forestry, and fisheries), and those self- or familially-employed in commercial, manufacturing, and service enterprises leaned toward the LDP; clerical and blue-collar workers (usually in large enterprises) went for the JSP. The pattern is one of conservative voting among relatively independent occupations, and leftist voting among clerical-manual employees. By 1983, the LDP coloration of the merchant-manufacturer-service stratum had declined significantly, but

TABLE 15.3   Voting Patterns for LDP and JSP, by Occupation (%)

	1963		1983		1990	
	LDP	JSP	LDP	JSP	LDP	JSP
Self-employed in primary sector	78	15	74	10	77	17
Self-employed in commerce, manufacturing, services	69	18	59	8	63	12
Employed in primary-sector family enterprise	61	24	81	4	79	10
Employed in family enterprise in commerce, manufacturing, services	74	17	58	10	60	16
Managerial employee	44	44	47	10	50	18
Clerical employee	34	53	31	29	36	33
Manual worker	35	50	39	21	36	33
Student	—	—	15	50	31	44
Housewife	56	31	40	16	39	30
Other/unemployed	56	28	56	13	51	29

SOURCE: Akarui Senkyo Suishin Kyōkai Zenkoku Chōsa, cited in Araki Toshio, "Tōhyō Kōdō to Shakaiteki Zokusei" (Electoral Behavior and Social Attributes), in *Senkyo* (Elections; special edition of *Jurisuto*), Yūhikaku, 1985.

otherwise the occupational contours of the LDP vote were almost unchanged. The JSP vote, by contrast, had changed markedly: the socialist tendencies of every occupational group had weakened. Thus, although the most significant change in Japan's occupational structure during these two decades was the dramatic decrease of the primary sector and the increase in the number of workers in commerce, manufacturing, and services, the JSP still lost strength. Still, the result of this socioeconomic change was that the primary sector's salience within the LDP electorate shrank, while that of the more working-class element increased.[4] On the other hand, the electoral base of the JSP became more unbalanced.

In light of these trends, it appeared that the LDP was becoming a "catch-all" party, gathering votes from all occupational groups, while the JSP was constricting into a "class" party unable to win the votes of any occupational group except clerical and manual employees. Actually, the JSP was not even the party of these occupations, since it did not even win as large a share of the votes of this stratum as the LDP! After the 1989 House of Councillors election, however, the JSP began both to increase and broaden its vote. In the 1990 general election, the JSP increased its support in almost every occupational group; moreover, its occupational imbalance was less than before, and indications that it, too, was becoming a catch-all party were evident.[5] But the JSP took a severe beating in the 1993 election, and its support base shrank once again.

Next, let us look at the relationship between socioeconomic status (SES) and voting behavior. The socioeconomic characteristics of voting behavior in Japan during the 1960s can be described as follows: first, no clear relationship was discernible between income and party choice. Second, the leftist tendency of the white-collar class was striking. Third, voting for parties of the Left increased directly with level of education. And, fourth, younger voters tended toward the Left, with older voters leaning toward the conservatives. These characteristics, with the exception of the fourth, form a pattern quite at odds with those found in the democracies of North America and Europe, where conservative voting tendencies grow progressively stronger as one goes up the SES ladder. Consequently, many observers feel that Japanese voting behavior is difficult to explain in terms of socioeconomic characteristics. Rather, it is suggested that Japan's politics is "cultural," that is, it reflects differences in people's values. The quality of political behavior is determined not by religious, economic, and status cleavages and differences, but rather by cleavages deriving from differences in people's value systems.[6] Thus, one may think of the LDP as representing people with traditional value orientations, while the JSP and the rest of the opposition, in contrast, represent those with more modern value systems.

Alternatively, some American scholars have attempted to interpret Japanese voting behavior using what they call a "social network approach."[7] According to them, a simple sociological approach premised on the existence of a Euro-American pattern of social cleavages is insufficient, and an understanding of Japanese political behavior requires that one incorporate into the sociological approach the complexity of social relationships. In Japan, group membership is a more important factor than abstract categories of income or class. Consequently, variables that reflect networks of social relationships, interactions, and communication—such as size of workplace, labor union membership, and length of residence in one's community—are more useful than broad sociological characteristics in explaining voting behavior. For example, labor union membership is an indicator of incorporation in a type of social network in which support for leftist parties is the norm; similarly, length of residence and home ownership are indicators of incorporation in neighborhood associations and other sorts of conservative social networks.

A tendency for social networks to determine voting behavior is distinctive in Japanese voting behavior, and this tendency is partly behind the extraordinary shift of voter support to the new parties in the 1993 election. Part of the shift was due to the new availability of a non-LDP conservative option, but part of the shift took place among former LDP voters whose social ties to specific politicians led them out of the LDP when these politicians defected, and who voted in 1993 for their longtime representatives as candidates of new parties.

THE PSYCHOLOGICAL APPROACH

Party Support

The psychological approach attempts to comprehend voting behavior by focusing on the relationship between psychological attitudes and behavior, that is, it aims to explain voting behavior in terms of the attitudes and feelings of voters. Among these attitudes, the most important is support for a political party. The phenomenon of individual feelings of attachment and partiality for a particular political party first attracted attention in postwar American analyses of voting behavior. Subsequently, feelings toward political parties were adopted as the singlemost important explanatory factor vis-à-vis voting behavior. In Japan, also, attitudes of party support are a stable and lasting component of the political consciousness of individual voters.[8]

In American scholarship, the term "party identification" (or "party ID") was used to denote psychological feelings of attachment or loyalty toward a political party. It was measured by directly asking voters if they were Republicans or Democrats. What was being measured here was neither formal party membership nor party activism nor actual voting behavior, but only the psychological attitude of the individual voter. In Japan, the question asked to determine party support attitudes is, "What political party do you usually support?"

Party support attitudes in Japan are similar to party ID in the United States. They are *ubiquitous*: of all political attitudes, party support is the one held by more individuals than any other. They are *stable*: relative to other political attitudes, they are less apt to change over time. And they are *prescriptive*: their power to influence other political attitudes and behavior is considerable. Party support serves both as a "cognitive screen" through which individuals evaluate and interpret policies and issues, and as a "guide" that leads voting behavior.[9] But it is not identical in Japan and the United States: the characteristics of party support in Japan are (1) a larger number of people professing *no* such support, (2) more *unstable* support, and (3) more people who *drift* between party support and nonsupport.[10]

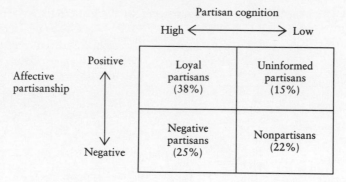

FIGURE 15.3   A Typology of Political Partisans
SOURCE: Miyake Ichirō, *Seitō Shiji no Bunseki* (An Analysis of Party
Support), Sōbunsha, 1985, p. 73.

Types of Party Support

Party ID in the United States has two elements: direction (*which
party* is supported) and strength (*how strongly* it is supported). By
contrast, in Japan, there are five major parties; consequently, the
direction of party ID cannot be depicted, as it can in the United
States, with a single continuum running from strong Democratic to
strong Republican ID. Moreover, as political scientist Miyake Ichirō
has found, even excluding direction of ID, there are in Japan two
other dimensions of party support. The first is partisan cognition or
awareness—nonjudgmental interest in and knowledge of political
parties. The other is affective partisanship, and includes negative or
positive orientation toward one or more parties. Combining these
two dimensions, as shown in figure 15.3 (the results of a national
opinion poll), one can divide party support feelings in Japan into
four categories, and then incorporate support for specific parties.

The first of these categories, accounting for almost 40 percent of
the respondents to the survey, are the "loyal partisans." They score
high in knowledge of and interest in parties and low in political
cynicism, and tend to vote faithfully for the party they support. They
are the parties' hard core, the stratum from which the activists come.
The "negative partisans"—one-quarter of the respondents—score
just as high as the loyalists in political knowledge but lower in interest, and are significantly more cynical. Their party support is
changeable, and they frequently vote for candidates from parties
other than the one they profess to prefer. They are the so-called floating voters.

The "nonpartisans"—roughly one-fifth of the sample—do not sup-

TABLE 15.4   Identification of Partisan Types, by Party, 1976 (%)

| | Partisan types | | | |
Party ID	Loyal partisans	Negative partisans	Nonpartisans	Uninformed partisans
LDP	52	24	11	13
JSP	54	29	9	7
JCP	64	26	9	0
Kōmeitō	66	14	6	13
DSP	48	38	11	4
NLC	41	45	8	5
Other party	0	100	0	0
No party supported	3	27	54	16

SOURCE: Same as figure 15.3, p. 75.
NOTE: Figures represent proportion of party's supporters accounted for by each type of partisan.

port any party or, if they do, their support is exceedingly weak. Neither their knowledge nor their interest is high, and they, too, are cynics. Many in this group do not vote at all; they are apathetic, but in a skeptical, modern way. And, finally, about 15 percent of the respondents are "uninformed partisans." They are ignorant of and uninterested in politics, but they trust parties and politicians and, if solicited, will vote; hence, despite their lack of interest, their voting rate is relatively high. They, too, are apathetic, but in a traditional, deferential way.[11]

Table 15.4 presents data on the party ID of each of these four types of citizens at the time of the 1976 general election. Over half of those voting for the LDP and JSP were loyalists, as were almost two-thirds of the highly disciplined JCP and Kōmeitō voters. Negative partisans accounted for only about one-quarter of the LDP, JSP, and JCP supporters—although defection of even these proportions may go far to explain the drop in both LDP and JSP votes in the 1993 election—and only 14 percent of the Kōmeitō's. The uninformed were relatively common among LDP and Kōmeitō voters. As one might expect, over half of those professing no support at all were in the nonpartisan category.

Next, let us look at the relationship between party support and voting behavior among these groups. Party support was the key to voting—the stronger the support, the more likely individuals were to vote, and the more likely they were to vote for the party they claimed to support. These relationships differed across categories, however,

TABLE 15.5 Voting Behavior, by Partisan Type (%)

	Loyal partisans	Negative partisans	Nonpartisans	Uninformed partisans
Percentage not voting for party of support	9	19	15	18
Abstention rate	3	10	20	11

SOURCE: Same as figure 15.3, p. 87.

as table 15.5 indicates. Almost all the loyalists voted, and fewer than 10 percent voted for candidates not from their parties of choice. By contrast, 20 percent of the nonpartisans abstained, and 15 percent wandered from their preferred party. Among both negative and uninformed partisans, roughly 10 percent did not vote at all and roughly 20 percent were unfaithful to their party.

Long-term Change in Party Support and Cabinet Support
Figure 15.4 presents data from the Jiji News Service monthly survey of party support attitudes from 1966 onward. We have added support for the cabinet (always dominated by the LDP during

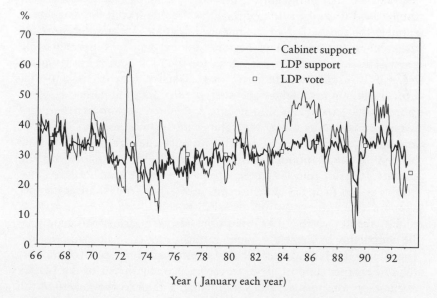

Year (January each year)

FIGURE 15.4 Cabinet Support, Party Support, and Vote for the LDP
SOURCE: Jiji Press Survey.

this period), and also the LDP vote in the House of Representatives elections.

In this figure, LDP support shows a gentle decline, albeit with fluctuations, after the mid-1960s. The support rate fell below 30 percent after 1971 and bottomed out at about 25 percent in 1974. Thereafter, it rose again and, in the 1980s, rose above 30 percent. (There are two exceptions to these trends: the rise in LDP support in 1970 is probably due to the return of Okinawa from U.S. occupation to Japanese control and to the end of the radical student movement of the 1960s; the 1976 drop can probably be attributed to the Lockheed scandal.) In the summer of 1988, party support dropped precipitously under the influence of the Recruit scandal, but revived with the establishment of the Kaifu cabinet and the 1990 general election. With the exception of these two very recent oscillations, the long-term pattern of LDP support is one of relatively gentle fluctuations. By contrast, support for the cabinet shows many more, and far wider, short-term fluctuations.

Moreover, during the 1960s, the two curves tended to fluctuate in tandem; since 1970, however, there have been large gaps between them. From this we can see how popular images of both cabinet and prime minister have grown more volatile since the 1972 Tanaka cabinet. But support for the cabinet is not the same thing as support for the LDP that dominates it; they are clearly perceived as different things. And it is probable that the gaps are due less to fluctuations in support for the LDP than to changes in cabinet images. Support for the cabinet appears to have become independent of support for the party. The data on electoral support for the LDP shown in the figure, however, are closer to the curve of LDP party support than to that for cabinet support. When one analyzes the data on cabinet support more closely, one finds that it cuts across party support: there are many people who support the cabinet but do not support the LDP, and many LDP partisans do not support the cabinet when it is headed by an unpopular prime minister. Thus, support for the cabinet does not translate directly into votes for the LDP. Party support is a far stronger influence on voting behavior than is cabinet support.

The result of the 1993 election also confirms this analysis. Although the Miyazawa cabinet rating dropped, LDP support declined only gradually. The electoral result was closer to LDP support than to cabinet support. Thus, it seems that the defeat of the LDP is attributed more to the party's performance than to the failure of the Miyazawa cabinet.

DETERMINANTS OF VOTER CHOICE

Party support, a relatively stable attitude, influences what party one votes for; there are, however, other determinants of voter choice as well. Miyake Ichirō has distinguished between three types of such determinants: party orientations, candidate orientations, and issue orientations. Party orientations, basically, center upon the party support we have been discussing. Party support exerts a relatively stable influence on one's vote, changing little from one election to another—its influence is a long-term determinant of voting behavior. There is, however, another component of party orientation—positive or negative party images, likes and dislikes—that can change rapidly from one election to the next on the basis of particular political conditions or events, and which exert a short-term influence on voter choice. For example, voter perceptions of a party's ability to govern and its financial probity are easily changeable.

Candidate orientations are influences on voter choice derived from evaluations of individual candidates; in a country with medium-sized, multimember election districts like Japan (until 1993), such considerations loom large. When there are several candidates from one party running in a single district, party orientations are of no help in choosing between them. For this reason, public opinion surveys include questions such as, "When you vote, do you vote on the basis of party, or on the basis of an individual candidate?" Until 1967, citizens voting on the basis of candidate outnumbered those voting on the basis of political party. This pattern was reversed in the 1969 election, but since then, party orientations have not intensified, and in recent elections they have been only slightly stronger. In fact, however, party and candidate orientations are not either-or influences: both are at work, often in a two-stage sequence. In a multimember district, many voters first choose according to party, and *then* choose from among their preferred party's candidates on the basis of individual qualities.[12]

Issue orientations are tendencies to decide how one will vote based on the policies presented by the different parties in an election and on the issues of major public interest at the time of the election. Issue orientations include not only the public promises made by each party but also general evaluations of the parties based on their performance to date and their track records in government and parliament. The ruling party's economic performance, as reflected in rates of unemployment, inflation, and economic growth, are also important. Positive evaluations of the government's performance push voters toward supporting the ruling party, while negative ones push them to-ward the opposition. Voting on the basis of issue evaluations is called issue voting, while voting on the basis of governmental performance is called performance or restrospective voting.

These three sets of orientations interact to influence voting behavior, with each exerting a different weight in combination with the others. Because in Japan election campaigns are organizationally based, with *kōenkai* activities at their core, candidate factors and campaign mobilization techniques have a major impact on individual voters' decisions. Since the outcome of general elections influences the subsequent course of politics for several years, however, one must also emphasize the importance of issue orientations. And party ID is ever operational.

NOTES

1. Kabashima Ikuo, *Seiji Sanka* (Political Participation), University of Tokyo Press, 1988, pp. 84–85.
2. This is the urban-rural typology used by the *Asahi Shinbun* newspaper in its analyses of electoral behavior. Here we have used the categories from the 1983 election in each case so that we are comparing the same groups of constituencies across all elections.
3. For a detailed discussion, see Kawato Sadafumi, "Nationalization of the Japanese Electorate," paper presented at the annual meeting of the American Political Science Association, Washington, D.C., September 1991.
4. Araki Toshio, "Tōhyō Kōdō to Shakaiteki Zokusei" (Electoral Behavior and Social Attributes), in *Senkyo* (Elections; special edition of *Jurisuto*), Yūhikaku, 1985, p. 174.
5. Ishikawa Masumi, "Nihonjin no Sentaku" (Electoral Choices for the Japanese), *Aera* 33 (1989).
6. Watanuki Jōji, "Dentō to Kindai no Tairitsu to shite no Nihon Seiji" (The Conflict of Tradition and Modernity in Japanese Politics), in Watanuki Jōji, *Nihon Seiji no Bunseki Shikaku* (Japanese Politics: An Analytical Perspective), Chūō Kōron, 1976, p. 196.
7. Scott Flanagan and Bradley Richardson, *Japanese Electoral Behavior: Social Cleavages, Social Networks, and Partisanship*, Beverly Hills, Calif., Sage Publications, 1977.
8. Kyōgoku Jun'ichi, "Seiji Ishiki Kenkyū no Ayumi" (A History of the Study of Political Consciousness), in Tōkei Sūri Kenkyū-jo, ed., *Seiji Ishiki no Kanjō Kōzō no Kenkyū* (A Study of the Attitudinal Structure of Political Consciousness), Tōkei Sūri Kenkyūjo Kenkyū Ripōto, no. 45, 1979, p. 1.
9. Miyake Ichirō, *Seitō Shiji no Bunseki* (An Analysis of Party Support), Sōbunsha, 1985, p. 4.
10. Miyake Ichirō, Kinoshita Tomio, and Aiba Juichi, *Kotonaru Reberu no Senkyo ni okeru Tōhyō Kōdō no Kenkyū* (A Study of Voting Behavior in Elections on Different Levels), Sōbunsha, 1967 pp. 116–18.

11. Scott Flanagan et al., *The Japanese Voter*, New Haven, Conn., Yale University Press, 1991, ch. 6.

12. Miyake et al., *Tōhyō Kōdō*, pp. 38–39; Bradley Richardson, "Constituency Candidates versus Parties in Japanese Voting Behavior," *American Political Science Review* 82 (1988): 713.

CHAPTER 16

THE KŌENKAI

THE KŌENKAI AND ELECTORAL STRATEGY

One extremely important aspect of elections and parties in Japan is the *kōenkai*, the personal support organizations maintained by candidates and elected politicians. One can see the types of activities that were performed by *kōenkai* in politics before the war; moreover, formal social organizations whose purpose is the support of particular individuals or organizations are not limited to politics. *Kōenkai* activities, however, as an organized, permanent part of campaign tactics, date from around the general election of 1958. At first, *kōenkai* were organized primarily by LDP candidates, but soon members of the JSP and other parties began to form their own. At present, almost every candidate for public office has some sort of personal support organization.

In the view of some, the emergence of the *kōenkai* is one aspect of the modernization of hitherto highly traditional campaign practices. In the words of Gerald Curtis, "What is significantly modern about the *kōenkai* [is] the use of a mass-membership organization with the function of organizing large numbers of the general electorate on behalf of a particular Diet candidate."[1] Of course, since the *kōenkai* are elements of grass-roots campaign strategy, they present a facade of being spontaneously organized by their members in order to support some candidate; in fact, the politician himself is the head of the organization and pays for almost all of the operational and personnel expenses of the *kōenkai* himself.[2] But, despite this populist charade, the *kōenkai* do represent a modern departure.

In general, Japanese election campaigns are organized on the basis of the so-called three *ban*: *jiban*, *kamban*, and *kaban*. *Kamban*, meaning "signboard," refers to a candidate's reputation, his appropriateness for public office as indicated by his status, academic credentials, personal record, and political persona. *Kaban*, or "satchel," refers to campaign funds. And *jiban*, "turf" or "stamping ground," refers to a physical area or organizational base in which the candidate can expect to win more votes than any other candidate. In contrast to the JSP and the DSP, which can count on the votes of organized labor, and the Kōmeitō and the JCP, which have highly mobilized party organizations, candidates of the LDP, Japan New Party, and Shinsei Party cannot rely on their party organizations. Consequently, it is imperative that they cultivate and defend a *jiban*.

Traditionally, a *jiban* was built through the efforts of local notables to mobilize the vote through the medium of organizations that exist at the level between local notables and the citizenry—neighborhood associations, farmers' co-ops, merchants' and businessmens' organizations, unions, religious organizations, women's and young people's organizations, and so forth. It was through the local notables, who thus mobilized the vote, that candidates for parliament won votes. Unsurprisingly, such notables became the core of politicians' local support structures.

The postwar democratization and land reform obliterated the traditional prewar stratum of local notables—the landlord class. The leadership stratum that replaced them was organizational notables—public officials in municipal and prefectural government. This new stratum of organizational notables won their own positions through election to office, and for this purpose had built their own *jiban*. In the postwar period, the dependence of regional governments on the central government has been high, and, for local politicians, obtaining subsidies and revenue-sharing funds has necessitated appeals to and liaison and cooperation with MPs. It was through this process that, under each MP, there grew up structured networks and hierarchies of local politicians, and layers of *jiban*. The MP guaranteed his reelection on the basis of votes gathered and handed over by the local politicians, and the local politicians maintained their offices and positions on the basis of the "pork" that the MP kept flowing into the local arena.

The *kōenkai*—which constitute a direct link between candidate and individual voter—stand in sharp contrast to this traditional sort of election strategy based on the mobilization of networks of MPs and local politicians. The local notables initially set themselves up as the officials of the *kōenkai*; in this respect, the *kōenkai* were no different from the old hierarchical type of campaign structure. The key aspect of the *kōenkai*, however, is not that local notables are the leaders, but that the memberships run in the tens of thousands.[3] In this respect, the *kōenkai* "represent an innovation in campaign strategies

and are to be contrasted with a strategy of reliance on local politicians and other community leaders."[4] They constitute a clear
challenge to the local politicians' old role in mobilizing the vote, and
signify an erosion of the functions performed by local politicians in
election campaigns.

One may cite two causes for the original creation of the *kōenkai*
by conservative candidates. First, the poverty of local finances during
the 1950s stimulated local administrative overtures to the central
government. Local politicians gave MPs access to their own *jiban* in
exchange for government largesse; as a result, local politicians became incorporated into the support networks of conservative MPs.
Second, the merger of the conservative parties in 1955 created a
situation in which LDP candidates in the same constituency had to
run against each other. Because each candidate thus became unable
to rely on the party organization to mobilize voters, it became necessary for each one to build his own vote-mobilization organization.
Within a given constituency, the fact that the targets of all the candidates' campaign efforts were the same LDP supporters only made
these rivalries even more intense. At first, the *kōenkai* were created
by incorporating the respective vote-mobilization organizations of
the local politicians under each MP as their components, but gradually they became transformed into autonomous organizations of
jiban cultivation that linked the MP and the voters directly, bypassing the local political middlemen.

ORGANIZATIONAL STRUCTURE OF THE KŌENKAI

Kōenkai consist of two parts. The core of the *kōenkai* is human, and
composed of tens of thousands of members. This membership core
must be expanded over time, slowly and steadily, following the link-
ages established through friendship and neighbors, workplace and
profession. This core is relatively permanent; it cannot be expanded
rapidly, but at the same time it is unlikely to deteriorate rapidly
either. It is, however, also deceptive—given a politician's desire for
"insurance," the number of members in a *kōenkai* is usually two or
three times the number of votes necessary for a candidate to get
elected. Consequently, the total memberships of all the *kōenkai* of all
the politicians in a constituency usually exceed the number of voters
there. Unsurprisingly, the *kōenkai*'s core includes everybody from
firm, loyal adherents of the candidate to those who are members in
name only.

Around the *kōenkai*'s core is an external, organizational belt. This
circumferential band comprises the old structure of local politicians

and the leaders of occupational groups such as farmers' co-ops, construction companies, merchants' associations and chambers of commerce, medical associations, and so forth. Among them are many individuals who are also parts of the inner core, but most participate in the *kōenkai* only as representatives of their organizations, for the purpose of furthering their own organizations' goals.

Unlike the general membership, the size of this external belt fluctuates sharply along with the fortunes of the MP—whether or not he becomes a cabinet minister, whether or not his faction or party is excluded from the ruling coalition—and with the particular policies he tries to push. In order to keep them on board, it is imperative for the MP to respond to their political demands and funnel benefits to his and their constituents.

The Clean Election League does a national opinion survey after each general election that includes questions about *kōenkai*. Table 16.1 includes such data from the 1986 survey, which indicates that only 18.2 percent of the national sample reported being members of *kōenkai*. On the other hand, 39.3 percent reported having been solicited to join. When one recalls that almost every candidate nowadays has a *kōenkai*, this participation rate seems quite low. It probably reflects the fact that relatively few people formally join *kōenkai* of their own volition.[5] All a politician really needs from the *kōenkai* is a list of the names of voters whose votes he hopes to count on; those who attend any *kōenkai* activity are likely to be counted among the membership, regardless of their own feelings. From such facts, it is not surprising to find that no more than about one in three of those reporting *kōenkai* membership report ever having paid the membership dues themselves.

When one looks at *kōenkai* membership rates among the different

TABLE 16.1   *Kōenkai* Membership, by Party Identification, 1986 (%)

Party ID	Respondent is *kōenkai* member	Respondent has been solicited to join *kōenkai*
LDP	26.5	41.4
JSP	15.3	45.2
Kōmeitō	33.9	45.8
DSP	20.5	53.4
JCP	17.4	36.8
Total	18.2	39.3

SOURCE: Akarui Senkyo Suishin Kyōkai Zenkoku Chōsa (Clean Election League Survey).

parties, participation is highest among supporters of the LDP and the Kōmeitō, but there are *kōenkai* members among the supporters of all the parties. In parties that do not have candidates running against each other in a single constituency, the party organization backs up candidates' *kōenkai* activities. In Japan, many voters resist joining a party formally; consequently, *kōenkai* are often surrogates for party organization, and often serve to organize those candidate-oriented rather than party-oriented voters who support a candidate as an individual rather than as the representative of a party. The JSP, for its part, views *kōenkai* as "undesirable from the perspective of party organization—they strengthen tendencies toward individual campaigns"; nevertheless, "in areas where party organization is weak, effective [*kōenkai*] are recognized as a necessary evil."[6] The JCP and the Kōmeitō conceive of them as "party *kōenkai*," incorporating them into their wider activities for the purpose of mobilizing support from a wider stratum of society not confined to actual members of the party and the Sōka Gakkai.

According to Gerald Curtis, *kōenkai* are most common in medium-size and smaller cities.[7] In the countryside, the vote-mobilization functions of traditional local notables are still functioning and *kōenkai* are thus unnecessary; in metropolitan areas, voters are so numerous and so mobile that organizational efforts are difficult and ineffective, and image-oriented campaign tactics are much more efficacious. According to 1967 survey data cited by Curtis, the *kōenkai* participation rate in medium-size and small cities is higher than that in either countryside or metropolis, lending his explanation plausibility. Long-term data, however, cast doubt on his argument. For example, data from 1986 suggest that the participation rate in metropolitan areas is the lowest, but that *kōenkai* are equally common in smaller cities and in towns and villages. (See table 16.2.) In-

TABLE 16.2	Participation in *Kōenkai*, by Degree of Urbanism of Place of Residence (%)

Place of residence	1967	1969	1972	1976	1979	1980	1983	1986
Metropolitan area	4.2	15.6	9.1	9.8	20.1	14.1	11.4	14.5
Medium-size or small city	6.4	10.5	9.9	14.9	20.9	14.6	16.0	19.3
Town or village	5.8	10.2	8.8	15.3	16.6	16.9	18.1	18.7

SOURCE: Same as table 16.1.

deed, insofar as these data are any indication, the relative frequency of *kōenkai* in different types of communities varies across time. They have increased in every type of community since the 1960s, and, in general, it is accurate simply to think of them as ubiquitous. The "modernity" of these organizations can most easily be inferred from their smooth and increasing fit with all sectors of contemporary Japanese society.

KŌENKAI ACTIVITIES

The purposes of the *kōenkai* are two: to strengthen and consolidate a politician's *jiban* over the long term, and to mobilize votes in the short run. Since the dissolution of parliament and calling of new elections are not predictable, it is necessary to keep one's *kōenkai* active all the time. The typical MP's schedule—going back to the constituency every weekend to consult with *kōenkai* members, and then back to Tokyo again on Monday—attests to the importance of *kōenkai* activities. In the case of most LDP MPs, for example, the number of staff in their local *kōenkai* offices is greater than the number of staff helping with their parliamentary duties in their offices in Tokyo. (See table 16.3.) They run the *kōenkai* while the MP is in Tokyo and manage his weekend schedule back home so that he makes contact with as many members as possible. The MP is kept literally on the run when in his district.

There are three broad areas of *kōenkai* activity. First, the *kōenkai* attend to and help with the demands of the locality for budgetary assistance for new facilities, road repairs, and other construction. Local mayors and assemblymen go through the local *kōenkai* office and through the MP's Tokyo office staff to appeal to him. The MP communicates these wishes to the relevant ministries and serves as a bridge between them and city hall, and also solicits his fellow MPs and faction leader, trying to apply pressure so that local projects find a place in the government's budget. Prime Minister Tanaka Kakuei, a master of the pork barrel, sent his staff home every summer to collect budget requests from the municipalities in his district—his own so-called *kōenkai* budget process. It is said that most of these items eventually appeared in the following year's national budget. Albeit in different degree, all of the faction and party leaders perform the same sort of local service, as do backbenchers as well.

Second, local *kōenkai* offices attend to the myriad requests and problems that local citizens bring to them. They are of a vast variety, many personal and nonpolitical: a child's admission to college or the search for a job, gifts for weddings and condolence money for funer-

TABLE 16.3   Personal Accounts of Ten LDP Members of Parliament, 1989 (¥1,000)

	A	B	C	D	E	F	G	H	I	J	Mean
Income											
Official allowance	18,800	18,800	18,800	18,800	18,800	18,800	18,800	18,800	18,800	18,800	18,800
From party and faction	8,374	10,000	12,390	8,000	8,000	13,000	13,000	7,000	7,000	17,000	10,376
Contributions	58,925	66,608	55,430	65,200	81,000	44,840	6,160	61,300	90,000	15,961	54,342
Fund-raisers/parties	40,000	—	20,000	—	—	36,000	38,126	20,500	45,000	4,447	20,407
Loans	7,400	38,800	—	33,060	10,000	—	—	27,000	30,000	5,179	15,143
Other	4,000	4,000	17,780	8,630	4,000	6,700	6,532	12,869	5,690	4,482	7,468
Subtotal	135,499	138,208	124,400	133,690	121,800	119,340	82,618	147,469	196,490	65,869	126,538
Expenses											
Personnel	39,485	33,987	37,692	45,360	33,000	25,710	21,942	51,674	86,500	22,930	39,828
Travel and communications	12,569	17,097	18,397	32,830	23,000	12,955	12,213	30,019	34,000	6,228	19,930
Commercial travel	2,815	3,817	3,500	3,600	1,000	2,157	1,965	6,036	12,000	1,634	3,852
Car expenses	1,461	3,840	3,435	11,500	5,000	2,914	3,362	11,600	5,000	1,577	4,968
Telephone/facsimile	2,097	4,290	3,690	4,670	4,800	2,520	617	4,833	7,200	1,115	3,265
Telegrams	392	285	512	6,110	3,200	1,194	332	2,904	2,400	964	2,147
Postage	5,804	4,865	7,260	6,950	9,000	4,170	5,937	4,646	7,400	938	5,697
Office expenses	13,957	19,048	6,375	8,720	8,000	5,034	5,883	15,340	31,000	5,886	11,924
Office rent	7,026	10,004	1,800	1,960	2,000	600	4,465	4,000	27,600	4,080	6,353
Furnishings/supplies	6,308	7,936	3,478	6,200	2,400	3,937	965	10,401	1,000	1,595	4,422
Utilities	623	1,108	1,097	560	3,600	497	453	939	2,400	211	1,148
Operations	24,280	63,064	50,536	44,740	47,500	31,622	59,486	58,608	37,500	30,356	44,769
Policy activities	12,243	573	33,292	3,010	12,000	3,558	3,325	17,547	1,200	5,297	9,204
Weddings/funerals	9,632	24,982	10,889	22,030	16,800	12,405	15,250	21,591	22,300	10,760	16,663
Kōenkai activities	2,405	37,509	6,355	19,700	18,700	15,659	40,911	19,470	14,000	14,299	18,900
Subtotal	94,731	133,196	113,000	131,650	111,500	75,321	99,524	155,641	189,000	65,400	116,452
Number of staff											
Tokyo office	3	4	8	4	3	3	2	2	6	2	3.7
District office	6	8	16	12	10	6	8	23	32	4	12.5
Offices: Tokyo	2	2	1	1	1	1	1	1	2	2	1.4
District	4	2	3	4	2	2	1	6	9	1	3.4

SOURCE: Jimintō Seiji Kenkyūkai, cited in Sone Yasunori and Kanazashi Masao, *Nihon no Seiji*, Nihon Keizai Shinbun, 1989, p. 127.

als, good offices in obtaining a business loan, resolution of traffic accidents, or mediation of a quarrel between two individuals or groups. Some of these are taken care of by staff, while others require the personal attention of the MP. The more personal the problem, the greater the effect, the more solid the vote.[8]

Third, the *kōenkai* provides its members with recreation, entertainment, and social life. Above all, the *kōenkai* is targeted to the votes of the membership, and it is important always to keep them attracted to the political patron. At every opportunity the *kōenkai* branches hold meetings, at all of which food and drink are served. The intimate atmosphere—a community centered on the MP—born of exchanging cups with one's legislator helps bind the *kōenkai* members together.[9]

And beyond this, the *kōenkai* puts on a variety of entertainment: movies for the general membership meeting, baseball games and marathon races for the youth division, chess tournaments and golf outings for the middle-aged, cooking classes for the housewives, volleyball for the women, *kimono*-wearing lessons, tea ceremony and flower-arranging classes, and on and on. They even organize tours for the members and trips to Tokyo, where, in exchange for a voluntary cleanup of a portion of the Imperial Palace gardens, they receive a kind word from the Emperor himself. And such trips always include a healthy dose of sightseeing.

MERITS AND DEMERITS OF THE KŌENKAI

The influence exercised by *kōenkai* vis-à-vis Japanese politics is considerable. First, a tremendous amount of money is necessary to set them up and run them. Even if all that participants at a *kōenkai* party get is a box lunch and a bottle of *sake*, as such gatherings multiply, the cost adds up. The *kōenkai* are a major cause of the high cost of politics in Japan, and, in turn, a cause of political corruption and popular political alienation. Table 16.3 presents the personal accounts for 1989 of ten LDP first-term MPs. Their average annual expenditure was ¥116 million, with a high of ¥189 million, and in these amounts *kōenkai* expenses figure prominently. Personnel expenses accounted for roughly a third of the total, and almost all of this went as salaries of *kōenkai* office staff. Every MP has at least one *kōenkai* office in his home district with permanent staff—some as many as thirty—to keep in contact with his constituents. Operational expenses are high, and among them wedding and funeral expenses rank high along with *kōenkai* activities. Constituents' funerals and weddings are extremely important—MPs offer to be go-betweens in weddings, and are assiduous in sending flowers and telegrams of condolence to funerals. As of February 1990, such congratulatory and condolence gifts and contributions were banned under the Public Office Election Law, unless the MP himself attended the ceremony, but, given the link between such activities and the vote, one may wonder whether this measure will have much effect.

Second, the consolidation of the *kōenkai* as campaign organizations, with all the expense and numbers of workers they require, constitutes a tremendous barrier to entry into politics and represents a severe constraint on the opportunities for new candidates to run for office. In recent years, the reelection rate of incumbent MPs has become very high, slowing the pace of generational turnover in the political world.

Third, because of the increasing cost of the *kōenkai*, new candidates for office tend increasingly to be individuals who are able to "inherit" the *kōenkai* of the politician retiring. This is the reason for the recent increase in the number of MPs who are either the sons of MPs or whose previous position was personal secretary to the MP whom they followed into parliament. Consequently, the *kōenkai*'s relationship with the MP as an individual has weakened, and it is the *kōenkai* members rather than the MP who are responsible for the survival of the *kōenkai*.[10] Moreover, the hierarchical order of the *kōenkai* has been reversed, with the MP being forced to cater to the special-interest demands of the local *kōenkai*. The result is a national politics of private advantage in which important national political issues are reduced to local benefits and private deals.

On the other hand, insofar as the *kōenkai* provide MPs with stable prospects of reelection, they are able to avoid the never-ending race of vote-hunting that consumes vast amounts of U.S. Congressmen's time. They are thus able to focus their attention on their primary function: the legislative process. And they do make politics responsive to constituent demands. It all depends on what the electorate wants of their representatives—and it looks as if the voters are more than willing to see the *kōenkai* stay. This is why one should not expect the new electoral system for the lower house, which combines single-member districts and proportional representation, to lead to the demise of the *kōenkai*. The new system eliminates one of the original forces leading to the creation of the *kōenkai*, that is, the need for candidates of the same party to run against each other. But the fact that politicians who do not run against others from the same party have also built their own *kōenkai*, and that the *kōenkai* perform valued functions for both MPs and citizens, suggest that changes in the electoral system alone will not immediately affect the role of the *kōenkai* in Japanese politics.

NOTES

1. Gerald Curtis, *Election Campaigning Japanese Style*, New York, Columbia University Press, 1971, p. 128.
2. Ishikawa Masumi and Hirose Michisada, *Jimintō: Chōki Shihai no Kōzō* (The LDP: The Structure of Long Political Rule), Iwanami, 1989, p. 128. Here, as elsewhere, we use masculine pronouns by design, to convey the male domination of parliamentary politics in Japan.
3. Curtis, *Election Campaigning Japanese Style*, pp. 129–30.
4. *Ibid.*, p. 129.
5. *Ibid.*, pp. 132–33.
6. Masumi Junnosuke, *Gendai Nihon no Seiji Taisei* (The Political System of Contemporary Japan), Iwanami, 1969, p. 231.
7. Curtis, *Election Campaigning Japanese Style*, pp. 136–37.
8. Tonooka Akio, "Seijika ni okeru Kane no Kenkyū" (A Study of Politicians and Money), *Bungei Shunju* (June 1975): 186.
9. *Ibid.*, p. 179.
10. Kitaoka Shin'ichi, "Jiyū Minshu-tō: Hōkatsu Seitō no Gōrika" (The LDP: Rationalizing a Comprehensive Party), in Kamishima Jirō, ed., *Gendai Nihon no Seiji Kōzō* (The Political Structure of Contemporary Japan), Hōritsu Bunkasha, 1985, p. 64.

CHAPTER 17

POLITICAL MOVEMENTS AND POLITICAL PARTICIPATION

MANAGED SOCIETY AND PARTICIPATORY DEMOCRACY

Political participation is an old, and a new, problem. In modern democratic states the central decision-making body is the legislature, comprising popular representatives who have been authorized at the ballot box to govern in the name of the people. Politics in the hands of legislators truly representative of all the people is, however, a fiction: upon the establishment of the modern state, the election of popular representatives—that is to say, the right to vote—was restricted to certain classes and strata. The rise of new conflicts of interest and the political maturation of the people that accompanied subsequent social and economic development gave rise to ultimately successful protest and massive movements in opposition to the restricted franchise. Thus it is that in contemporary democratic states all the people, generally without regard to social class, gender, religion, race, and so forth, are guaranteed the opportunity to participate in politics.

In light of this development, one might be tempted to say that the problem of political participation has been resolved. In the late 1960s, however, a movement for participatory democracy erupted in Japan and the other advanced industrial nations, and the proper form of political participation again became the focus of debate. In France, the movement grew out of the student-led "May Revolution" of 1968. In the United States, it arose out of the anti-Vietnam War, environmental protection, and civil rights movements. But regardless of the specific catalyst, there lay behind all of these movements a common reason and significance, in that "participatory democracy" was everywhere the banner of a movement in pursuit of a new politics for this era. That is, one cause behind these movements was the advance of "managed society" and the over-concentration of power in advanced industrial societies. The advance of bureaucratization is inevitable in contemporary society, but, even conceding this, the centralization of decision-making has advanced in *all* types of social groups to which individuals belong, to the point that humans have become the objects of management or domination by the central leadership of even ostensibly democratic organizations.

The world of politics is no exception. The distance between political leaders and citizens has become greater and greater, and voters tend to become little more than objects of mobilization for the purpose of endowing political leaders with legitimacy. And, in addition to contributing to popular alienation from political decision-making, the economic dimension of managed society—highly advanced and rapid industrialization under the control of vast, impersonal corporations—destroys the human environment. It was the deepening of these conditions that gave rise to movements that rethought the quality of organizational power and popular political participation.

If one accepts the argument that these were the origins of the movement for participatory democracy, one can see why the movement developed simultaneously in support of decentralization of economic and political power and protection of livelihood. The breakup of centers of concentrated political power, and the facilitation of popular participation therein, were ways to overcome alienation and the destruction of a livable environment. This is the reason why participatory democracy is predominantly debated in the context of local politics.

Participatory democracy is not simply an add-on to representative democracy, however, nor does it urge a return to direct democracy. Moreover, the organizational institutionalization of expanded opportunities for participation is not its goal either. Participatory democracy does represent each of these functions partially. Participatory democracy is at heart, however, a sort of unstructured, generalized expression of aspirations, a philosophy and movement seeking decentralization in all spheres of social life, fulfillment and protection of the human living space, and an unceasing questioning of the quality of political participation.

ERUPTION OF RESIDENTS' MOVEMENTS AND POLITICAL CULTURE

It was in this context that, around the end of the 1960s, a host of "residents' movements" (*jūmin undō*) arose in Japanese politics. The issues that gave rise to them were myriad—there were movements against pollution, environmental destruction, and massive regional development projects, and movements for the enhancement of social infrastructure such as schools, water and sewers, roads, parks, and welfare facilities. In addition to these sorts of movements, whose causes lay in the structure of local society, there were also broader citizens' movements (*shimin undō*), such as the antiwar and consumer protection movements. In light of the proliferation of these sorts of movements, the possible transformation of political culture itself became the subject of debate: these movements differed in quality and structure from previous types of mass movements based on political parties, labor unions, or other types of functional organizations. These "old social movements" had been led by movement professionals within the hierarchical frameworks of particular organizations; residents' and citizens' movements were natural, spontaneous movements led democratically by amateurs, and their organizational control of their memberships was loose. Moreover, they were novel in that their goals were rooted in the livelihood of the individual members.

Discussions of the transformation of political culture did not, however, emerge simply from the explosive growth of this organizationally new type of movement. Viewed broadly, the significance of the residents' movements was the same as that of the worldwide movement for participatory democracy already noted. As the same time, they were significant as a rejection of the sort of traditional political mores summed up in the phrase "Let them in, but don't let them touch,"[1] and against the village-like political conditions in which traditional grass-roots social groups continued to wield political influence.

We have argued that the movement for participatory democracy particularly emphasized the local sphere. The objectives of residents' movements were many and varied. Nevertheless, it is significant that they arose at the end of the 1960s, in a context of government-sponsored rapid economic growth. Under the rapid economic growth policies of the 1960s, the motto of "local government with a pipeline to Tokyo" was highly realistic; consequently, local governments were excessively aligned with the central government, and were pushing regional and urban development regardless of local feelings. As a result, although the GNP grew, pollution and environmental degradation did also, to the extent that in some instances they threatened human life itself. Moreover, the spread of suburbanization at a rate faster than infrastructural development could keep pace with only brought more instability to human and community life.

The residents' movements were movements of local people literally compelled to resist this constellation of inconveniences and environmental dangers. Accordingly, the targets of resistance were the elected executives and administrative institutions of local government. Many observers looked askance at the radical attacks of these movements on traditional authority, and criticized them for their self-centered local egotism and raids on the public purse in disregard of longer-resident citizens who actually paid most of the local taxes. In such cities as Anan in Tokushima prefecture and Numazu and Mishima in Shizuoka prefecture, however, massive movements in opposition to the construction of huge petrochemical complexes provided opportunities for a fundamental rethinking of such concepts as local government, self-government, and development. Moreover, one may say that the ubiquitous movements in pursuit of infrastructural development also made major contributions to the systematic creation of a foundation for civilized metropolitan living. Not only that, but residents' movements hastened reform of the procedures and rules of policy decision-making in local government. Thus, the eruption of residents' movements shows, in multiple ways, a progressive transformation of political culture.

INSTITUTIONALIZATION OF PARTICIPATION AND REFORM OF LOCAL GOVERNMENT

In local elections nowadays, essentially every candidate for office flaunts the banner of "politics in accord with citizen participation." This political situation is of relatively recent origin, however, dating as it does from the late 1960s.

Galvanized by the upsurge of residents' movements, mayors all over the country began calling for city government in accord with citizen participation. Most of these mayors were supported by parties and organizations of the Left; however, these organizations were not necessarily supported by the citizens, who exerted their own independent influence directly on local government. Originally, residents' movements performed two functions: resistance to politics-as-usual and participation in policy planning. They attempted to push policy change through over stiff resistance and to make such policies possible by participating in political planning processes. In any case, the mobilization of residents' movements in pursuit of political participation helped to bring into existence—through election and persuasion—a host of local executives with a completely new political style.

The "progressive" executives who appeared in this way sought to build the basis of their political and policy operations not on the traditionalistic groupings of local society or the local assemblies composed of their representatives but on the broad citizenry. For this reason, in the early stages of their administrations they worked to build a dialogue with the citizens through such mechanisms as "discussion meetings" and "citizens' assemblies" for the purpose of expanding public hearing and public information functions, and to improve the performance of information-dissemination functions. In addition, they endeavored to institutionalize citizen participation in the process of both long-term planning and operational planning in local government. The concrete forms of participation they instituted were many and varied, including everything from an expanded role for advisory councils to broad-scale delegation of policy planning to citizens' committees and citizens' councils. In addition to setting high standards for citizen participation in policy and overall planning, local governments also attempted in the case of specific projects to incorporate residents' participation in the form of consultations involving those living in the immediate vicinity of the project. The primary objects of this process were "nuisance facilities" such as roads, waste treatment plants, crematoria, garbage dumps and incinerators, and so forth.

The question of how much this institutionalization of popular participation actually enhanced the political influence of administratively inexperienced citizens must be answered case by case. In the most general sense, however, as a result of these myriad attempts to institutionalize participation, the attitudes and behavior of local government and politics have been reformed in a variety of respects that are today undeniably and irreversibly part of the local political scene. One such reform, which came about through this sort of participation, was the discovery of the local executive as a representative organ of the people, not simply the head of an administrative structure and puppet of Tokyo. There has always been, in Japanese local administration, a tendency for the intentions of a strong-willed executive to become those of local government. Given this, having input into the process by which an executive forms his intentions amounts to having influence over the workings of government. The community-building discussed in chapter 8, made possible by "living law," is one example of this.

Second, although popular political mobilization, once achieved, gradually lost its radical edge, it still continued on a high level, and local executives were put in the position of having to continue to promote processes of wide-ranging citizen participation regardless of their personal views on the subject. Accordingly, neighborhood associations and all kinds of local functional groups as well as the local power structures in the hands of local notables were seriously weakened.

Third, the destruction of old, elitist patterns of political participation and the political mobilization of the mass of the people led toward the emergence of new patterns of neighboring in an urbanized society. Through participation in local government planning and operations, citizens attempted new forms of community-building. Moreover, they broadened the sorts of links of spontaneous solidarity exemplified by volunteer activities. This was the first time in its modern century that Japan had experienced the formation of a citizen-based culture of politics and administration.

CITIZEN PARTICIPATION AND THE STRUCTURE OF LIVELIHOOD

One occasionally hears nowadays the argument that the era when residents' movements and citizen participation were the focal point of politics has come to an end. And, unquestionably, the number of movements that embody radical resistance to and demands upon local government has declined. To a large extent, however, this is because local governments have simply incorporated the movements, setting their policy priorities through participatory citizen planning and working toward the full construction of basic social capital. It is also because, with the increasing dependence of Japan's economy on high-tech, information-intensive, and knowlege-based enterprise, the attractiveness of huge, complex, heavy-industrial development projects has diminished, and with it the source of many citizens' grievances. The fact that movements of intense resistance to development projects have not disappeared, however, is attested to by the conflicts presently raging about the construction of nuclear-powered electric generation facilities.

What is also happening, however, is that citizen participation and citizens' and residents' movements are becoming focused on the structure of their own livelihoods and lifestyles as a totality and an attempt to come up with original ideas for community relationships appropriate to an urban, postindustrial society. One example— already common, but one of the first steps in this transformation—is the "construction agreement." These are covenants concluded by residents in a particular area for the purpose of protecting the residential environment and that establish mutually accepted behavioral standards for the residents of that area. In addition to these, afforestation agreements, consumers' movements for the cooperative purchase of chemical-free food, and recycling movements are also multiplying. Such movements emerge and operate as autonomous citizen groups, and in turn put pressure on government to enrich the political soil in which more such movements may grow. Moreover, movements for citizen administration of community facilities, for voluntary—instead of state-guided and government-run—social education activities in areas such as health and citizenship, and for the preservation of the historical and natural environment through foundations and land trusts, among others, have also become active. None of these are simply appendages of the activities of the local administration but are examples of the people building up their own living spaces with their own hands.

CIVIC POLITICAL CULTURE AND
CITIZEN PARTICIPATION

Since the initial eruption of residents' movements in the late 1960s, citizen participation in local politics has attained considerable maturity. Given the increased levels of popular education and increased leisure time at the disposal of the people, one may anticipate that the preconditions for the building of living spaces by the citizens themselves and the reform of local politics and administration will be further consolidated in the future.

On the other hand, and partly because of this, there are still many unresolved issues. One is the disclosure and dissemination of information. As of April 1990, 177 local governments (37 prefectures and 140 municipalities) had enacted public information disclosure ordinances, but, even in these instances, the basic criteria and conditions of disclosure have not always been fully worked out. The explicit specification and liberalization of the conditions of open disclosure of information are essential conditions of participatory local government. At the same time, local administrations must formulate and disseminate policy information that enables all citizens to evaluate accurately the condition of the community and its quality of life. But this sort of disclosure and dissemination of information cannot simply be left to the judgment of local administrators—it is important that the people themselves seek and generate it.

If attempts such as these accumulate, the enthusiasm for autonomously creating a rich environment and an open polity as parts of community culture will become even stronger among more and more citizens. And this in turn will contribute to the transformation of local political units under a centralized political and administrative structure into local *governments* in both name and substance.

NOTE

1. The Japanese phrase *yorashimu beshi, shirashimu bekarazu* is, more literally, "incorporate the people under political authority but don't let them participate in politics."

CHAPTER 18

THE POLITICAL FUNCTION OF THE MASS MEDIA

THE MASS MEDIA AND POLITICS

It is impossible to conceive of politics in the modern era in the absence of the mass media of communication. Politics most commonly unfolds in the context of huge state and local collectivities and organizations, but such phenomena occur on a level far beyond the scope of direct human experience. Consequently, before people can come to know these phenomena or make judgments about them, some vehicle is essential to communicate them to the people. The most important such vehicle in the contemporary era, without question, is the mass media.

For this reason, of the political functions of the mass media, the first to note is that of the reporting of political reality. At first blush, the reporting of facts may seem like a simple operation, but, in truth, it is hardly so. In the first place, the very determination of what the facts are entails sticky questions. Politics, in particular, is a realm of large-scale, complex problems. The way such problems appear usually differs depending on one's viewpoint, as does, indeed, reality itself. Moreover, the decision as to which, from among an unlimited universe of facts, will be extracted and reported is in the hands of the mass media. In a sense the mass media, through their selective inclusions and exclusions of the facts to be reported, communicate a particular viewpoint. In other words, the reportorial function of the mass media serves not simply to report the facts, but also to lead public opinion in particular directions.

The opinion leadership function is performed not only through the reporting of facts, but also through the deliberate propagation of specific opinions. This, which we shall call the editorial function, is the second political function of the mass media. In addition to reporting the news, it is common for newspapers, television and the like to add commentary or analysis in order that the facts be understood; insofar as this commentary is influenced by the subjectivity of the commentator, one may subsume it also occurs under the editorial function, along with the explicitly opinionated sort of material already found on the editorial page. In any case, because the media are able to influence public opinion through both their reportorial and editorial functions, it is well to think of them as a type of political authority, a wielder of political influence.

The influence of the media on public opinion is not, however, exerted simply through such activities as reportage, interpretation, and editorializing. The contemporary mass media exist, above all, to provide popular entertainment. Especially in the case of television, the proportion of programming devoted to entertainment far surpasses that devoted to the news. The more interest people show in entertainment, the less they usually show in politics. Moreover, even in regard to reporting, material related to people's entertainment interests far outweighs that related to politics. In a sense, the "recreationalization" of the news takes place. In this way, the mass media serve to direct popular interests away from politics. Thus, one may cite the media as one of the causes of political apathy in contemporary society.

CHARACTERISTICS OF THE PRESS

At the same time that the contemporary mass media are becoming ever more variegated, it is accurate to say that the press, politically at least, still occupies the central position among the media. What, then, are the distinctive political features of the Japanese press? First, Japan's major national daily newspapers are situated firmly in the top bracket of the world's press by virtue of their circulations of several million copies apiece. These mass-circulation newspapers are delivered to households nationwide through an elaborate delivery system. Because most families have neither the time nor the money to subscribe to multiple newspapers and compare their content, the great majority of citizens tend to subscribe to a single paper over a long period of time. Consequently, the differences in content among the major dailies are meaningless to the average reader.

The tendency for differences among the dailies to disappear and for them to become increasingly uniform is also promoted by conditions on the side of the publishers. The fact that the readership of each paper is in the millions means that the readership is highly heterogeneous in terms of age, income, occupation, education, beliefs, and so on. Consequently, there are powerful incentives for the publishers to produce a product that will satisfy all elements of this varied readership.[1] As a result, all of the dailies present their readers with a content that is of a muchness. Moreover, every publisher expends a tremendous amount of effort avoiding being scooped by the others on major news items. The result of this fixation, in combination with the desires of government agencies to guide public opinion, is the distinctively Japanese institution of the press club.[2] Press clubs—an exclusivistic system in which coverage of an organization and collection of information regarding it are limited to the accredited members of the club—are attached to every agency in the executive branch of government and also to parliament and major private-sector organizations. Accordingly, the reporters who are members of a given press club are guaranteed that they will not be scooped, and the government agencies acquire a privileged position vis-à-vis the guidance of public opinion. The consequence is that the content of all the dailies is becoming increasingly similar.

The second characteristic of the press (with the exception of the official newspapers of the political parties) is a nonpartisan, unbiased neutrality. In the foreign press, many newspapers take specific political positions, but in Japan all of the major dailies are politically neutral. If one presumes that both the reportorial and editorial functions presuppose some, at least tacit, point of view, then it is clear that the self-proclamation of political neutrality does not necessarily guarantee absence of bias in a newspaper at all. But the illusion of neutrality in the press, at least, is quite strong.

One example of this is the fact that the overwhelming preponderance of newspaper articles are without bylines. By contrast, almost all articles in European and American newspapers are signed. The assignment of authorship to an article conveys a warning, in advance, that the subjective judgment of the author is included therein. The reader thus can keep in mind in advance the tendencies of the author as recalled from his or her past writings and read the article accordingly. In this way, it is precisely the public clarification of subjectivity that constitutes the effort to ensure objectivity. In Japan, however, the fact that most articles are unsigned emphasizes the unity of the newspaper company as a whole over the responsibility of each individual reporter and, by denying the subjectivity of each reporter, asserts the objectivity of the reality reported. If one assumes that no article can completely transcend the subjective limitations of the reporter, however, then this "objectivity" is a pretense, and serves only to support the illusion of neutrality.

TELEVISION AND POLITICS

Today, television is the mainstream of the mass media. According to studies of popular lifestyles, the average Japanese watches an average of 3 hours of TV daily, and 3 hours 40 minutes on Sundays, while devoting only 35 minutes on average to reading newspapers, magazines, and books.[3] Of course, since the natures of broadcast and print media differ, one cannot say that TV has completely replaced the press, but it is certain, at least, that popular interest is directed overwhelmingly toward TV.

Television, like the press, performs both reportorial and editorial functions, but, in fact, the proportion of programming devoted to the news is slim. According to a 1986 study, on the average day, entertainment programming accounted for 47 percent of the total; by contrast, educational and cultural programs accounted for 36 percent and news for only 15 percent.[4] In the evening prime-time hours, entertainment accounted for 59 percent of what people watched, with education and culture following with 20 percent and news with 21 percent. Needless to say, this reflects the preferences of the viewers. According to one study of popular expectations regarding TV, by far the most common—held by 52 percent of the respondents to the survey—was a "restorative" one: "I want a lift for my spirits, a little relaxation." A substantial, but much smaller, 33 percent wanted TV to illuminate the world around them, agreeing most strongly with the statement: "I want to learn about the trends and events of the world." And 12 percent seemed to be seeking self-improvement in agreeing with the statement: "I want to absorb some culture, to improve myself."[5]

Consequently, when one considers the political implications of television, one must recognize its entertainment function as being much more important than its informational one. One distinctive feature of Japanese TV is that the proportion of young viewers is exceptionally large. Because of this, programmers have to try to produce shows that can simultaneously appeal to a broad age stratum, running from elementary and junior high school pupils to the elderly. Consequently, programming standards tend to regress to the level of the preferences of the youngest viewers. Given this trend, dramas and documentaries that aim at social critique are not welcomed, and mindless dramas and movies filled with sex and violence form the mainstream of programming. One cannot say that this sort of TV entertainment has any particular political influence *per se*, but, insofar as it does not provoke criticism of the social or political status quo, it serves to reinforce this status quo.

In its informational function, the faithfulness to life and immediacy of TV give it a strength unmatched by the print media and an influence that cannot be ignored politically. It is easy, however, for television viewers to see reportage, too, as another form of entertainment, and for news show producers to pander to this tendency. Thus, even in the news, the apolitical tendencies of the mass media are particularly apparent in TV. This apolitical tendency is manifest here in the communication of information about political events and issues in a nonpolitical form; this process includes such practices as isolation, fragmention, and privatization issues.[6]

"Isolation" refers to the taking of political and social events out of their historical and social context and the presentation of them along with episodes and attendant phenomena completely unrelated to the true nature of the event. "Fragmentation" refers to the technique of breaking news events up into tiny bits and presenting them—in the form of news flashes, sound bites, comments, and summaries instead of imparting comprehensive understanding and evaluation of matters related to one other. And "privatization" refers to the treating of politicians and political events without emphasizing their public significance but, rather, viewing them simply as "private" aspects of those involved. In particular, Japanese TV news devotes an extraordinary amount of effort to revelations about the private lives of show business personalities and other famous people; one cannot deny that this tendency serves to concentrate people's interest on private things, even when the famous personalities in question are political actors.

THE MASS MEDIA AND PUBLIC OPINION

The editorial function, along with the reportorial, is one of the major functions of the mass media. If the commentaries of the media could alter the views of large numbers of people, public opinion would change. But public opinion, though by definition a public phenomenon, does not exist in objectively clear form. Rather, except for infrequent demonstrations at the ballot box, public opinion becomes clear only a bit at a time, through the public's responses to other agencies' efforts to influence it. In this sense, the mass media are a medium for the clarification, if not leadership, of public opinion. Of course, the reporting of events also influences the shape of public opinion. Vis-à-vis the formation and presentation of public opinion, however, it is probably accurate to say that the decisive role is performed by the editorial function.

Regarding the influencing of public opinion, one of the most important agencies is the commentaries published in the press. These include editorials and opinion pieces, and also letters to the editor and individual commentaries and analyses by critics and experts. Since such editorial material (in the broadest sense) stresses particular viewpoints, it need not be nonpartisan. In general, during the years of LDP rule, the press tilted toward the activities of the opposition parties and the politics of the Left; in international politics, it follows a relatively dovish line.[7]

This tendency is sometimes criticized as journalistic bias. On the other hand, however, from the perspective of maintenance of some sort of balance in politics as a whole, the oppositionist tendencies of the press have played an important role in restraining the authority of government. Particularly in a country like Japan, where a single conservative party dominated government and the party system for decades, one may say that the leftist, oppositionist, pacifist coloration of the press is rather to be appreciated.

Unfortunately, the editorial function of the press has in recent years significantly atrophied. One reason for this is to be found in the tremendous growth of newspaper circulation. When the objective is to sell newspapers to millions of different readers, there is a temptation to provide content that is satisfying to all and offensive to none. Because of this, the press gives priority to "objective, truthful reporting" over editorial material that can easily slide into support for particular political positions.[8] Moreover, the conservative and apolitical trends among the general public also invite conservatism in the press. The fading of the oppositionist tone of the press represents a strengthening of the unbiased, nonpartisan, neutral image of the press. This situation raises the danger, however, that the press, through its reportorial function, may manage public opinion surreptitiously. Particularly in the case of Japan, as long as the press clubs serve as the major channel of communication between the press and the government, one must admit the possibility of newspapers, in practice, degenerating into public relations sheets for the government.

Formerly, the press, along with the "comprehensive magazines,"[9] constituted the acme of political journalism; together they played a leadership role in the formation of popular political opinion. Amid the conservatization of the electorate, however, this journalistic elite has continuously lost influence. The circulations of the comprehensive magazines have declined precipitously, as has the editorial function of the newspapers.[10] Among the reasons for this is certainly the swing of popular interest from the print to the broadcast media, but one should note that the *total* circulation of magazines has risen sharply. The current boom in comic books and slick show-business magazines is one factor behind this rise, but a flood of superficial, *People*-type weekly magazines is another striking characteristic of today's magazine journalism. The problem is that these weeklies, many of which are published by newspaper companies, serve no critical, analytical, or even informative political purpose at all—on the contrary, they contribute exclusively to the *de*politicization of the journalistic world. In the United States—which differs not at all from Japan in regard to the dominance of mass culture—magazines such as *Time* and *Newsweek*, whose main content is news and comment, still sell in massive numbers and compete successfully with their flashier rivals; one may see in this one of the differences between Japanese and American democracy. In any case, it is a difference that should lead Japanese political journalists to some self-reflection.

THE MASS MEDIA AND POWER

The mass media, as we have noted, performs significant—either more or less beneficial—functions in the political process. The question is: Does this mean that the media themselves constitute a center of political power? A propos of this one should note the results of a 1980 study that analyzed the class structure of influence in Japanese society.[11] In this opinion survey, the institution that respondents cited as being the *most* influential of all was the media: the press, television, radio, and so forth. The respondents in this study were themselves leaders from all sectors of society—including the civil service, political parties, business, labor, academia, cultural fields, and social movements—and, in response to the question of which groups in society were most influential, they responded almost unanimously: the mass media were number one. It is clear that these respondents, at least, consider the media as a separate center of power.

Such evaluations are, of course, not unique to Japan. The study just cited was repeated in the United States and Sweden; in those countries, too, the media were ranked number one. Thus, in many countries, the mass media are considered as a group that wields power sufficient to influence policy decisions at least indirectly. Because evaluations such as these are simply an aggregation of the subjective images of those surveyed, there are those who argue that they have no objective validity; on the other hand, since power itself depends on others' subjective perceptions of it, any group perceived by society's elites to be highly influential already possesses much of the raw material for exercising power.

Rather, the question is the concrete meaning of media power. The media is by definition a vehicle of mass communication. Of course, being a vehicle does not mean that the media consists simply of physical buildings and equipment—they include the people who make the equipment work. Accordingly, there are two meanings in the statement, "The media is a center of power." First, there is the sense in which politicians and commentators use the media as a vehicle, exercising and enhancing their own influence *through* the media. A typical example of this is the way Prime Minister Nakasone and President Reagan boosted their popularity through the skillful use of television. In such cases, the power of the media does not exist independently; rather, it exists insofar as it augments the power of the prime minister and the president.

Second, there is the intrinsic influence exercised by press and television reporters and commentators through their statements in the media. This factor—the independent political influence of newspaper articles and television shows—in some cases is critical. For example, not only is it probable that neither the Watergate nor the Recruit scandals would have come to light in the absence of the thoroughgoing investigative reporting of the press, it is also unlikely that the massive Japanese demonstrations in opposition to the renewal of the U.S.–Japan Mutual Security Treaty in 1960 would have come to such a sudden end had not the seven major newspaper publishers agreed among themselves to abate the tone of their coverage of the movement. In general, however, although the activities of the media can exert tremendous influence in such major public crises, and in the event of political corruption and scandal, by appealing to the morality of the people, in regard to the daily occurrence of political events, it is rare that newspaper articles and TV programs exert an influence superior to that of the parties and bureaucracy.

When one thinks about the future of the relationship between the media and power, the role of the media as an instrument of power seems more important than its intrinsic power. Of particular note is its function in the "image games" that unfold on TV. As a means for political powerholders seeking to improve their images, TV has many more attractions than does the press. In particular, images transmitted by the press are unavoidably indirect and abstract; those transmitted by TV are direct, vivid, and concrete. Moreover, on TV, leaders are able to present themselves with considerable freedom. In 1972, Prime Minister Satō provoked considerable public criticism when, on the occasion of his resignation, he held a press conference at which he attacked the print media and showered compliments on the TV networks. But the event, in retrospect, could be seen as an omen for the future relationship between the different media and those in power. In contemporary American elections, it is said that one's skill in using television determines whether one will be elected or not. In Japan, too, one suspects that such a day is not far off.

NOTES

1. Kyōgoku Jun-ichi, *The Political Dynamics of Japan*, University of Tokyo Press, 1987, p. 201

2. *Ibid.*, p. 197

3. Yamamoto Akira and Fujitake Akira, eds., *Zusetsu: Nihon no Masu Komyunikeishon* (Japanese Mass Communication Illustrated), 2nd ed., Nihon Hōsō Shuppan Kyōkai, 1987, p. 105.

4. *Ibid.*, p. 106.

5. Uchikawa Yoshimi and Arai Naoyuki, eds., *Nihon no Jaanarizumu* (Japanese Journalism), Yūhikaku, 1983, p. 140.

6. Maruyama Masao, "Seijiteki Mukanshin" (Political Apathy), in Heibonsha, ed., *Seijigaku Jiten* (Dictionary of Politics), Heibonsha, 1954, pp. 746–48.

7. Kyōgoku, *The Political Dynamics of Japan*, p. 200.

8. *Ibid.*, p. 201.

9. The comprehensive magazines, or *sōgō zasshi*, are a distinctively Japanese genre of monthly magazine that combines news; short stories and essays; historical, social, cultural, and political commentary; book, music, theater, and film reviews; and economic analysis, in issues running to 200 to 300 pages.

10. Kyōgoku, *The Political Dynamics of Japan*, p. 202.

11. Miyake Ichirō, Watanuki Jōji, Shima Kiyoshi, and Kabashima Ikuo, *Byōdō o Meguru Eriito to Taikō-eriito* (Elites, Counter-elites, and Equality), Sōbunsha, 1985, pp. 137–38.

PART 5

THE POLITICAL CULTURE

CHAPTER 19

DEMOCRACY AND LIBERALISM

ORIGINS OF DEMOCRACY IN JAPAN

One can trace the origins of democracy in modern Japan as far back as the Freedom and Popular Rights Movement of the Meiji era. The movement—which began in 1874 with a petition to the throne for the establishment of a popularly elected assembly and ran through the movement for the establishment of a national parliament to the establishment of the Liberal and Progressive parties in the 1880s— was clearly a democratic movement aimed at expanding political participation for the people. The objectives of the movement included demands for the establishment of popular sovereignty, as stated by Ueki Emori, one of the leaders of the movement, in his *Proposal for a Japanese Constitution* (*Nihon Kokken An*, 1881). Emori argued in favor of "state sovereignty," asserting that sovereignty inheres in the state because it is the collectivity of the people; and he argued further that if a government forgot its mission to exercise the authority entrusted to it *by* the people for the benefit *of* the people, or abused this authority, then the people had the right to resist such a government.[1] Within the context of the Freedom and Popular Rights Movement, Ueki's was a radical position. In fact, for the most part, the movement went no further than demanding the establishment of a parliament elected by male property owners within a monarchical framework. Nevertheless, the fact that over 200,000 people participated in the 1880 petition movement for the establishment of a parliament shows clearly that the movement enjoyed the support of a large segment of the Japanese population.

With the establishment of imperial absolutism under the Meiji Constitution, democratic movements of this type collapsed. There were democratic elements in the Meiji Constitution, but in practice only very limited elements of democracy were able to survive within the framework of the imperial state. For example, the constitutional guarantees of the rights of subjects—incomplete though they were—and the establishment of a popularly elected parliament were democratic elements of the constitution. As the standards for daily morality, emphasizing docility and obedience and symbolized by the Imperial Rescript on Education—proclaimed in the name of the emperor—made clear, however, the imperial state sought to control even people's innermost thoughts. Thus, the political rulers were at the same time moral rulers; the people were made not only politically powerless but morally powerless as well. Moral independence is a prerequisite for independent individual attitudes and behavior. Without any prospect whatsoever for the emergence of an independent moral order, one could hardly hope for the development of individualistic values independent of those officially prescribed. In other words, popular sovereignty was categorically rejected by the Meiji state.

TAISHŌ DEMOCRACY

The Meiji Constitution established the principle of absolute imperial sovereignty; in operation, however, constitutional ambiguities led to tension between parliament, the civil bureaucracy, the military, and the councillors around the throne, creating room for veto power and freedom of maneuver for each. Thus, the Constitution led to a governing process approaching that of a constitutional monarchy. For this reason, efforts to emphasize and broaden the democratic aspects of the Constitution were able to democratize politics to a certain extent under the Meiji Constitution. The era of "Taishō democracy" (1912–26) was also such a time in which efforts were made, in the spirit of this multi-centered constitutional structure, to enhance the democratic aspects of Japanese politics.

When pressure from the army led to the downfall in 1912 of the civilian cabinet of Premier Saionji Kinmochi and the formation of a new cabinet under General Katsura Tarō, a wave of popular resentment against the unconstitutional actions of the new government led to a powerful movement for protection of the constitution, and the Katsura cabinet fell after only three months. In the ensuing years, a number of party politicians attained the premiership; during the last years of the Taishō era, bureaucratically led cabinets made a short-lived comeback, but in 1924 a military-led cabinet was brought down by a second movement for protection of the Constitution, and the establishment of a cabinet under Premier Katō Kōmei, supported by three constitutionalist parties, ushered in a decade of rule by civilian cabinets led by party politicians. Under the Katō cabinet, the longstanding proposal for universal male suffrage was realized and the rights of the people to participate in politics were expanded dramatically.

Even the democratic movement of the Taishō era was, however, unable to effect changes in the Meiji Constitution itself; rather, it involved various democratic elements expanding their power *within* the framework of that constitution. Thus, from the very beginning the realization of popular sovereignty was unthinkable. In an essay entitled "The Essence of Constitutional Government and the Path to its Perfection," Yoshino Sakuzō, a representative theorist of Taishō democracy, coined the term *minponshugi*, or "people as the basis," as a translation of the word "democracy":

> *Minponshugi* sets aside and does not address the issue of exactly where sovereignty resides as a question of legal theory. Rather, as regards the exercise of sovereignty, it is an ideology that fervently exhorts the sovereign to establish as its highest priority the solicitous consideration of the well-being and dispositions of the general public.[2]

Thus, for the time being, Taishō democracy shelved the question of whether sovereignty should reside in the monarch or the people and attempted, instead, to establish a political process that would permit the people to participate and aim to realize the popular welfare.

In the 1930s, party government, confronted by Japan's economic crisis, collapsed. In its stead the military seized political power and, suppressing to the best of its ability the democratic elements of the Meiji Constitution, established a militaristic, totalitarian state. In the process there were attempts made to curb the recklessness of the military. In 1936, in the immediate aftermath of a failed military coup, MP Saitō Takao made a speech in parliament calling for a purge of the military; in 1937, MP Hamada Kunimatsu—again on the floor of parliament—criticized the military for meddling in politics and offered to commit suicide if the military could substantiate its accusations that the civilian politicians were disloyal Japanese. If they couldn't, he suggested, the army minister should kill *him*self. But most public figures stood on the sidelines, and some even attempted to advance the interests of their parties by actively ingratiating themselves with the military. In any case, the fact that, during the abject retreat of Taishō democracy in the face of the military, hardly any signs of a popular resistance movement appeared shows clearly the limits of Taishō democracy.

POSTWAR DEMOCRACY

The democratization program of the U.S. Occupation abolished the Meiji Constitution and decisively promoted the democratization of Japan. The fact that democracy was imposed on Japan from outside rather than taking the historically normal path of indigenous, autonomous development, however, imposed certain crucial conditions on democracy in Japan. In particular, under the impact of the intensifying Cold War in Asia, the democratizing thrust of the Occupation soon became diverted into a program of strengthening Japan, politically and economically, against the threat of communism. Thus, before the attitudes of the Japanese people had been adequately transformed, a reaction against democratization had begun. As a result, many traditional elements originating in the Meiji state survived the Occupation, and contributed to Japanese democracy a number of distinctive features not seen in Euro-American democracy.

First, Euro-American democracy assumes that the most basic constituent units of society are individuals and that human society is consciously constructed by and in accordance with the will of individuals. In Japan, society is thought of much more as a naturally occurring, organic creation than a composite of purposive individuals. The model social group in Japan is the family or the village; both are naturally occurring primary groups within which, ideally, individuals lead amicable lives of harmony. Other types of social organizations are modeled on these sorts of primary groups, and the state is no exception. The obligation of leaders in such groups is to interact with the members on the basis of warm, parental feelings; the obligation of followers is to maintain the harmony of the group by all living together intimately. In such a cultural context it is not at all strange for democracy to be defined as everyone participating in group activities in order to cultivate intimate relationships and thus maintain harmony.[3]

Second, Euro-American democracy is a strictly political concept. The function of politics is to resolve conflict; democracy, too, must serve this purpose. In Carl Becker's words, "Democratic government rests upon the principle that it is better to count heads than it is to break them."[4] In Japan, however, since the state was originally conceived of as a surrogate family (in the idea of the "family state"), the state was inevitably thought of as a social collectivity in which conflict and opposition simply would not occur. In the absence of conflict, there is no place for politics; in a word, the Japanese state was ideally an apolitical state.

The fact that, ever since the Meiji Restoration, Japanese politics presupposed the harmony of groups, meant that conflict and quarrels were illegitimate—something to be eliminated from the world of politics. The proper state of affairs was an absence of conflict and confrontation; if they should by chance occur, this was treated as an exceptional and deviant event. Consequently, the Japanese have never excelled at dealing with conflict and disputes as routine occurrences. What the Japanese *are* expert at is strategies designed to avoid conflict and confrontation, such as *nemawashi*. In accord with this distinctive feature of Japanese politics, democracy, too, is seen less as a means for resolving conflict and disagreement and more as a technique for avoiding it. The result is that in Japan a "democratic" decision is defined in principle not simply as majoritarian but as unanimous.

POLITICAL ETHICS AND DEMOCRATIC POLITICS

Contemporary Japanese democracy has for long rested ultimately on the distribution of benefits. The vote-mobilization strategy of LDP candidates has been to distribute concrete benefits to the voters through the mechanism of the *kōenkai*; the policies of the LDP as the party of government were also intended to attract the support of the electorate by making them beneficiaries of the distribution of subsidies and so forth. To the extent that this sort of distribution of benefits is emphasized, the people come to evaluate politicians only in terms of their ability to "produce pork," and pay little attention to things like politicians' responsibilities and ethics. And the politicians, for their part, pay attention to little except caring for the "home folks" and spend little time thinking about issues like accountability and ethics. The fact that although, on the one hand, democratic politics is becoming firmly established in Japan and, on the other, political scandals like Lockheed and Recruit never seem to stop is probably not unrelated to these two types of unconcern.

The fact that the issue of political ethics has rarely been taken too seriously is also partly the result of the absence, in Japanese democracy, of a republican tradition. The idea of democracy in the West signified the autonomous and conscious creation, by the people, of a political order. In order to invest the idea with real meaning, however, it is necessary for every citizen to possess the capability of becoming a political actor. In other words, it is necessary for them to possess the capability to create order in their own lives autonomously and independently. This sort of capability is deeply related to individual ethics; together they comprise what has been described by political philosophers since ancient Rome as the "virtue" of the citizen.

Republicanism, in contrast to monarchism—which invites despotism and corruption—emphasizes that the way to realize wholesome politics is through the autonomy of a citizenry possessed of virtue. In its emphasis of citizen virtue, republicanism differs from democracy, which stresses undiscriminating equality; it contributes a valuable supplementary element to democratic impulses, which tend to ignore ethics. The intense reaction of American democracy to cases of political corruption such as Watergate can be looked upon as the result of America's retention of a republican tradition.

Postwar Japanese democracy arose under the influence of American democracy; it received, however, almost no influence from America's republican tradition. This was because the emperor system was retained, albeit in symbolic form, thus cutting off the possibility of the establishment of republicanism. In Japanese democracy, opportunities for individual citizens to become autonomous bearers of political order have always been few and far between. Most people are satisfied with the political benefits they receive; in return they support the long-term rule of the conservative party. In this way, single-party dominance by the conservatives is maintained, and, as a result, the soil is prepared in which political corruption grows. Moreover, insofar as concern for one's own benefits becomes the primary motivation for political behavior, interest in public issues weakens and people cease to care about exerting effort to strengthen political ethics. Consequently, political corruption has ceased to be simply an infrequent, incidental occurrence and has become built into the structure of Japanese politics under the LDP.

In order for political corruption to be eradicated, it is necessary that efforts be made to raise politics from a standard of individual benefit to one of public interest, to make issues of social justice and ethics the focus of political debate. This is not a problem that can be resolved through the simple aspirations of politicians; rather, it relates fundamentally to the political posture of the people. In other words, it is a problem related to whether or not the people possess the virtue appropriate to creators and guardians of an autonomous order. Such civic virtue is different from the sort of short-term popular outrage over scandal and reform which drove the LDP from power in 1993. In order to nurture such virtue over the long run, there is no real alternative to the individual acquisition of autonomy through education. Contemporary Japanese education is, however, in the stultifying grip of Tokyo bureaucrats more interested in controlled than civic education, and there appears little immediate prospect of major change in this situation.

ORIGINS OF LIBERALISM IN JAPAN

We have sought to establish the origins of Japanese democracy in the Freedom and Popular Rights Movement. Can we do the same with liberalism? Indeed, the movement demanded various civil rights along with the establishment of parliamentary government and the right of political participation. The focus of the movement was, however, unquestionably less on protecting the personal freedom of the individual from unreasonable interference and infringement by authority than it was on wresting political power from the hands of a minority and securing it in the hands of the people through the realization of participatory rights. The real zeal of the movement was for the establishment of democratic political processes that facilitated the freedom to *attain* power rather than for liberalism, which emphasizes each citizen's freedom *from* power. As it went in a popular song of the day, "Even if the citizen isn't free, if politics is, that's fine with me."

Fukuzawa Yukichi criticized this tendency of the movement, saying, "A society in which private rights are not yet guaranteed, which is so ambivalent that both violators thereof and those whose rights are violated are indifferent, and which rather concentrates all its efforts on [the competition for] political power cannot avoid the accusation that it has its priorities backward."[5] Fukuzawa's critique presupposes the logic of modern liberalism, that is, it is precisely in order that individual freedom may be protected from the encroachments of authority that decisive political power must reside ultimately in the hands of the people, not the other way around.

Thus, although the Freedom and Popular Rights Movement was clearly the origin of the democratic movement in Japan, there is room for doubt that it is also the origin of Japanese liberalism. Indeed, liberalism was at the time doubly handicapped. If one interprets liberalism as the demand for the expansion of individual civil rights through the independent efforts of individuals, there is precious little hope for liberalism in a society in which collectivities such as the state, the community, and the family take overwhelming precedence over the individual. Moreover, liberalism is not simply a demand for private self-indulgence; rather, only free individuals can, through rational action, create an autonomous civil society. Thus, liberalism demands that the freedom of the individual be held in high esteem. Unfortunately, the words "freedom" and "liberty" were

originally rendered in Japanese by the word *jiyū*, which had overtones of selfishness and licence.[6] *Jiyū* is still widely used for these
words; consequently, some people still understand them in light of
the traditional meaning of *jiyū* and, by extension, still misinterpret
the term *jiyūshugi*, or liberalism.

THE IMPERIAL STATE AND LIBERALISM

With the promulgation of the Meiji Constitution, the publication of
the Imperial Rescript on Education, and the establishment of the imperial state, the prospects for liberalism became more and more un-
favorable. The constitution provided for the rights of subjects, who
enjoyed "liberty in regard to residence and change of abode (Article
22)"; "freedom of religious belief (Article 28)"; and "liberty in regard
to speech, writing, publication, public meetings, and associations
(Article 29)." All of these rights were, however, conditional, to be exercised "within the limits of the law." Rights regarding people's religious beliefs were hedged about even more strongly: they were free
only "within limits not prejudicial to peace and order, and not antag-
onistic to their duties as subjects." Unsurprisingly, once the Meiji
Constitution was established, debates about freedom and liberty
faded from the scene.

Even during the period of Taishō democracy, there were no liberal
developments worthy of notice. Statism simply retreated a little; even
if one can recognize some *de facto* expansion in individual freedoms,
there was still no possibility of civil liberties being accepted in principle. Rather, with the end of the Taishō era and the beginning of the
Shōwa era (1926–89), a trend toward criticism of the modern, constitutionalist aspects of the Meiji Constitution as *jiyūshugi* emerged.
Some critics went further, asserting that, being egotistical, liberalism
served only to preserve the status quo and lacked the potential for
bringing about emergence from Japan's political, economic, and
diplomatic crises; what was needed to break out of the status quo
was the firm hand of totalitarian dictatorship.[7]

With defeat in 1945, the Japanese people were presented with a
spendid chance to seize freedom with their own hands. The Japanese
people, however—unable to establish a liberal tradition since the
Meiji era—were once again unable to establish civil liberties through
their own efforts. Even the most basic demands for liberalism—
abolition of the repressive Peace Preservation Law and the Special
Higher Police (the "Thought Police") and legalization of criticism of
the emperor system—were realized for the first time in a SCAP decree of October 1945, entitled "Removal of Restrictions on Political,
Civil, and Religious Liberties."[8] There was almost no sign of any

spontaneous effort to advance such reforms in advance of this decree. For example, one day before the announcement of the decree, Home Minister Yamazaki Iwao, in an interview with a Reuters correspondent, said, "I consider all those who call for change in our form of government, especially abolition of the emperor system, to be communists, and they will be arrested under the terms of the Peace Preservation Law."[9]

The halfheartedness of postwar liberalism can be seen even among those reputed to be liberals. The *Asahi Shimbun*, historically thought of as a liberal newspaper, stated in its "Vox Populi, Vox Dei" column the day after the issuance of the SCAP decree, "We can understand the suppression of extremist thought, but we cannot accept the proscription of viewpoints moderately at odds with those of the powers that be. Moreover, we cannot comprehend an arrangement under which petty bureaucrats are authorized to investigate intellectuals of high position in regard to important questions of state."[10]

In response to this, Fujita Shōzō, a historian of political thought, inquired, "Why is someone who can accept governmental control of thought itself—be it 'extremist' or 'respectable'—a liberal?" adding, "The Special Higher Police were evil not because they sent 'petty bureaucrats' to investigate 'intellectuals of high position' but because they investigated 'intellect' (and religious faith) in the first place." As he put it, prewar Japanese liberalism was "*nothing more than the anxiety* to avoid the *so-called* extremist path and choose the *so-called* temperate path."[11] In retrospect, his critique was right on the mark.

LIBERALISM AND THE MISSING INDIVIDUAL

One of the characteristics of Japanese liberalism is the fact that it does not presuppose the existence of heterogeneous individuals. If freedom is meaningful only in the context of reciprocal relationships between individuals, then efforts are necessary to avoid collisions between different individuals' freedoms or, where such collisions occur, to resolve the conflicts to which they give rise. On such occasions, exactly where freedom lies and whose freedom takes precedence is not self-evident. At such times, the balancing of freedoms is the key issue; moreover, this issue naturally implies the question of how to create rules that enable the avoidance of the collisions between one freedom and another freedom—that is, how are social order and the freedom of the individual to be made compatible? In addition, when the effort is made to resolve collisions of freedom with freedom, it becomes necessary to clarify the internal priorities of freedom. For example, in a collision between an enterprise's freedom to pursue profit and the public's right to freedom from pollution, it becomes necessary to address the questions of which deserves to take precedence, why, and by how much?

The predominant attitude in contemporary Japan, however, views freedom as a self-evident reality and does not seriously grapple with such questions. Of course, even in Japan the collisions of different individuals' and groups' respective freedoms is an everyday occurrence. When this happens, however, the typical response is to ignore the collision per se and either tacitly let the freedom of the stronger party overwhelm that of the weaker, or the reverse: to give unconditional support to the freedom of the weaker party. What is lacking here is any attempt to resolve the problem by establishing rules for compromise or conflict resolution.

By "establishment of rules" we mean the creation of systems essential for the maintenance of social order through the subjective actions of the constituent members of society. This process was completely lacking in prewar Japan. Social order on the local level was nothing more than the natural extension of the family and the village; moreover, on the supralocal level—the state—it meant simply the structures of bureaucratic administration. The notion of creating social order through the autonomous actions of individuals was utterly nonexistent. Even in regard to today's younger generation, so unblushingly self-absorbed in their affluence, one may doubt whether there is any inclination toward a social order based on individual autonomy. In that the subjective creation of objective norms by individuals who are either repressed by collectivities *or* hedonistically self-absorbed is impossible, there is an eerie continuity between the prewar and postwar eras.

"Freedom," in contemporary Japan, is less a value to be realized through the unremitting efforts of human beings than it is simply a condition in which people are living tranquilly by coincidence. Of course, resistance to the encroachments of authority can spring also from this sort of self-centered "freedom for its own sake," but sustained resistance is impossible. One of the reasons that all of the myriad, recurring postwar movements of resistance to authority flourished briefly and then ended in collapse is the absence of the conviction that freedom is a value to be actively striven for.

ECONOMIC LIBERALISM

Along with political liberalism—the pursuit and consolidation of individual liberty vis-à-vis the government—there is economic liberalism, the pursuit of governmental noninterference in the economic activities of private individuals. In advanced industrial societies where capitalism developed smoothly out of the demands of the bourgeoisie, it was common for a laissez-faire economic philosophy to be adopted. In such societies, small and cheap government was preferred, and if it maintained the legal order internally and national security externally, it was seen as adequately performing its proper functions. In Japan, however, capitalist enterprise developed under the solicitous care, protection, and stimulation of a government bent on rapid modernization; from the very onset of development, the bourgeoisie was heavily dependent on the government. Therefore, until the end of World War II, it was impossible for laissez-faire to become the dominant political current.

After the war, however, as the immediate postwar chaos came under some degree of control and the business community began to regain its self-confidence, economic liberalism came for the first time to be purposefully pursued. It was the second Yoshida cabinet, inaugurated in October 1948, that began the strong promotion of liberal economic policies.[12] The establishment of this regime is often thought of as the beginning of the so-called reverse course of "reactionary" policy, but in fact what characterized Yoshida's government was not an attempt to restore the prewar system but rather a groping toward a laissez-faire policy line. This can clearly be seen from its firm adherence to balanced budgets from 1949 through 1952, and from the steady decline in government expenditures as a proportion of the GNP through the cutting of taxes and reduction of the scale of government finance. Under this laissez-faire policy line, on the one hand, full employment policies were rejected vis-à-vis labor; on the other, protectionist policies benefiting industry were also suppressed, and many aspects of economic coordination were left to the workings of the competitive free market.

This sort of laissez-faire policy did not always enjoy strong support even within the conservative camp. Indeed, the conservative Kishi and Ikeda cabinets (1957–64) pursued egalitarian policies aimed at full employment and the expansion of social welfare. These egalitarian policies led, however, to the growth of government; as budget deficits and the national debt ballooned, arguments for small government became stronger—especially in the business community, but also among a growing proportion of the population that had become dissatisfied with their tax burden. The conservative cabinets of prime ministers Suzuki and Nakasone (1980–87) responded to this sort of small government argument with plans for administrative reform, privatization of public corporations, and the stimulation of private-sector enterprise through the abolition of government regulations and so forth. Clearly, these sorts of policies constituted a return to economic liberalism and had much in common with a laissez-faire policy line. The ultimate goals of the welfare state and the influence of the administrative bureaucracy were not lost, but one can still see that supporters of laissez-faire had come to constitute a force that could not be ignored.

This laissez-faire type of economic liberalism expanded its influence greatly during the 1980s. Under the slogan of small government, policies of deregulation and privatization were pursued by the U.S.'s Reagan administration and the U.K.'s Thatcher government; the core of this so-called neoconservatism was in fact a laissez-faire liberalism stressing freedom of choice. Even if one cannot discern laissez-faire immediately behind the liberalizing reforms that swept Eastern Europe like wildfire in 1989, one cannot deny that a thirst for political and economic freedom of choice was at the heart of the whirlwind. In any case, it is a fact that all over the globe liberalism, and laissez-faire, in particular, have regained the influence previously lost in the face of challenges from socialism and egalitarianism; in many advanced industrial societies they are regaining a position of ideological predominance. The fact that the LDP is trying to regain lost ground by stressing liberal ideology after its heavy defeat in the 1989 House of Councillors election is evidence of the breadth of support for a laissez-faire type of liberalism that also exists in Japan today.

Notes

1. Ienaga Saburō, ed., *Minshushugi* (Democracy), *Gendai Nihon Shisō Taikei* (An Outline of Modern Japanese Thought), vol. 3, Chikuma Shobō, 1965, p. 14.
2. Oka Yoshitake, ed., *Yoshino Sakuzō Hyōron Shū* (Collected Reviews by Yoshino Sakuzō), Iwanami, 1975, p. 45.
3. Jun-ichi Kyōgoku, *The Political Dynamics of Japan*, University of Tokyo Press, 1987, pp. 125–26.
4. Carl Becker, *Modern Democracy*, New Haven, Conn., Yale University Press, 1941, p. 87.
5. Fukuzawa Yukichi, "Shiken-ron" (Theory of Individual Rights), quoted in Nihon Seiji Gakkai, ed., *Kindai Nihon no Kokka-zō* (Images of the Modern Japanese State), Iwanami, 1983, p. 5.
6. Yagyū Akira, *Hon'yakugo Seiritsu Jijō* (A History of Translation Terminology), Iwanami, 1982, pp. 175–91.
7. Ishida Takeshi, *Nihon Kindai Shisō Shi ni okeru Hō to Seiji* (Law and Politics in Modern Japanese Political Thought), Iwanami, 1976, pp. 241–55.
8. SCAPIN 93, October 4, 1945.
9. Fujita Shōzō, *Tenkō no Shisōshiteki Kenkyū*, (A Study of the Intellectual History of Conversion), Iwanami, 1975, p. 252.
10. *Ibid.*, p. 253.
11. *Ibid.*, pp. 253–56.
12. Ōtake Hideo, "Sengo Hoshu Taisei no Tairitsu-jiku" (Conflict in the Postwar Conservative System), *Chūō Kōron* (April 1983): 143–45.

CHAPTER 20

EQUALIZATION AND EGALITARIANISM

EGALITARIAN SOCIETY

One political problem facing all of today's advanced industrial societies is that of equalization and egalitarianism; Japan is no exception. Equalization, or leveling, is a concept indicating the real, concrete extent of equality in a society. Equality is a universal *value*; equalization refers to the actual *attainment* of this value. In societies where equalization is advanced, differences in the distribution of social values, such as income, education, and prestige, shrink, but it is impossible that they be completely equalized. Even apart from the natural differences in people's qualities and abilities, the range of differences in the social values obtained by different individuals is produced by a wide variety of accidental factors. Consequently, equalization is always a matter of degree and in all societies, no matter how equalized, there is always room for further improvement.

In contrast to equalization, an empirical concept, egalitarianism is a normative concept that refers to the attitudes of people who wish to see a more equal condition or for whom the pursuit of equalization of some type is a primary consideration. Egalitarianism and equalization thus belong to different dimensions—belief and reality—but, at the same time, there is an intimate relationship between them. In the first place, in strongly egalitarian societies, equalization tends to be pushed forward. At the same time, the progress of equalization to a certain point is also a precondition for the firm rooting of egalitarianism. In societies where extreme inequality exists, it is very difficult for egalitarianism to take root. But where equalization has made significant progress and the most glaring forms of inequality have begun to be eliminated, it is common for powerful demands for further equalization to appear.

Once equalization has progressed even farther, however, it is not at all clear that egalitarianism will necessarily become even stronger.

In regard to such factors of great importance to egalitarians as the distribution of wealth and the extent of social mobility, for example, it is difficult to determine in principle precisely what constitutes full or acceptable equality. Indeed, in all likelihood it is impossible for anyone to make that determination without the metaphysical perceptions of a Platonic philosopher-king. This impossibility introduces an element of permanent disagreement and instability into egalitarian societies. Moreover, this egalitarianism not only produces a force pursuing ever greater equalization but also, in reaction, gives rise to demands for greater stability at the expense, if necessary, of equality.

In this way, equalization and egalitarianism are different, but mutually and intimately related, concepts. Egalitarian societies are societies in which equalization is far advanced *and* egalitarianism is dominant. Such societies are found today in all of the advanced industrial countries; accordingly, one of the most important issues in each is how to adapt politics to the demands and implications of egalitarian society. This is because egalitarianism and equalization are at the same time dearly held ideals *and* a source of conflict and tension in democratic society.

EQUALIZATION IN JAPAN

The beginnings of equalization in Japan are to be found in the Meiji Restoration. In general, the Meiji monarchy abolished the entire, elaborate Tokugawa hierarchy of intermediate statuses and the special privileges pertaining to status, and elevated into preeminence the absolute power of the emperor. All people became equally the subjects of the emperor, and his authority alone was raised to a higher plane. In this way, under the absolute monarchy, the medieval class system was destroyed and, with the exception of the monarch, everyone was placed in the equal status position of "subject." The democratic revolutions of Europe and America were generically similar: they simply pushed equalization farther, replacing imperial sovereignty with popular sovereignty and equality as subjects with equality as citizens.

The formation of the Meiji state was premised more modestly on quite the same logic. On the one hand, an absolute monarchy was established and the divinity of the emperor asserted; on the other, the merger and equalization of the four Tokugawa strata of people was stressed. In particular, under the emperor—the patriarch of the family state—all people were considered equally to be "children of the emperor." On one level, this is closely analogous to the equality among subjects of the absolute monarchies of Europe. *Within* the

Meiji state, however, the hierarchical ordering of positions was heavily emphasized; in particular, within the administrative bureaucracy and the military the obedience and loyalty of subordinates to superiors was stressed. Moreover, because the militarization of Japan in the 1930s led to the permeation of all spheres of society by military values, equalization overall was severely limited.

After World War II, however, equalization was promoted in many spheres of society; moreover, the sorts of egalitarian movements that had been rigorously suppressed in prewar Japan appeared throughout society. The most striking forms of equalization involved income and education. There had been extraordinary economic inequality in the prewar society, but the democratization policies of the postwar period resulted in large-scale changes in the social structures that had produced these inequalities. Moreover, the economic growth that began in the 1960s dramatically decreased income disparities. As a result, in terms of the working class's share of the nation's income, Japan became a country of great equality even by international standards; moreover, with their increasing nonfarm incomes and agricultural subsidies, the total income of farm households came to surpass that of working-class households.

Levels of education also increased dramatically, with the proportion of junior high school graduates going on to high school increasing from 42.5 percent in 1950 to 95.0 percent in 1992. In addition, the proportion of high school graduates going on to college increased from 9.8 percent in 1956 to 38.8 percent in 1992. Along with the overall trend toward higher levels of education, income differences among groups with different educational achievements have also been gradually decreasing; it seems clear that increasing levels of education have the effect of advancing the equalization of society in general.

Egalitarian movements—of which the labor movement, the early postwar farmers' movement, the *buraku* liberation movement (discussed later in this chapter), and the women's liberation movement are but a few concrete examples—have also become active. Moreover, during the years of LDP rule all of the opposition political parties became more egalitarian, and it was not uncommon for them to criticize the government from an egalitarian position. And, because even among the supporters of the LDP there were strong voices calling for the correction of inequities, it became common for government policies also to manifest egalitarian intentions. Given all this, it is less surprising that, even under conservative rule, social welfare policy expanded significantly. It can be argued, however, that despite this equalization, inequality of wealth is as great as ever;

nevertheless, one should not ignore the fact that the expansion of the social insurance system has, for the poor, the effect of providing them with the equivalent of a certain amount of assets.

Thus arose the phenomenon seen in contemporary Japan where the great majority of people see themselves as middle class. The proportion of people categorizing themselves as such rose from 73 percent in 1959 to 91 percent in 1979;[1] although this proportion declined somewhat subsequently, it has again risen to above 90 percent even in the 1990s. Granted, there are those who argue that this middle-class consciousness is nothing but an illusion, but regardless of whether or not it is an illusion, one cannot deny that this consciousness has come to exert an influence on the behavior of most citizens.

Since the late 1980s, differences in property ownership have grown as a result of the skyrocketing of land prices, and a process of stratification contrary to equalization has spread. Indeed, it is a fact that since the mid-1980s equalization has stagnated. Equalization is, however, a very long-term process, and one cannot necessarily equate a short-term stagnation with the termination of the process. Even more important, equalization has meant not only economic leveling; it has brought in its train homogenization and uniformity in culture and values, and the recent phenomenon, sometimes labeled stratification, has certainly not included class-based fragmentation in the realm of culture and values. And, whatever the case, there has been no change in the importance of egalitarianism as a motivating force in contemporary politics.

THE POLITICS OF EGALITARIAN SOCIETY

One may count among the following the major characteristics of politics in an egalitarian society. First, equalization inevitably brings a diminution of authority. The basis of power is, ultimately, force. Authority, by contrast, rests on the unconditional approval of the ruled, their acceptance of the legitimacy of the rulers. It presupposes an *unequal* relationship between those who possess authority and those who accept and obey it. Equality contradicts and destabilizes this order, thus leveling the social basis of authority. Because government depends on both authority *and* power in maintaining its rule, the decay of authority causes an extraordinary decline in the government's capacity to govern.

Second, this decay of authority is visible not simply among people or government officials—it spreads among all types of institutions and to moral standards. Such systems and standards, to function effectively, require authority. After eroding the authority of individuals and public offices, however, equalization also diminishes the authority of the social structures and values that stand behind them and undergird the contemporary social system as a whole. The result of this is increasing "permissiveness," which is really nothing more than the dissolution of systems and standards. Some of the concrete manifestations of this trend include the increase in crime, the breakup of the family, and the chaos surrounding education in many contemporary societies.

Third, egalitarian society always entails major difficulties in the generation of popular acceptance of the differentiation between leaders and people. Consequently, it becomes increasingly hard for leaders to exercise effective leadership. Not only are leaders who attempt to exercise strong leadership in many cases looked upon with suspicion by the people, but also opposition forces can easily take advantage of this popular suspicion to criticize such leaders. As a result, leaders in an egalitarian society, in performing their roles, must unceasingly emphasize their oneness and community with the people. And in constantly demonstrating their oneness with the people, not only do the leaders find it difficult to exercise strong leadership, but it is also difficult for them to rise above popular prejudices and traditions.

Fourth, there is a tendency in egalitarian society for a passion for further equalization to take root among many. In such instances, it is common for egalitarian elements, borrowing the government's own ideals, to bring pressure to bear on government to realize a more— even an impossibly more—equal society. Moreover, it is typical for equalization to entail an extraordinary increase in the level of public education, which in turn leads to broadened political participation and demand-making. Thus, in an egalitarian society, the pressures and demands upon government increase without end. The fiscal and personnel resources at the government's disposal are, however, finite—no government can fulfill all the demands placed upon it. Consequently, if the demands placed upon government go beyond a certain level, it is impossible to avoid a sudden and precipitate drop in the people's evaluations of government performance and thus in their own feelings of efficacy.

Thus, although the demands and pressures on government follow an unswerving upward path, the authority of government and institutions, and that implicit in standards, decreases and the independence of leadership weakens; inescapably, the governability of society declines. A particularly striking example of such a decline was the

United States in the 1960s and 1970s. In the case of Japan, an overall decline in governability has not yet occurred. But the symptoms of such a decline have already appeared.

Originally, as has already been discussed, the primary form taken by equalization in postwar Japan involved the redistribution of profit for the purpose of remedying disparities in income. Equalization is, in this regard, an issue of major concern in Japanese politics. But one means of income redistribution is government subsidies, and the proportion of government expenditures accounted for by subsidies is, by international standards, extremely high. With reduction of government size as the primary purpose of administrative reform, one might have expected that it would from the very outset have aimed to control subsidies, but in fact such was hardly the case because subsidies were a major instrument for the maintenance of the power of the LDP, and a large segment of the public are themselves their beneficiaries. Unsurprisingly, it was impossible for the government, or for the political elite, to set forth on a course of broad-gauged regulation of subsidies. Moreover, amid the functions of contemporary politicians, the allocation of benefits (including these sorts of subsidies) occupies the most important position. Even if a politician does nothing more than provide an adequate level of such benefits to the voters, he can usually induce them to tolerate even his most egregious violations of political ethics. Given all of the above, it is not necessarily off the mark to suggest a decline in governability in Japanese politics.

DISCRIMINATION IN AN EGALITARIAN SOCIETY

In the sense that an egalitarian society promotes the realization of the universalistic principle of equality, it has many admirable aspects. At the same time, however, it has its pathological aspects. One of these is discrimination. Needless to say, regardless of equalization, inequality does not cease to exist. The self-evident reality of human existence is, rather, *in*equality. Today's human beings are completely and mutually unequal in respect to a wide variety of capabilities. One might even say that it is precisely *because* of the reality of inequality that it is necessary to demand equality as an ideal.

Egalitarianism seeks, insofar as possible, to eradicate inequality, but, unless one is a radical egalitarian, it is common to accept a certain degree of inequality in practice. In most cases, as long as equality is guaranteed as a legal right, it is considered inevitable that social and economic inequality will exist to a certain degree. When such inequalities are not limited to particular spheres, however, but have a cumulative impact on the lives of members of certain groups in a variety of the domains of their lives, this is incompatible with the principle of equality. This is discrimination.

Discrimination thus involves the differential treatment of a certain group on the basis of their characteristics and behavior in a way that denies to that group its desired equality of respect and treatment. Typical examples of groups subject to discrimination are, in the United States, blacks and native Americans, and, in Japan, the *burakumin*, Koreans, and Ainu. In Japan, as in the other advanced industrial countries, equalization has made impressive strides; on the other hand, one can still see clear examples of discrimination.

How is it that equality and discrimination can coexist in a society? In the first place, putting a discriminated-against group in an economically and socially disadvantaged position contributes to the economic and social benefit of other groups. For example, if the living standards and educational level of a group are low, when members of that group are employed it is possible to keep their wages low. Along with this economic reason there is, however, undeniably, a psychological reason at work. Although egalitarianism can serve as the impetus for one's feeling it intolerable to be inferior to others, it can also easily slide over into an impulse to want to be superior to others in some way. Therefore, paradoxically, the stronger egalitarianism is, the stronger also is the impulse toward discrimination. If this is to be overcome, it is necessary that egalitarianism be supported by a truly universalistic sense of human rights.

ELIMINATION OF DISCRIMINATION

As we have already noted, despite the extraordinary advance of equality, discrimination still does not cease to exist. In the case of Japan, the three most striking examples of groups subject to discrimination are the *burakumin*, Koreans, and women.

Despite almost 70 years of effort by the *buraku* liberation movement, the residents of the *buraku* are still unable to escape discrimination. The word *buraku* means "village" (*burakumin* means "people of the *buraku*"), and refers to the areas of residence of the descendants of the Tokugawa-era outcast class, whose status derived from their involvement in occupations such as slaughtering, tanning, and butchering, which were considered unclean by Buddhism. In 1871, the Meiji government issued the Outcast Liberation Ordinance, which decreed that the residents of the *buraku* were henceforth to be equal to all other citizens in status and occupation. This act, however, contained no provision whatsoever for liberating them from the reality of discrimination and poverty; consequently, social discrimination continued without interruption. In 1922, the *burakumin* organized their own, independent liberation movement, the Suiheisha, or Levelers' Society; after the war it reorganized as the Buraku Liberation League (Buraku Kaihō Dōmei) and launched a variety of campaigns for the total elimination of discrimination. Following upon the activities of this movement, an Advisory Council on Integration Policy was formed in 1960 and, in accord with its recommendations, a Law on Special Measures for Integration Policy Operations was passed in 1969. This special measures law was to remain in effect for 10 years, but it was extended until March 1982 and, in accord with the terms of the subsequent Law on Special Measures for Regional Improvement, the continuation of ongoing projects of central and local governments in the *buraku* areas (legally referred to as *dōwa chiku*, or integrated districts) was recognized until 1987. Moreover, in April 1987, parliament passed the Regional Improvement Finance Law, considered the "final integration policy act," which provided for the continuation until 1992 of financial assistance to the integrated districts for the purpose of improving their environments and employment and educational situations.

As the result of over 20 years of integration policy, aspects of the physical environment of the *buraku* such as substandard housing and roads have been considerably improved, and there is a trend toward decreasing the disparities visible in working conditions and education. In the area of employment, however, most *burakumin* still work in public offices and medium and small enterprises, while the number employed in major corporations is still extremely small. In the area of education, although the disparity in rates of children going on to high school has narrowed greatly, problems such as the high school dropout rate are as serious as ever. Intermarriage with persons from outside the *buraku* has increased rapidly, but matrimonial discrimination still survives in a variety of forms. Given this situation, there are among the *burakumin* organizations strong voices calling for the passage of a Basic Law on Buraku Liberation, a general legal affirmation of the equality of all of the populace similar to the Fourteenth Amendment or the proposed Equal Rights Amendment to the U.S. Constitution. But, in any case, it is difficult to eradicate discrimination against the *burakumin* simply through improvement of the physical environment. What is necessary is a fundamental transformation of the political culture, which is so liable to exclusion of minorities and those with unconventional beliefs.

The largest group of foreign residents in Japan is the Korean minority, which numbers some 660,000. The great majority of them are individuals who moved or were forcibly brought to Japan between 1911 and 1945 when Japan ruled Korea and who stayed after the liberation of Korea, and their descendants. The Korean minority does not enjoy a favorable standard of living; they are engaged primarily in such businesses as pachinko parlors, Korean barbecue restaurants, money-lending, scrap iron, and day labor, and very few have found employment in major corporations or the specialized professions. The great majority of them have permanent resident status, but no matter how long they live in Japan and no matter how many taxes they pay, they do not enjoy rights of political participation. With a few exceptions, they cannot become public servants. This is because these rights are reserved only for Japanese citizens. Moreover, although a great number of Koreans were sacrificed to Japan's war effort as either soldiers or laborers, the benefits of the Pension Act, the Law for the Assistance of Families of Those Wounded or Killed in War, the Law for Special Assistance to Wounded Veterans, and similar laws are only available to Japanese citizens.

In addition to this sort of discrimination, a major issue of discrimination against foreigners concerns the requirement that they be fingerprinted as part of the alien registration process. According to the Alien Registration Act enacted immediately upon Japan's regaining of independence in 1952, all aliens over the age of 16 residing in Japan are required to be fingerprinted; the objective was the maintenance of civil order. In opposition to this discriminatory system, a number of resident Koreans and other foreign supporters began during the 1980s to refuse to be fingerprinted; in 1985 the number of such persons grew larger, and the problem became a major social issue. Accordingly, in 1987 and 1992 the law was revised so that the previously required quinquennial fingerprinting became unnecessary for most foreigners. The fingerprinting process, as a means of controlling aliens, remains in place, however, and the issue is not yet resolved.

Gender discrimination is also a serious problem. In contemporary Japan, great disparities still exist between men and women in a variety of areas, such as education, employment, professional advancement, income, and wealth. The areas in which gender-based disparities are most striking are the workplace and politics; employment inequality between the sexes has attracted special attention. In every aspect of employment—recruitment, hiring, placement, promotion, training, benefits, and retirement—obvious disparities between men and women exist. In contemporary Japan, with the number of working women growing rapidly and the competence of the female labor force far advanced, it is unsurprising that voices calling for the full achievement of an egalitarian working environment have become stronger. It was in this climate that, in April 1986, the Equal Employment Opportunity Act was passed. Although this law banned discrimination in the areas of education and training, benefits and welfare, and retirement and termination, it left a number of gaps—going only so far, for example, as to say that "special efforts" should be made to achieve equal opportunity in recruitment, hiring, placement, and promotion. Nevertheless, this law is at least a starting point for the realization of gender equality in the workplace.

Inequality in politics is also striking: as of 1993 there were only 14 women in the House of Representatives (2.7 percent of its membership) and 37 in the House of Councillors (14.7 percent). Not only are less than 2 percent of all local assembly members women, but only 9.6 percent of the members of national government advisory councils and 7.2 percent of those of local governments are women. And women make up only 1.4 percent of all the members of the boards of education, election boards, and other prefectural and municipal citizens' committees set up in accord with the Local Autonomy Act. Women in executive office have also been extremely rare: only 11 have been cabinet ministers since the war, and at present 2 mayors are the only female municipal executives in the country. One can only say that, in an age in which female prime ministers and presidents have been active in such countries as Britain, Norway, and the Philippines, the overwhelming domination of politics by men bespeaks Japan's backwardness. Omens of change are not, however, entirely absent. In the July 1989 Tokyo prefectural assembly election, women won 18 (or 14 percent) of the 128 seats, and, in the House of Councillors election held three weeks later, women won 22 (17.4 percent) of the 126 seats contested. In combination with the fact that in 1989, for the first time, the proportion of female high school graduates going on to college surpassed that of males —albeit by a small margin—it may be that 1989 will become a year to remember in the history of the eradication of gender inequality in Japan.

EDUCATION IN AN EGALITARIAN SOCIETY

Education-related issues also can be considered comprehensively only in relation to egalitarian society. In general, education is a powerful instrument for advancing equalization. In particular, if one considers equality of opportunity to be the core of equality, then the fact that education is the key to opportunity means that education is almost the only way to realize equality. It is common knowledge that, by promoting equalization through education, postwar Japan has achieved major results.

Nevertheless, it is also a fact that certain detrimental influences of egalitarian education have attracted attention. One of these is that egalitarian pressures have driven the competition for school advancement to destructive extremes. In contemporary Japanese education, entry into schools with top reputations has a decisive importance in determining whether or not one attains a lucrative career and a superior social position. Consequently, the competition for entry into top-rated schools is ferocious. In the background are the facts that, due to equalization, there are today (1) a very large number of individuals capable of entering colleges and universities, and (2) an egalitarian expectation that if one is successful in entering such a school, one will move upward socially. In addition, one cannot overlook the fact that "when society becomes a mass society in which equality of educational opportunity is general, . . . then the desire for employment and success in the world after graduation [fades relative to] a growing desire to get into a school with high social prestige, so that both parents and children can enjoy a sense of psychological satisfaction."[2]

Egalitarianism is related to many other phenomena viewed as weaknesses of contemporary Japanese education. For example, the stronger egalitarian inclinations are, the deeper is the despair of those unable to achieve "average" attainments and those who drop out along the way. Egalitarianism is thus a partial cause of such problems as violence in schools and children's refusal to go to school. Moreover, spreading equalization erodes the authority of the teacher in the classroom. For teachers who have lost their authority, the most effective way to lead a large number of pupils is to "manage" them impersonally, in accordance with administrative rules. And in egalitarianism thus also lies one of the causes of the appearance of bureaucratically managed education in Japan.

Long ago, Plato observed of human beings in democratic society that "the father will acquire the habit of imitating his children; he will fear his sons. The sons, in turn, imitate the father, showing their parents neither deference nor fear. . . . Teachers fear and flatter their students, the students feel contempt for their masters and tutors."[3]

This statement describes vividly one aspect of Japanese society today. Without question, overcoming the pathologies of egalitarian society is the greatest challenge facing Japanese education today.

NOTES

1. Inuta Mitsuru, *Nihonjin no Kaisō Ishiki* (Class Consciousness in Japan), PHP Kenkyūjo, 1982, p. 16.
2. Amano Ikuo, "Gakkō to wa Nani ka?" (What Is School?), *Asahi Shimbun*, 2 April 1985, evening ed.
3. Plato, *The Republic*, Richard Sterling and William Scott, trans., New York, Norton, 1985, p. 254.

CHAPTER 21

NATIONALISM

ORIGINS OF NATIONALISM

Nationalism refers to ideas and movements directed toward the unity, independence, and development of a nation. The word "nation" derives from the Latin verb *natio*, "to be born." Originally it was used to describe a group of people born in the same place. Today, the term is most commonly used to refer to a body of people living in the same place and sharing language, customs, and culture. In premodern times, the lives of most people were subsumed under communities of very restricted geographic scope; consequently, no meaningful regional society existed beyond the scale of the community. It was when such communities began to dissolve and the boundaries of human life began to expand that the modern state was formed. Sooner or later, all modern states sought the form of the nation-state, which signifies the fact that the concept of nation has developed in intimate relationship with the institutional structure of the modern state.

In Japan, the formation of a nation-state began with the Meiji Restoration; consequently, it is accurate also to say that Japanese nationalism began with the Restoration. Embryonic nationalistic phenomena had, however, already appeared before the Restoration. One example of such phenomena is the ideology of "expelling the barbarians" (*jōi*). *Jōi* was a body of thought that sprang up in the 1850s in response to the appearance, and military and political threat, of foreigners; propounded by the ruling class, it called for the protection from foreign aggression with force. According to Maruyama Masao, this "protonationalism" had two characteristics.[1] First, because it was an ideology of the ruling class, it implied almost no sense of popular solidarity or unity—on the contrary, within the ruling class, there were many who looked upon both the common people *and* foreigners as enemies. The term "evil subjects and crafty foreigners" (*kanmin kōi*), which appears in the nationalistic literature of the day, exemplifies the point. Second, because the ruling class looked at international relations with eyes accustomed to a domestic world of hierarchical, class-based relationships of domination, they tended to see relationships between states as a matter of subjugating or being subjugated. Among the states of Western Europe there existed universalistic standards of international conduct, which served to make nationalism more rational; in Japanese protonationalism, by contrast, there was a strong element of irrationalism.[2]

When this sort of protonationalism came face to face with the overwhelming industrial, technological, and military superiority of the Western powers, Japan was forced in self-defense to arm itself with the civilization of the "enemy." In other words, modernization became an imperative task. If modernization—with all its egalitarian and constitutional implications—were to penetrate into politics, however, the power structures supporting the ruling class would be threatened. What the government sought, therefore, was a modernization restricted to "material civilization," with the utmost possible exclusion of any influence from Western philosophical or political ideas.[3] Contemporary slogans such as Western scholar Sakuma Shōzan's "Eastern morality, Western arts" and "Japanese spirit, Western technology" exemplify this attitude. And at least in economic and military terms, the Meiji government succeeded to a significant extent in this attempt at "compartmentalized" modernization.

NATIONALISM IN THE MEIJI STATE

Because the Meiji state was created for the purpose of resisting the aggression of the Western powers, one of its crucial tasks was to imbue the people with patriotism and inculcate a sense of nationalism. How did the Meiji state accomplish this? First, loyalty to the emperor was linked to allegiance to the state. At the time of the Restoration, the people did not think of themselves as a nation; moreover, their sense of attachment to the state was as yet exceedingly weak. Implanting a sense of direct patriotism in such a people was extraordinarily difficult. Therefore, the government tried to stimulate loyalty to the concrete person of the emperor rather than the abstraction of the state and to use loyalty to the throne as a substitute for patriotism. Thus, the idea of equating "loyalty and patriotism" (*chūkun aikoku*) was established.

Second, in order to strengthen loyalty to the emperor, the parallelism of family and state was propounded: as the family has a father,

Nationalism   227

so does the state have an emperor. And, as children in a family obey the father and fulfill the obligations of filial piety to their parents, so do the people fulfill the obligations of loyalty to the emperor. This moralistic approach to nationalism was encapsulated in the slogan *chūkō itchi*, or the "unity of imperial loyalty and filial piety."

Thus, the nationalism of the Meiji state was founded on the two moral principles of *chūkun aikoku* and *chūkō itchi*; what this meant was that the concept of the state in nationalism was intimately linked to the primary group (such as the family or village). Consequently, love of country appeared as love of one's hometown. In the short run, this made nationalism easier to cultivate; at the same time, however, the government also feared that parochial local and familial consciousness could conflict with a unified national spirit. Indeed, the poet Yosano Akiko's bitterly antiwar poem, "Don't Die for the Throne"—which urged the young to think of family first—expresses the contradictions of nationalism built on a familial fiction.

It is impossible for nationalism linked with intimate, almost mythic groups like family and village to avoid a tendency toward irrationalism and emotionalism. One means of tempering nationalism is to link it with individualism and democracy. This is because one can expect, when nationalism is built on a foundation of independent individuals, that nations will be less likely to go off on collective crusades on behalf of race, *volk*, or fatherland in which doubting individuals are swept aside by the herd. But, at the same time, such nationalism can actually be stronger insofar as it draws upon the active commitment of millions of citizens. Fukuzawa Yukichi, the pioneer of Westernization, expressed this relationship as "through the independence of each individual the country becomes independent."

The first attempt to reach a synthesis of nationalism and individualism, free of emperor and state, was the Freedom and Popular Rights Movement. Almost all of the participants in this movement were statists—exponents of state power and prestige—but they felt that in order to achieve international independence it was necessary for every citizen to feel pride in their support for the state, and called accordingly for the establishment of popular rights.[4] They were acutely aware that the world's greatest industrial and military powers lay in the individualistic and often democratic West. With the collapse of this movement, however, the link between statism and popular rights was broken, and a statism unencumbered by any consideration of individualistic rights became dominant.

Another attempt to link nationalism, individualism, and democracy during the Meiji era was the "Japanism" movement propounded by the journalist Kuga Katsunan and political commentator Shiga

Shigetaka through the magazine *Nihonjin* (The Japanese) and the newspaper *Nihon Shinbun* (The Japan News).[5] This movement resisted the government's top-down modernization, which really amounted to imposed Westernization, contrasting it with the idea of indigenous, "national" modernization pushed by the people from below, free of state manipulation. In the words of Kuga: "National politics demonstrates to the outside world the excellence and independence of the people; domestically, it signifies their unity. What national unity essentially means is that all matters pertaining to the people should be dealt with by the people. Therefore, one should say that national politics is, in this respect, . . . politics in accord with the popular will."[6]

The Japanism movement, however, was also unable to reverse the trend of decaying support for popular rights, and Japan entered the twentieth century with a nationalism based on a glorified, mythologized family-state whose infallible virtues and expansionist needs were open to question by none.

TRANSITION TO ULTRANATIONALISM

Nationalism, still untempered by any element of individualism or democracy, encountered a period of temporary stability during the period of Taishō democracy, but, as the country sank into an economic quagmire early in the Shōwa era, its irrational and emotional aspects came to the fore. As the military seized political power from the political parties, this irrational nationalism contributed to an ideology of totalitarianism which served to mobilize the people for the war effort. At this point, as nationalism, it lost all sense of proportion. Outside observers described it as ultranationalism or extreme nationalism.

Why were such prefixes attached to the term? Briefly, because Japanese nationalism had a qualitatively different character from that of other countries. That is, the state had an absolutist quality that kept an iron grip even on the hearts and minds of the people.[7] Because the modern states of Western Europe had experienced the horrors of the religious wars that had followed the Reformation, they tended not to interfere in the innermost thoughts of people—their philosophies, their religious faith, and their morals—choosing to concentrate exclusively on regulating their external behavior. The modern state that arose in Japan, however, sought to subject even individual thoughts and beliefs to the will of the state. We have already noted how even morality was foisted upon the people in the form of orders from the monarch.

Of course, there was ultranationalistic potential in the Meiji Constitution ever since its promulgation. From the very beginning, elements of constitutional monarchism and "ultra-absolute" monarchism coexisted in the system created by the constitution. If the former was emphasized during the years of Taishō democracy, then ultranationalism was the gross exaggeration of the latter. Just as the concept of the state that took shape under the Meiji Constitution was familial, with the emperor as the paterfamilias of one great national family, so also was the ultranationalism of the Shōwa era built on a familial fiction.

This ideology functioned as a totalitarian ideology under the military dictatorship. In this sense, Japanese totalitarianism was a sort of "familial totalitarianism." For example, contemporary writers encouraged the family paradigm by such statements as: "The Yamato race [that is, the Japanese race] is a family with the emperor at its center; it is established on the relationships of one great blood kin group, on the relationships between the branches of a family, so to speak"; and of Japanese totalitarianism "a totalitarianism in which all are of one heart and body, originating from the blood relationships of the Japanese race."[8] Moreover, a representative political scientist of the day, Yabe Teiji, referred to Germany as "racial totalitarianism," Italy as "state totalitarianism," and Japan as a "familial, communal state, . . . possessing, and manifesting, family relationships that truly epitomize the relationships of the intimate social group."[9] Thus, one can see, at least in the realm of ideology, an extraordinary continuity between the Meiji state and the Japanese totalitarian dictatorship of the 1930s and 1940s.

COLLAPSE OF NATIONALISM

Japan's defeat on August 15, 1945, put an end to the military dictatorship. Simultaneously, Japanese nationalism, too, witnessed a precipitate collapse. That in some cases military defeat has, rather, caused a flareup of nationalism is clear from such examples as Prussia after its defeat by Napoleon, France after the Franco-Prussian War, and China after its bitter defeat in the Sino-Japanese War. There was, however, no such swelling of nationalism in postwar Japan. This was partly because Japanese nationalism was founded on military supremacy. Having relied upon the fact that "the emperor's armies are ever-victorious and the territory of the divine nation has never been invaded," it received a mortal blow from military defeat.[10] Moreover, the distinctive nature of the state was attributed to its unique, imperial national polity, or *kokutai*; this *kokutai* was based ideologically on a fusion of all Japanese values. That the political impetus behind the Japanese people's "sense of mission was [so] comprehensive meant that the spiritual void produced by its collapse was vast"; herein lies another reason why nationalism did not rise up after defeat.[11]

Because Japanese nationalism had originally been intimately linked with primary social groups like family and village, the collapse of nationalism also served to disperse people's feelings of belonging and identification, and refocus them on groups like family, village, and small local associations, which had previously been linked to the state. For a short while after surrender, quasi-criminal groups proliferated all over the country, performing police functions within their localities by default; it appears that many demobilized soldiers were absorbed by such groups.[12] These sorts of organizations, built as they were on fictive kinship relations, served to absorb the dispersed residue of nationalist sentiment. Moreover, one can see how the mass nationalism that had previously burst out over the military victories of the Japanese empire was redirected after the war into wild enthusiasm over victories in the world of sports. In this sense, the passionate popularity of the 1964 Tokyo Olympics was the curtain raiser for a new type of postwar Japanese nationalism.

What relationship does this contemporary nationalism bear with its prewar predecessor? If one accepts that earlier nationalism was based on intimate collectivities like the family and the village, in today's Japan, where the family and village have lost their communal similarities and are ceasing to be the objects of people's feelings of belonging, the conditions for the revival of traditional nationalism in that form are absent. This does not mean, however, that prewar nationalism has utterly vanished. Although the reality of the familial and village communities has disappeared, nevertheless, as fictions, they live on in many types of collectivities. For example, corporations have become the objects of strong feelings of identity and belonging, similar to those of a family, for their employees. Moreover, school alumni associations, from elementary school to university, have become the medium for the cultivation of local affections similar to those of the traditional village. The sense of belonging felt toward these sorts of collectivities is, however, apolitical and does not function in the same way as political nationalism. In order for traditionalistic feelings of belonging to be remobilized as political nationalism, some national symbol is necessary.

FLAG, ANTHEM, EMPEROR

The most important element in any attempt to revive traditional nationalism is the revival of popular symbols like the Rising Sun flag and the anthem *Kimigayo*, which eulogizes the reign of the emperor. The Nakasone government, established in 1982, wanted to wind up the era of "postwar" politics once and for all. To this end it initiated a variety of policies, one of which was an attempt to promote nationalism. It is not difficult to see the connection between this goal and such activities as Prime Minister Nakasone's unprecedented and controversial official visit to the Yasukuni Shrine, where the souls of Japan's war dead are enshrined, and expansion of the military budget beyond its long-respected limit of 1 percent of the GNP. But most important, in terms of the scope of its influence, was his policy of requiring the raising of the Rising Sun flag and the singing of *Kimigayo* at public elementary, junior high, and high school ceremonies nationwide. This policy was premised on the idea that the Rising Sun is the "national" flag, and *Kimigayo* the "national" anthem, although in fact there is no law that makes them so. The government argued strongly that the flag was "national" on the basis of customary law, as a matter of popular belief, but in fact there are a great many Japanese who do *not* recognize the Rising Sun as the national flag nor *Kimigayo* as the national anthem because of their associations with the prewar military dictatorship.

Nevertheless, along with the Nakasone government came a policy of forcing the Rising Sun and *Kimigayo* on schools throughout the nation. This was most vividly exemplified by its imposition even in the schools of Okinawa where, because it was savagely devastated during the war, many people have an antipathy toward both flag and anthem far more intense than that of mainland Japanese. There is good reason to see in this policy, which was nothing but a symbolic, nationalistic appeal to the emotions, a serious danger of revived, irrational nationalism. Nationalism is, to be sure, a universal phenomenon, and one may make the argument that in both Western and Asian nations national flags and anthems are the objects of extreme respect. From the perspective of the irrationality of nationalism, however, whether it be a case of the American flag or the French anthem, going overboard with idolatry of flag and anthem is hardly desirable. And one must not forget that the Japanese flag and anthem are particularly and inextricably interwoven with offensive memories lingering from a war of aggression.

As a national symbol, the emperor system is even more effective than the Rising Sun flag or *Kimigayo*. According to the present Constitution the emperor is a "symbol of national unity"; nevertheless, popular feelings of veneration for the emperor are still strong. The illness and death of the Shōwa emperor in 1988 to 1989 demonstrated the fact that popular emotions vis-à-vis the emperor are still powerful. From the perspective of seeking to revive nationalism, these popular emotions have a tremendous potential utility; one may, however, entertain a number of doubts on this score.

First, according to the Constitution, the emperor "shall not have powers related to government." It is doubtful that the emperor could legitimately be used as a national symbol in a political context, in light of the letter and spirit of the Constitution. Second, since there are always divisions and conflicts among the people, national unity is unthinkable in the absence of some process for generating political integration. Therefore, it would be difficult for the emperor to serve as a "symbol of national unity" and yet avoid participating in such a political process. The Constitution seeks to maintain a very delicate balance between the emperor and politics. Third, under the basic principles of the Constitution, the freedom to criticize the emperor and the emperor system are recognized unconditionally. Given this, one can only describe as a gross violation of the fundamental principles of the Constitution the actions of the Liberal Democratic Party when it disciplined the Liberal Democratic mayor of Nagasaki, Motoshima Hitoshi, for stating that the Shōwa emperor bore responsibility for the war. In any case, using the emperor as a symbol for the purpose of reviving traditional nationalism would amount to destroying the balance inherent in the Constitution.

INTERNATIONALIZATION AND NATIONALISM

Among the distinctive features of contemporary Japanese nationalism, the most important is the inevitability of internationalization and, simultaneously, the loud exclamations of nationalism it produces. Every aspect of the lives of the Japanese people is exposed to international influences: in the area of everyday food, clothing, and shelter, almost nothing is provided for completely with domestically produced items. The vast flood of information that pours in hourly comes from all over the world. Unprecedented numbers of people travel abroad and observe foreign scenes and manners. At the same time, great numbers of foreigners come to Japan to stay for short or long periods, including refugees who drift onto Japan's shores and seek permanent settlement. Internationalization is already an inescapable reality.

Why, then, is nationalism emphasized so in an age of internationalization? Basically, it is rooted in demands for the protection of Japanese identity amid a torrent of internationalization that seems to show no signs of abating. The impulse is cultural, but it is at the same time economic: national unity is seen as essential in order both to protect a wide variety of domestic interests built up by the Japanese with great effort and at great cost and to resist the foreign pressures that are part of the friction arising from Japan's advance abroad. Internationalism is the natural outcome of economic logic; nationalism, however, is also the natural outcome of economic interest.

It can be argued that a healthy nationalism is an essential condition for popular democracy in the modern world. Even granting some validity to this view, one must also, at the very least, allow for the following two qualifications. First, there is no justification for a nationalism that is not "relativized" by internationalism, that is, made flexible and empathetic through close cooperation with other peoples. Second, it is impossible to anticipate either rationalization or internationalization in Japanese nationalism if, from the beginning, it is generated on the basis of a national flag, a national anthem, and the emperor system. To the extent that national identity is seen as necessary by the Japanese, the sole appropriate way of achieving it is by creating solidarity among the citizens. If society is a network created through popular solidarity, then what is needed at present is a civil society on a plane quite apart from that of the state. In the past, the Japanese experienced the parochial fusion of family, village, and state, but they have never experienced universalistic social solidarity. One of the most glaring gaps in contemporary Japanese education is the absence of any effort to instill the meaning of civic solidarity in young people. What is essential is the creation of national solidarity independent of the state. It is only in this way that the Japanese will ever arrive at the point where they can speak of solidarity with other peoples or of the internationalization of Japan.

NOTES

1. Maruyama Masao, *Gendai Seiji no Shisō to Kōdō*, Miraisha, 1946, pp. 156–57. For an English version of this essay, see Maruyama Masao, *Thought and Behavior in Modern Japanese Politics*, Ivan Morris, ed., London, Oxford University Press, 1963, ch. 4.

2. Rationalism, as used here, refers to the reasoned calculation of how best to achieve the nation's goals given the resources at its disposal and the goals and resources of other nations with which one's own nation may disagree. The presence of international standards of conduct makes it far easier to predict the behavior of other nations and thus to decide rationally how to achieve one's own ends. Japan, however, set itself apart from other nations and was frequently unable to predict how other nations would react to its own international behavior and unable to calculate a rational path toward its own goals.

3. Maruyama, *Gendai Seiji no Shisō to Kōdō*, pp. 157–58.

4. Maruyama Masao, *Senchū to Sengo to no aida* (Between Wartime and Postwar), Misuzu Shobō, 1974, pp. 214–15.

5. *Ibid.*, pp. 283–88.

6. Kuga Katsunan, *Kinji Seiron Kō* (Thoughts on Contemporary Politics), Iwanami, 1972, p. 83.

7. Maruyama, *Gendai Seiji no Shisō to Kōdō*, p. 16.

8. Ogura Kenji in *Zentaishugi no Honshitsu* (The Essence of Totalitarianism, 1938), quoted in Shibata Toshio, "Zentaishugi" (Totalitarianism), in Kuwahara Hiroshi et al., *Nihon no Fashizumu* (Japanese Fascism), Yūhikaku, 1979, pp. 203–4. Here again we see the roots or irrationalism in Japanese foreign policy: the state could not be questioned, and therefore goals or diplomatic or military strategies which ignored Japan's weaknesses or other countries' strengths could not be criticized.

9. Yabe Teiji in *Zentaishugi Seijigaku* (The Politics of Totalitarianism, 1943), quoted in *ibid.*, pp. 207–8.

10. Maruyama, *Gendai Seiji no Shisō to Kōdō*, p. 165.

11. *Ibid.*, p. 166.

12. *Ibid*, pp. 166–67.

SUGGESTED READING

For the reader who has time for but one book, the best single introduction to contemporary Japanese history, society, economy, and politics is still Edwin Reischauer's *The Japanese Today* (Cambridge, Belknap Press, 1988). On the American Occupation of Japan, Kazuo Kawai, *Japan's American Interlude* (Chicago, University of Chicago Press, 1960), has similarly stood the test of time, while Andrew Gordon, *Postwar Japan as History* (Berkeley, University of California Press, 1993), puts the postwar period in a perspective not usually seen in snapshots of Japan at the contemporary moment.

Overviews of the political system are found in two books by J.A.A. Stockwin: *Japan: Divided Politics in a Growth Economy* (2nd edition; London, Weidenfeld and Nicolson, 1982) and *Dynamic and Immobilist Politics in Japan* (London, Macmillan, 1988). The institutions of national government are examined by Hans Baerwald in *Japan's Parliament* (Cambridge, Cambridge University Press, 1974), T.J. Pempel in *Policy and Politics in Japan* (Philadelphia, Temple University Press, 1982), Chalmers Johnson in *MITI and the Japanese Miracle* (Stanford, Stanford University Press, 1982), B.C. Koh in *Japan's Administrative Elite* (Berkeley, University of California Press, 1989), and Richard Samuels in *The Business of the Japanese State: Energy Markets in Comparative and Historical Perspective* (Ithaca, Cornell University Press, 1987), and the role of law in politics and society is examined by Frank Upham in *Law and Social Change in Postwar Japan* (Cambridge, Harvard University Press, 1987), and John Haley in *Authority Without Power: Law and the Japanese Paradox* (New York, Oxford University Press, 1991). For an example of the dramatically different ways in which Japanese politics have been evaluated, one should look at Ezra Vogel's laudatory *Japan as Number One* (Cambridge, Harvard University Press, 1979) and then

at Karel Van Wolferen's dyspeptic *The Enigma of Japanese Power*
(New York, Vintage, 1989).

Local government receives its due in Kurt Steiner, *Local Government in Japan* (Stanford, Stanford University Press, 1965), Steven
Reed, *Japanese Prefectures and Policy Making* (Pittsburgh, University
of Pittsburgh Press, 1986), and Richard Samuels, *The Politics of Regional Policy in Japan* (Princeton, Princeton University Press, 1983).
And community-level society and politics, rural and urban, are intimately and vividly presented in R.P. Dore's *Shinohata* (New York,
Pantheon, 1978) and Theodore Bestor's *Neighborhood Tokyo* (Stanford, Stanford University Press, 1989), respectively.

The Japanese policy process is the focus of John Campbell in two
books—*Contemporary Japanese Budget Politics* (Berkeley, University of California Press, 1977) and *How Policies Change: The Japanese
Government and the Aging Society* (Princeton, Princeton University
Press, 1992)—and of Gary Allinson and Yasunori Sone in *Political
Dynamics in Contemporary Japan* (Ithaca, Cornell University Press,
1993) and Samuel Kernell, ed., *Parallel Politics: Economic Policy-
making in Japan and the United States* (Tokyo, Japan Center for
International Exchange/Washington, D.C., Brookings Institution,
1991). And foreign and security policy in particular are dealt with in
Kenneth Pye, *The Japanese Question* (Washington, D.C., AEI Press,
1992), Takashi Inoguchi, *Japan's International Relations* (Boulder,
Westview, 1991), Gerald Curtis, *Japan's Foreign Policy after the
Cold War* (Armonk, M.E. Sharpe, 1993), and Clyde Prestowitz,
Trading Places: How We Allowed Japan to Take the Lead (New
York, Basic Books, 1988).

On the subject of political participation, the authoritative work on
electioneering is Gerald Curtis, *Election Campaigning Japanese Style*
(New York, Columbia University Press, 1971), and Scott Flanagan,
Shinsaku Kōhei, Ichiro Miyake, Bradley Richardson, and Jōji Wata-
nuki have done the same for political attitudes and voting behavior
in *The Japanese Voter* (New Haven, Yale University Press, 1991).
Political parties and the electoral and party systems are the focus of
Gerald Curtis, *The Japanese Way of Politics* (New York, Columbia
University Press, 1988), Ronald Hrebenar, *The Japanese Party Sys-
tem* (Boulder, Westview, 1986), and Hans Baerwald, *Party Politics in
Japan* (Boston, Allen and Unwin, 1986), while Nathaniel Thayer, in
How the Conservatives Rule Japan (Princeton, Princeton University
Press, 1969), Haruhiro Fukui, in *Party in Power* (Berkeley, Universi-
ty of California Press, 1970), and Kent Calder, in *Crisis and Com-
pensation* (Princeton, Princeton University Press, 1988), examine the
Liberal Democratic Party in particular. And, for less conventional

forms of participation, Ellis Krauss, Thomas Rohlen, and Patricia Steinhoff look at *Conflict in Japan* (Honolulu, University of Hawaii Press, 1984) and Margaret McKean analyzes *Environmental Protest and Citizen Politics in Japan* (Berkeley, University of California Press, 1981).

Political culture is covered best in Takeshi Ishida's *Japanese Political Culture* (New Brunswick, Transaction Books, 1983), Jun-ichi Kyōgoku's *The Political Dynamics of Japan* (translated by Nobutaka Ike; University of Tokyo Press, 1987), and chapters 4–6 of Bradley Richardson and Scott Flanagan's *Politics in Japan* (Boston, Little, Brown, 1984), while the particular qualities of Japanese democracy are the focus of attention in Nobutaka Ike's *A Theory of Japanese Democracy* (Boulder, Westview, 1978) and Takeshi Ishida and Ellis Krauss's *Democracy in Japan* (Pittsburgh, University of Pittsburgh Press, 1989).

INDEX

Abe Hitoshi, 45
Ad Hoc Advisory Council for the Promotion of Administrative Reform (Gyōkakushin), 97; Second, 99; Third, 99–100
Ad Hoc Commission on Administration (Rinchō): First, 92–93; Second, 96–97, 98, 99
administrative guidance, x, 35–36, 37, 100
administrative reform, xii, 89, 92–100, 218
advisory councils (*shingikai*), x, 22, 39–45, 186
agent delegation, 60, 61, 64, 66
agriculture, 132, 161, 215
Aiba Juichi, 170
Ainu, 219
alien registration, 221
Allinson, Gary, 236
Amano Ikuo, 224
anthem (*Kimigayo*), 231, 233
Anti-Monopoly Law, 99
Arai Naoyuki, 198
Araki Toshio, 170
Asia-Pacific region, 110, 111, 112
authority, 216–17

Baerwald, Hans, 235, 236
Bank of Japan, 84
Becker, Carl, 204, 212
benefits, political, 124, 174, 180, 205, 206, 218
Bestor, Theodore, 236
bicameralism, 15
Board of Audit, 84, 85
bubble economy, 98
budget, xii, 43, 44, 73, 74, 83–91, 177
burakumin, 215, 219–20

bureaucracy, xii, 11, 33–38, 39–40, 48, 49, 76, 88
bureaucrats, 22–23, 39, 40, 41–42, 43, 45; power of, 24–25, 27
business community, xii, 47, 49, 211

cabinet, 18, 19, 20, 27–28, 84, 85, 168; Meiji, 7, 27, 33
Cabinet Legislative Bureau, 22
cabinet ministers, 19, 30–31
Calder, Kent, 236
Campbell, John, 91, 236
cities. *See* municipalities
civil servants. *See* bureaucrats
civil service, 33–38, 40, 48
coalition government, 31, 88, 123, 131, 132, 133, 134, 136, 151
Cold War, 101, 102, 137, 204
committees, parliamentary, 18–19, 21–22, 23, 120, 126
community, 3, 5, 6, 68, 186–88, 207
conflict, 3, 4, 5, 6, 12, 40, 49, 67, 69, 98, 187, 204, 205, 209, 210
Constitution: 10–11, 12, 15, 27, 29, 83, 84, 231–32; Article 9, 102, 106, 111. *See also* Meiji Constitution
consumption tax, 71, 120, 130
corruption, political, xii, 36, 48, 50, 91, 98, 122, 132, 136, 139, 150, 151, 179, 206. *See also* Lockheed scandal; Recruit scandal; Sagawa scandal
courts, power of, 15
cultural politics, 163
Curtis, Gerald, 154, 172, 176, 181, 236

defense, xiii; budget, 89, 97, 104–6. *See also* military; national security
Defense Agency, 97, 103, 104
Defense Council, 97, 98

239